INSPIRE / PLAN / DISCOVER / EXPERIENCE

GREECE
ATHENS AND THE MAINLAND

GREECE
ATHENS AND THE MAINLAND

CONTENTS

DISCOVER 6

EXPERIENCE 64

Athens 64

Mainland Greece 142

NEED TO KNOW 248

Left: Ceremonial guards outside the Greek Parliament, Athens
Previous page: The small port of Geroliménas village, Máni
Front cover: The lively Monastiráki square in the heart of Athens

DISCOVER

Moni Rousánou amidst rocky pinnacles, Metéora

WELCOME TO
GREECE

Taverna-lined city streets and buzzing bars. Ancient temples, mountains that were home to the gods and museums filled with treasures. Idyllic stretches of golden sand lapped by turquoise waters. Whatever your dream trip to Athens and mainland Greece includes, this DK Eyewitness travel guide is the perfect companion.

1 A café and taverna in Athens's Pláka district.

2 Locals enjoying a hearty traditional meal.

3 A beach on the Sithonia peninsula, Halkidiki.

4 The ancient theatre at Epidaurus, still in use today.

Kissed by three seas and stretching from the barren peaks of the northern Pindos to the sunny vineyards of Attica and the Peloponnese, mainland Greece is stunningly diverse. Sun-worshippers can bask on the sandy beaches of Halkidikí, while outdoor adventurers can trek the Víkos and Loúsios gorges and climb the craggy peaks of Mount Olympos. Iconic archaeological sites such as Delphi and Olympia attract vast numbers of visitors, but Greece is also rich in lesser known relics of the ancient world at Dodona and Dion, as well as romantic castles and imposing fortresses from later epochs such as those at Mystrás and Monemvasiá.

The cities, too, will not disappoint. The serene marble columns of the Parthenon, silhouetted above Athens as the sun sinks, sum up Greece for many visitors. This is Europe's oldest city,

but it also offers a youthful vibe and buzzing nightlife, where upmarket restaurants stand alongside traditional grill restaurants and old-school *ouzeris* jostle with the trendy cocktail bars of newly hip urban neighbourhoods. Thessaloníki, Greece's second city, is similarly vibrant. It seduces visitors with its array of Byzantine churches, an impressive roster of great museums and authentic street food.

This guide divides Athens and mainland Greece into easily navigable chapters, with detailed itineraries, expert local knowledge and colourful, comprehensive maps to help you plan the perfect trip. Whether you're staying for a weekend, a week or longer, this DK Eyewitness travel guide will ensure that you experience the very best that Greece's capital and its hinterland have to offer.

REASONS TO LOVE
GREECE

Magnificent temples, forbidding fortresses, the serene hush of centuries-old monasteries, exquisite local cuisine and wines, gold-sand beaches and breathtaking mountain scenery – there are so many reasons why visitors fall in love with mainland Greece. Here are some of our favourites.

1 STUNNING MONASTERIES

A visit to Greece's monasteries should be on any visitor's itinerary, from the extraordinary clifftop structures of Metéora *(p196)* to the Monastery of Daphni with its magnificent mosaics *(p128)*.

THE ACROPOLIS 2

Standing watch over Athens, the Acropolis *(p94)* is a landmark of Western civilization. The great marble masterpieces on the "Sacred Rock" epitomize Athens in all its glory.

3 GLORIOUS LOCAL FOOD

From traditional grills and fresh fish and seafood to meze sharing plates and a plethora of cheeses, Greek cuisine uses seasonal produce from Aegean shores, village gardens and mountain pastures.

VIBRANT ATHENS **4**

In Greece's capital city buzzing cafés, tavernas and markets rub shoulders with ancient ruins and Byzantine churches, while museums display millennia of art from ancient to modern.

THE WILD MÁNI **5**

Spend several days in this beautiful rugged peninsula *(p178)*. Almost untouched by the modern world until the 20th century, it remains little explored.

GODS AND HEROES **6**

The Greek myths are some of the greatest stories ever told. Admire the splendour of gods, goddesses and heroes embodied in marble and bronze at ancient temples and museums.

HIKING THROUGH THE VÍKOS GORGE 7

The path through the boulder-strewn ravine bed of the Víkos Gorge *(p218)*, up through forests of beech, maple and chestnut, offers some of Greece's most stunning scenery.

UNEARTHING THE PAST 8

With Mycenaean citadels, Classical temples, Byzantine monasteries, Ottoman mosques and Venetian fortresses, Greece is a treasure trove of historical sites and stupendous art.

9 WINE TASTING

Discover the rich variety of Greek wines on a tasting tour. From Halkidikí *(p230)* in the north to Nemea *(p183)* in the south, you'll find vineyards that tantalize your palate.

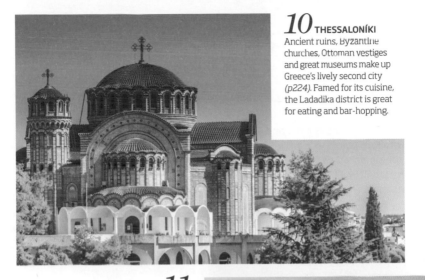

10 THESSALONÍKI
Ancient ruins, Byzantine churches, Ottoman vestiges and great museums make up Greece's lively second city *(p224)*. Famed for its cuisine, the Ladadika district is great for eating and bar-hopping.

ANCIENT DELPHI 11
Surrounded by a natural amphitheatre of soaring cliffs, Ancient Delphi *(p200)* is a must-visit. Here, visitors can imagine the spiritual centre of the ancient Hellenic world in its heyday.

TRADITIONAL MUSIC 12
Bouzouki, the most famous sound of Greece, dominates folk music and the rebel beat of *rembetiko* (blues). Live performances take place in clubs, bars and open-air festivals across the country.

EXPLORE
GREECE

This guide divides mainland Greece into four colour-coded sight-seeing areas, as shown on the map below. Find out more about each area on the following pages.

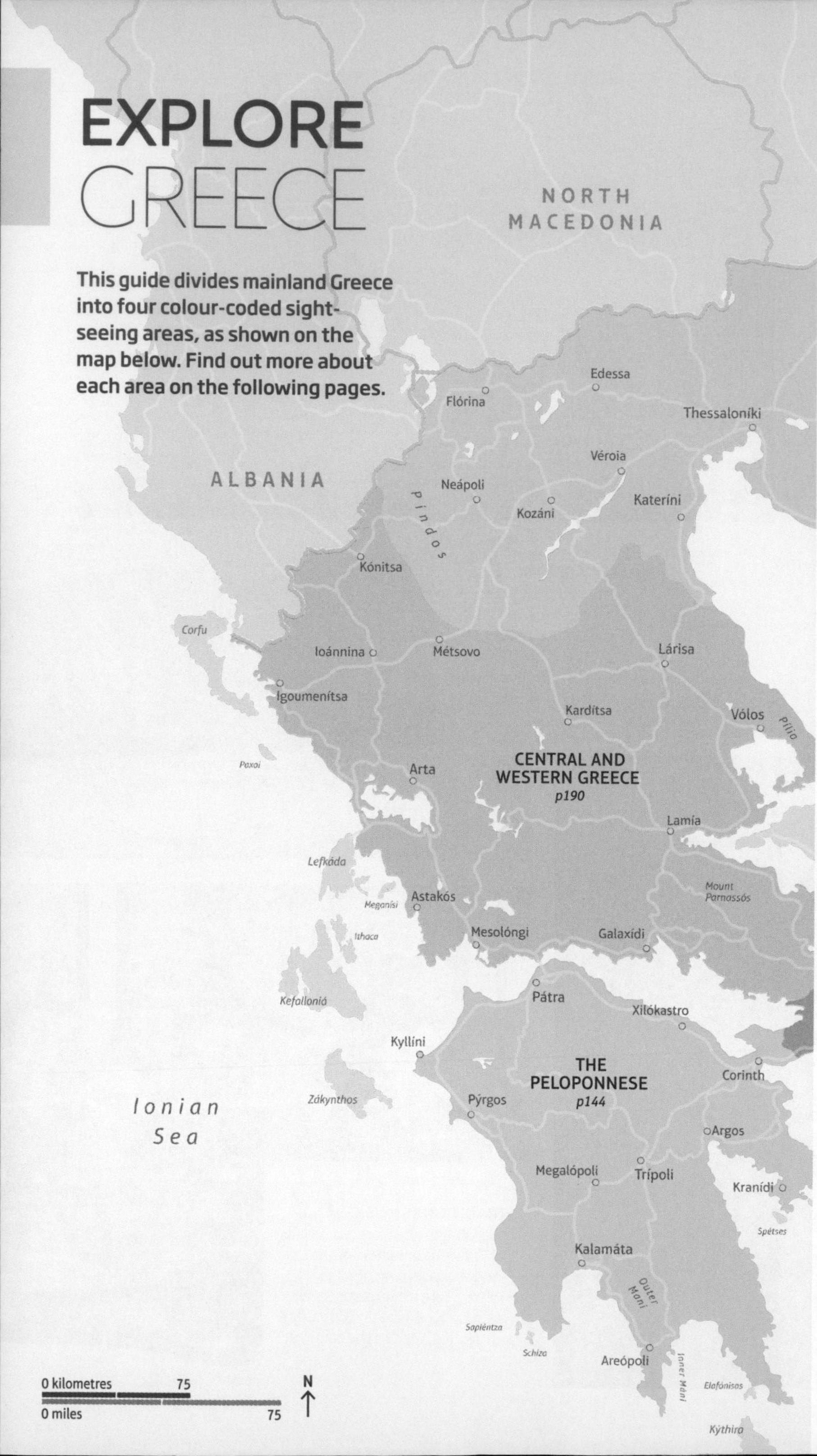

NORTH MACEDONIA

Edessa

Flórina

Thessaloníki

ALBANIA

Véroia

Neápoli

Kateríni

Kozáni

Pindos

Kónitsa

Corfu

Ioánnina

Métsovo

Lárisa

Igoumenítsa

Kardítsa

Vólos

Pilia

Paxoí

Arta

CENTRAL AND WESTERN GREECE
p190

Lamía

Lefkáda

Mount Parnassós

Meganísi

Astakós

Ithaca

Mesolóngi

Galaxídi

Kefalloniá

Pátra

Xilókastro

Kyllíni

THE PELOPONNESE
p144

Corinth

Ionian Sea

Zákynthos

Pýrgos

Argos

Megalópoli

Trípoli

Kranídi

Spétses

Kalamáta

Outer Mani

Sapléntza

Schíza

Areópoli

Inner Mani

Elafónisos

Kýthira

0 kilometres   75

0 miles   75

N

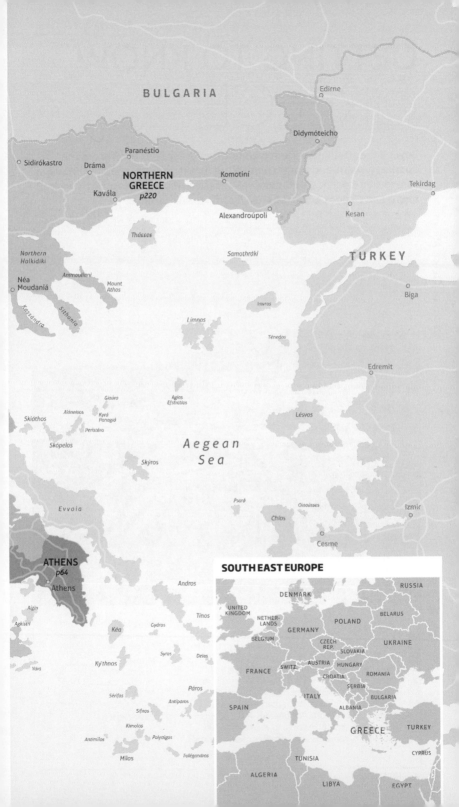

GETTING TO KNOW
GREECE

Beyond the stunning ancient wonders that Greece has to offer are the bustling bazaars and vibrant nightlife of Athens and Thessaloníki, fabulous, sun-soaked beaches, untamed wetlands, wild mountains and little-visited towns and villages where age-old traditions still survive.

ATHENS

PAGE 64

For most visitors, Athens is all about ancient temples, but Europe's oldest city is in so many ways its youngest too. It may be famous for ancient buildings and museums filled with treasures of the Classical era, but don't miss out on open-air cafés, nightlife under the stars and quirky contemporary art galleries. Beyond the city centre, the beaches of the Athens Riviera offer clear blue seas and white sand, while evocative ruins nestle among trees on verdant slopes.

Best for
Ancient monuments, amazing museums, great street food

Home to
National Archaeological Museum, Museum of Cycladic Art, Benáki Museum, Acropolis, Ancient Agora, Mikrí Mitrópoli

Experience
Dinner with a view of the Acropolis from a rooftop restaurant

PAGE 144

THE PELOPONNESE

Stretching from the Aegean to the Ionian Sea and from the Gulf of Corinth to the southernmost tip of mainland Greece, the Peloponnese is a land of rugged ranges and fertile plains. Frankish fortresses crown hilltops and watch over mountain passes, while Venetian castles gaze out to sea from impregnable crags. Scattered around this richly varied region are some of the most evocative relics of Greece's earliest civilizations. Dramatic river gorges offer trekking and rafting, while for a change of pace there are vineyards where Greece's finest vintages can be sampled.

Best for
Dramatic scenery, archaeological sites, medieval castles

Home to
Ancient Corinth, Ancient Olympia, Loúsios Gorge, Mycenae, Náfplio, Epidaurus, Monemvasiá, Mystrás, Máni

Experience
A drive around the rugged Máni peninsula to the southern tip of Greece

$\rightarrow$

CENTRAL AND WESTERN GREECE

The awesome scenery of the Pindos mountains, towering over Central and Western Greece, stands in stark contrast with the gentler farmlands of Thessaly and the lushly wooded slopes and charming hill villages of the Pílio peninsula. Heritage-steeped harbours and charming seaside villages are dotted around the shores, while high above the silvery Gulf of Corinth Ancient Delphi gazes out over a sea of olive groves. Pílio and the Víkos Gorge provide a plethora of outdoor adventures, while the monasteries of Metéora and Osios Loukás offer glimpses of Byzantine grandeur.

Best for
Epic mountains, clifftop monasteries, traditional villages

Home to
Ioánnina, Metéora, Monastery of Osios Loukás, Ancient Delphi, Pílio

Experience
Walking on age-old cobbled trails in the forests and orchards of Pílio

PAGE 220

NORTHERN GREECE

Embracing dramatic summits and gentler valleys cloaked in woodlands and vineyards, the hinterland of Northern Greece is fabulously varied, while around its coasts some of the finest beaches in the country are interspersed with wild wetlands. Vast, tranquil lakes and expanses of virgin forest that provide refuge for rare birds and butterflies are a delight for nature-lovers, while Thessaloníki, Greece's second city, serves up vibrant streetlife and an array of historical treasures.

Best for
Historical sites, sandy beaches, mountain walking

Home to
Thessaloníki, Halkidikí

Experience
A boat trip around Mount Athos

→

1 Visiting the Parthenon.

2 Lively Adrianou Street in the Pláka district.

3 *Evzones* guarding the Tomb of the Unknown Soldier.

4 Lykavittós Hill overlooking Athens at sunset.

Whether exploring Athens on foot or embarking on an epic journey of discovery around the mainland, Greece offers a treasury of ancient marvels, quirky cities, stunning landscapes and natural wonders. These itineraries will help you make the most of your visit.

2 DAYS
in Athens

Day 1

Morning Start your journey of discovery at the Acropolis (p94), where the city's story began. Some 2,500 years of history have taken their toll on its great temples, but passing through the Propylaia (p96) to climb to the top is nevertheless an awe-inspiring experience, as is the panoramic view of the city. Marvel at the magnificent columns of the Parthenon (p98) and Erechtheion (p96), before heading to the dazzling Acropolis Museum (p100). The glass-roofed Parthenon Gallery is the highlight here. The air-conditioned interior is also a delightfully cool haven on a hot day. Pause for refreshment in the terrace café, then stroll along traffic-free Dionysíou Areopagítou to admire the Temple of Olympian Zeus (p118) and Hadrian's Arch.

Afternoon Walk to Kydatheinon for lunch in the cool surroundings of O Damigos (Kidathineon 41). The signature dish in this historic tavern is *bakalarakia* – cod in crispy batter, served with a pungent garlic sauce. Afterwards, follow pedestrianized Adrianou through Pláka to wander around the vast Ancient Agora (p106). Then make your way through the colourful clutter of the Athens Flea Market (p111) to Plateía Monastiráki.

Evening Dine al fresco at O Thanasis (Mitropoleos 69), where the kebab platters are the best in town. Finish the evening with drinks at Couleur Locale (p45), a lively rooftop bar.

Day 2

Morning Spend the morning at the National Archaeological Museum (p74) for a stunning overview of the glories of the ancient world. Then hop on a bus or trolley to Plateía Syntagmá to admire kilted *evzones* on guard outside parliament (p119).

Afternoon From here it's a short walk to Kolonáki, where Dexameni (Plateia Dexamenis) is a perfect lunch stop with outdoor tables next to an open-air summer cinema. After lunch, take your time browsing the eclectic collection of arts and decorative crafts at the Benáki Museum (p82). Finally, discover eerily modern-looking relics of the deep past at the Museum of Cycladic Art (p80).

Evening Take the funicular to the summit of Lykavittós Hill (p84). Watch the sun set over the city, then dine at the elegant Orizontes Restaurant (p84) at the hill's summit while enjoying a glorious view of the floodlit Acropolis.

←

1 Mikrolimano marina in Piraeus.

2 The ancient Temple of Poseidon, Cape Sounion.

3 Fresh fish at a market stall in Ráfina port.

4 Schinias sandy beach near Marathónas.

3 DAYS
around Athens

Day 1

Morning Start from Athens early with a visit to the Monastery of Daphni (p128), around 30 minutes' drive from the city centre, to admire glittering Byzantine mosaics. Drive back through Athens to Piraeus (p130) for a fabulous seafood lunch on the harbourside deck at Jimmy's Fish (p131). Try the steamed mussels, or the octopus in red wine sauce.

Afternoon After lunch, follow the Attic Coast to elegant Vouliagméni (p139). Take a dip in the mineral waters of Vouliagméni Lake, then check in at the oh-so-chic Margi (www.themargi.gr).

Evening For dinner, take your pick of the Margi's multiple restaurants, where chefs create Med-fusion delights using ingredients from the hotel's organic farm.

Day 2

Morning It's a half-hour drive to Cape Sounion, the southern tip of Attica, where the Temple of Poseidon (p138) gazes over the Aegean. Admire the view and seek out Lord Byron's signature, carved by the poet into one of the columns.

Afternoon Drive up Attica's east coast, past Lávrio, to Avlaki, just south of Pórto Ráfti, where you can take a dip and enjoy lunch by the beach at Prima Plora (Akrotiriou 4). Drive on to Ancient Brauron (p134) to explore the ruins of its Temple of Artemis.

Evening Carry on to the lively port town of Rafína (p137) for an overnight stop and dinner in one of the bustling seafood restaurants beside its fishing harbour.

Day 3

Morning Grab a typical Greek breakfast of coffee, freshly squeezed orange juice and yoghurt with honey at a sunny seaside café, then drive to Marathónas (p136), scene of the world-shaping Battle of Marathon. Pay your respects to the hoplites who defeated Darius's Persians, then take a quick look at the Marathon Archaeological Museum and its finds from the battlefield. Back in the modern world, drive to Schinias, about 5 km (3 miles) from Marathónas, to discover one of Attica's finest beaches, where you can swim and eat lunch by the sea at one of half a dozen friendly tavernas.

Afternoon After lunch, head north to Ramnous (p137), where the remnants of a Classical holy city cover a hillside above the sea. Your next stop is the Amphiareio of Oropos (p136), where an impressive marble theatre stands above a valley fragrant with pine trees and wild herbs.

Evening From here, it's a quick drive down the E75 motorway to cool Kifisiá (p141), on the northern outskirts of Athens, where you'll find a plethora of upmarket restaurants and some lovely boutique hotels – perfect for the final evening of your journey around Attica.

7 DAYS
in the Peloponnese

Day 1

Start at the Corinth Canal *(p182)*, gateway to the Peloponnese. Pause to watch yachts passing beneath the bridge before carrying on to Ancient Corinth *(p148)*. Wander among the ruins of the once-great Roman city, then carry on to Dimitsána village on the lip of the awesome Loúsios Gorge *(p156)*. For lunch, try the traditional local cuisine at Drimonas *(p159)*, then burn off calories with a walk to the cliffside Moní Aimyalón monastery *(p157)* – it's around 6 km (4 miles) there and back. Afterwards, drive on to Andrítsaina *(p185)* to spend the night in this sleepy hillside town.

Day 2

Breakfast early to enjoy Andrítsaina's morning market at its best, then set off for Ancient Olympia, a 90-minute drive. You'll need the rest of the morning to absorb the wonders of the birthplace of the Olympic Games and its museum. Relax over lunch at Bacchus *(Archaia Pisa 27065)*, in nearby Miráka, a five-minute drive from Ancient Olympia, where the menu features local cuisine. Next, follow the Ionian coast

toward Pýlos, a two-hour drive. Pause to explore the ruins of Nestor's Palace *(p188)*, then treat yourself to a sybaritic night at Costa Navarino with its luxurious restaurants and hotels *(www.costanavarino.com)*.

Day 3

Start your exploration of Pýlos *(p189)* with a visit to the museum inside the Turkish Niókastro; take a peek at finds from ancient shipwrecks and admire the view of Navarino Bay. Then head south along the coast to Methóni *(p189)*, a fairytale-like sea-castle. Your next stop, about 45 minutes away, is Koróni *(p188)*, another Venetian fortress. Admire the panorama from its ramparts, then stroll to the palm-lined waterfront for a seafood lunch at Peroulia *(www.peroulia.gr)*. Afterwards, take a leisurely drive up the coast to Kalamáta, a pretty seaside town, to stay overnight.

Day 4

Today's journey takes you through mountainous Máni to Cape Tainaro, the southernmost tip of Greece *(p180)*, a two-

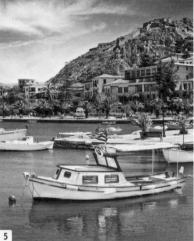

① The Corinth Canal, between the Peloponnese and the Greek mainland. ↑

② Alfresco lunch in Monemvasiá.

③ Octopi drying in the sun at Geroliménas harbour.

④ Visiting the ruins of the Temple of Hera in Olympia.

⑤ Náfplio harbour with the Palamadi Fortress in the background.

and-a-half-hour drive. Take lunch beside the harbour at tiny Geroliménas before driving up the vertiginous east coast, pausing at Vátheia (p181), the most spectacular of Máni's villages. It's around an hour's drive to pretty Gýtheio (p180), where you can stop for coffee by the harbour. From here, drive for 80 minutes to Monemvasiá (p170), where you have your pick of fabulous hotels, restaurants and bars. Chrisovoulo (p173) is the favourite for fine dining.

Day 5

Wander through Monemvasiá's maze of alleys. If you're feeling energetic climb the zigzag path to the deserted upper town. There's a sweeping view of the coast to north and south. Take a quick dip at the Portillo, a tiny bathing place beneath the ramparts, then eat an alfresco lunch at To Kanoni inside the medieval castle before setting off for Mystrás (p174), a two-hour drive. Spend the afternoon exploring its Byzantine marvels, and watch the breathtaking sunset over the mountains of Taigettus. Stay overnight at the luxurious Euphoria Retreat in Mystrás (p175).

Day 6

Drive for about an hour from Mystrás through the fertile fields and vineyards of the Evrotas Valley to Ancient Tegea (p185), stopping for a quick look at the ruins of its Doric temple. Next, an hour's drive along the E65 motorway will bring you to enthralling Ancient Mycenae (p160) where you can imagine Homer's swaggering heroes in their glory. Then head 30 minutes to Náfplio (p166) to arrive in time for a late lunch, stopping en route at the Cyclopean walls of Ancient Tiryns (p186). Spend the afternoon exploring pretty Náfplio and the Palamidi fortress. The old town centre is replete with restaurants – Omorfo Tavernaki (p167) is a top pick for dinner.

Day 7

Drive one hour to Epidaurus (p168), where the best-preserved ancient stone theatre in Greece awaits. Test its perfect acoustics. For a dip and a lazy lunch, head for Palela Epidavros, a 10-minute drive away, where you'll find a small, palm-lined beach and laid-back restaurants – the perfect setting for the end of your Peloponnesian tour.

7 DAYS

in Central and Western Greece

▌ Day 1

Start your tour by exploring the evocative sacred site of Ancient Delphi *(p200)*. After a bite to eat, drive to Fterolakka, close to the summit of Mount Parnassós *(p215)*, where there are panoramic views. From here, it's a one-hour drive north downhill to the sea. Pause for a photo at the roadside burial mound of the 300 Spartans who fell at the Battle of Thermopylae *(p216)*, then drive on for a further 90 minutes to the lively harbour town of Vólos *(p204)*, where you'll find a plethora of *tsipouradika* serving fresh seafood and glasses of local firewater.

▌ Day 2

Set off to explore the Pílio *(p204)*, driving over slopes to Vyzitsa. Pause for lunch on the village square. Carry on to Milies and discover the region's history in the Folk Museum. Drive across Mount Pílio to wind your way above a turquoise sea, through Tsagaráda, and detour to Agíos Ioánnis for a dip in the water. Follow the road back over the flank of Mount Pílio to stay over-night in Portaria, where Kritsa Gastronomy Hotel *(Portraria Pelion)* serves local cuisine.

▌ Day 3

Leave the Pílio for a drive across the fields of Thessaly, the hottest part of Greece. Breeze for two hours across this burning plain to Tríkala *(p212)*, with the summits of the Pindos looming ever larger as you head west. Pause for lunch at Panelinion *(Plateía riga Feraíou)* in the bazaar area, then stroll through the old quarter to the hilltop Byzantine castle. Continuing on, the scenery becomes more dramatic as you approach the monoliths of Metéora *(p196)*. If you have time to visit only one of its six monasteries, make it the pinnacle-poised Rousánou. From here, drive to cooler Métsovo *(p210)*. Try metsovone cheese with Katogi, the local wine, at one of the tavernas before turning in for the night at Katogi Averoff hotel and winery in Métsovo.

▌ Day 4

An hour's drive brings you to Ioánnina *(p194)*. Stroll around its Ottoman fortress and visit the Byzantine Museum. Take a boat trip to the tiny island of Nisí in Lake Pamvotis for lunch in one of the cafés that

1 Agiou Nikolaou in Vólos.

2 Agios Ioánnis beach, Pílio.

3 Varlaám monastery in Metéora, seen from Trikala.

4 Houses lining Párga harbour.

5 Ancient Roman sculpture at the entrance to Eleusis.

specialize in river fish from nearby mountain streams. Then stroll around the shore and visit the Agíou Panteleímonas monastery. Dine at Fysa Roufa (p195) and stay at the fabulous Frontzou Politeia (Lofos Agias Triadas), both in Ioánnina.

Day 5

The high point of today's adventure is around 30 minutes' drive from Ioánnina. Wander around the scattered stones of Ancient Dodona (p210) and its vast ancient theatre to imagine it in its heyday, when the Oracle of Zeus rivalled the Sibyl of Delphi. Then head for the coast and Párga (p212), a 90-minute drive, for lunch and an afternoon on the beach. There are plenty of places to stay in this little resort, and tavernas line its crescent quayside.

Day 6

This morning, drive south to the riverside grotto of the Nekromanteion of Acheron (p212), believed by the ancient Greeks to be an entrance to the Underworld. Then head down the coast to explore the

foundations of the ancient city of Kassope crouched on a low hill. Stop off in charming Préveza, at the mouth of the Amvrakikos Gulf, for lunch at a taverna in its market area. In the afternoon continue south, skirting the Amvrakikos Gulf, then around coastal lagoons to Mesolongi (p216), famed for its role in the War of Independence; stop to pay your respects to the martyrs to the cause. Your journey now takes you west, along the Gulf of Corinth (p217), to Náfpaktos for dinner and an overnight stay in its Venetian harbour.

Day 7

Before leaving Náfpaktos, make for the upper citadel to enjoy a fine view across the Gulf. Drive along the coast, then through the vast expanse of olive groves to reach the great medieval monastery of Osios Loukás (p198). Marvel at its glittering mosaics and richly coloured frescoes. A two-hour drive from here brings you to Ancient Eleusis (p132) and the outskirts of Athens. Explore the scattered remains of the ancient site to wind up your epic road trip.

7 DAYS
in Northern Greece

Day 1

Start your tour in Thessaloníki *(p224)* with a stroll around the Modiano market followed by lunch at Ouzerie Lola *(p226)*. Then walk along the waterfront before visiting the Archaeological Museum. Cross over to the Byzantine Museum for a peek at its glowing icons, then walk back to the centre in the footsteps of Roman legionaries by way of the Rotónda *(p227)* and Arch of Galerius *(p226)*. Spend the evening bar-hopping while snacking on meze in Ladadika.

Day 2

A 45-minute drive west takes you to Ancient Pella *(p244)*. Admire the mosaic floors which once graced its royal villas. A further 70-minute drive brings you to Vergína *(p242)*, where finds from the Royal Tombs are the must sees. Drive west to Edessa *(p243)*, and stroll the grounds to see the Great Waterfall (Karanos) before dinner.

Day 3

Lakes and mountains are highlights of today's westward journey. The drive skirts

the shore of Lake Vegoritida on the way to Florina, 70 minutes from Edessa, where you can take a break before carrying on to Psarades, gateway to the Préspa Lakes *(p238)*. Take a boat trip for a glimpse of two lakeshore churches and Prespa's resident birds. At nearby Kastoriá *(p241)* you can dine on fresh fish from the lake and stay in the 19th-century Orologopoulos Mansion *(www.orogopoulos.gr)*.

Day 4

Drive to the small town of Siátista *(p241)* to stroll around its streets, lined with half-timbered houses before carrying on to Véroia *(p243)*, a one-hour drive. Admire 14th-century frescoes in the church of Christos, then turn east before heading south to Kassándra *(p230)*, the western-most of the three Halkidikí peninsulas. Stay overnight at Sani, where you can swim at the beach before dinner in the marina.

Day 5

Drive back across the Kassándra isthmus to surprisingly little-visited Ancient

1 The Roman Arch of Galerius in Thessaloníki.

2 Beach on the Sithonía peninsula.

3 Fresco in the Protaton church in Karyes on Mount Athos.

4 Ancient Hellenistic columns at the archaeological site of Philippi.

5 Cityscape of Kávala.

Olynthos *(p231)* to explore its foundations and admire its mosaics. Then continue around the gently curving shore of the Gulf of Kassándra to the thickly wooded Sithonía peninsula *(p231)*. Near its neck, on the east coast, you'll find Vourvourou. The perfect place for a lazy afternoon and evening, this small, low-key resort sits on a calm bay. Rent a motorboat (no licence required) for a self-drive cruise to the tiny islands that lie dotted around its lagoon.

Day 6

Set off early, heading east, to Ouranopoli, gateway to Mount Athos *(p231)* and its amazing monasteries. Without a pilgrim's permit, you can only view the fortress-like, centuries-old religious foundations scattered around the mountain's rugged shores by boat, but along the west coast many of the monasteries lie close to the shore and can be admired from the sea. Most cruises depart between 9am and 10am and last 3–4 hours, returning you to Ouranopoli in time for lunch. In the afternoon drive east along the coast, heading for Kavála *(p244)*, but just before

you reach Eastern Macedonia's biggest city and seaport take a detour inland to the remarkable archaeological remains of the ancient city of Philippi *(p244)*. Wander around its ruins before reaching Kávala, a 20-minute drive, where there are plentiful options for eating and staying overnight.

Day 7

Stroll through Kávala's old Panagia quarter and its busy market for a view of the harbour from the hilltop castle. Admire the Ottoman aqueduct before dropping into the Archaeological Museum. Then drive into the thickly forested Nestos Valley before crossing the river into Thrace, Greece's easternmost region. Head past Xánthi *(p245)*, where beech-cloaked hills give way to fields of maize, cotton and tobacco, to Ancient Maroneia *(p246)*, where a stone theatre stands among olive groves. From here, the drive to the last stop, Alexandroúpoli *(p246)*, takes less than an hour. Join locals for a stroll along the waterfront before ending your pilgrimage around Northern Greece with dinner at Nisiotika, which is right behind the port.

Changing Seasons

Thanks to its varying climate, Greece offers rich, changing landscapes throughout the year. Head for the lower slopes of Olympos in spring to see a rainbow of wildflowers, or visit in winter for a surprising side to Greece, when summits are snow-capped.

←

Beautiful vivid red poppies at the foot of Mount Olympos in spring

NATURAL BEAUTY

Monumental mountains, deep canyons carved by snow-fed rivers and wildflower meadows: Greece is a land of rugged beauty. The sheer variety of landscapes on offer is almost as impressive as the vistas themselves, so venture beyond the city limits to delight in mother nature.

TOP 4 NATIONAL PARKS

Parnassós National Park
For a taste of the wild within sight of Ancient Delphi, head to Parnassós (p215).

Mount Olympos National Park
Treeless peaks rise above thick forests around Greece's highest mountain (p240).

Northern Píndos National Park
You might glimpse a bear in mainland Greece's largest national park (p208).

Préspa Lakes
Beautiful woodland surrounds a mirror-calm expanse of water at this national park (p238).

Mighty Mountains

With mountains covering three-quarters of the land, you'll have plenty to keep you on cloud nine in Greece. Mount Olympos (p240) is particularly impressive, its highest peaks often mysteriously obscured by clouds or outbreaks of thunder. From the summit you can look west towards the misty silhouette of the Pindos (p208), the fearsome massif that looms over the northern mainland.

→

Hikers exploring the paths of the monumental Mount Olympos in the north

PICTURE PERFECT
Grand Gorge

Head out on a hike to
the Beloi Viewpoint,
above Vradéto *(p209)*
village, for the most
incredible eagle's-eye
shot of the Víkos Gorge.

Grand Canyons

Nothing is more dramatic
than the canyons that carve
their way through Greece.
The Voidomatis river flows
through the 915-m- (3,000-ft-)
deep Víkos Gorge *(p218)* amid
the most awesome land-
scapes in the north, while the
Loúsios Gorge *(p156)* provides
a more unique vista, with
medieval monasteries
clinging to wooded cliffs.

↑ Clouds forming over
the thickly forested
Víkos Gorge

Limpid Lakes

Greece's coastline may hog the headlines,
but enchanting lakes offer some of its most
spectacular scenery. Hundreds of rare, shy
pelicans paddle and nest on the still green
waters of the Préspa Lakes *(p238)*, a vast
expanse of water and reedbeds. At Nisí
(p194), an islet in Lake Pamvotis, you can
sample freshwater fish from the lake in a
row of tempting waterside restaurants.

←
Clouds reflecting on the peaceful,
turquoise Préspa Lakes

Wild Wetlands

Around mainland shores,
little-visited wetland regions
await explorers. Wildlife
enthusiasts should not miss
the wonderful saltpans
around Mesolóngi *(p216)*,
which attract egrets, herons
and other wading birds. If
you're looking to catch a
glimpse of glossy ibis, storks
and purple herons, head to
northern river mouths like
the Axiós and Evros deltas.

→
Elegant pink flamingos
in the waters of the
Evros Delta

Browse a Market

Greece's city food markets are a world unto themselves. In the heart of Athens, the Central Market is famed for its greengrocers' section, its stalls piled high with vibrant fruit and vegetables. In Thessaloníki's Modiano market, look out for eels and trout from northern rivers and barrels overflowing with pungent herbs and spices.

←

Choosing from an array of colourful fruit at the Central Market in Athens

FLAVOURFUL FOOD

Thanks to a new generation of chefs, Greece is going through a culinary renaissance, with a resurgent pride in deep-rooted culinary traditions. Whether browsing for produce, sampling Greek dishes or even donning the chef's hat, foodies will have a plethora of experiences to indulge in.

TOP 5 TYPICAL GREEK DISHES

Kleftiko
Slow-cooked chunks of lamb or goat.

Mayieritsa
Hearty soup made with sheep offal, eggs, lemon, rice and herbs.

Keftedes
Fried balls of minced meat flavoured with mint and parsley.

Papoutsakia
Dish of aubergines filled with tomatoes, onions and herbs.

Stifado
A hearty stew made with rabbit or veal.

Tasting Plate

There's nothing more Greek than a meze platter – multiple delicacies served all at once. Common dishes include *melitzánosalata* (aubergine salad), *tyrokafteri* (cheese mash), and *fáva* (yellow split pea purée). Feeling more adventurous? Try *pastourma* (dried spiced beef) or *sujuk* (spicy sausage).

→

An array of typical, delicious meze

Indulge Yourself

Greeks love their traditional sweetmeats. Every city neighbourhood and village has its own *zacharoplasteio* (patisserie) full of cakes and pastries like *baklava* and *kataifi*, while the village *galaktopoleio* (milk shop) brims with creamy desserts like *ryzogalo* (rice pudding).

→

Honey-drenched *baklava* made of layers of filo

Cook Up a Storm

Want to re-create some of your favourite Greek dishes? In Athens, The Culinary Centre *(www.mathimatamageirikis.gr)* offers professional-level tutoring from top chefs. For an authentic, traditional course, head to Karaiskos Farm *(www.karaiskosfarm.gr)* just outside Portaria to learn about Pilion produce, or try out Mama's Flavours *(www.mamasflavours.gr)*, an eco-farm near Kalamata, to unlock the secrets behind dishes from Messenia.

←

Rolling vine leaves filled with rice, a traditional Mediterranean dish

Walk and Taste

Savour the flavours of Greece with a city food tour. Athens Walking Tours *(www.athens walkingtours.gr)* lead you off the beaten track to discover street food in the Psyrri neighbourhood, while Eat and Walk *(www.eatandwalk. gr)* offers tasty walks around Thessaloníki's market area.

→

Koulouri (bread rings) for sale at a kiosk in the centre of Athens

Golden Age

Under Pericles Athens enjoyed its greatest period of building. The marble columns of the Parthenon, Erechteion and Temple of Nike *(p94)* are a token of the city's power and glory during this golden age, while the ruins at Delphi *(p200)* are reminders of the Classical world's greatest sacred site. The acoustics of the theatre at Epidaurus *(p168)* are still perfect after almost 2,500 years.

→

The remarkably well-preserved ancient theatre at Epidaurus

UNEARTHING THE PAST

Classical, Roman, Byzantine and Ottoman relics lie in wait throughout Greece. Ramparts surround Mycenaean palaces and medieval strongholds glower over mountain passes. From the splendours of Periclean Athens to the Venetian castles of the Peloponnese, a journey into the deepest past awaits.

TOP 4 HISTORY MUSEUMS

National Museum
Superb museum of ancient artifacts *(p74)*.

Acropolis Museum
The glories of Periclean Athens *(p100)*.

Museum of Byzantine Culture
The Byzantine Empire portrayed from its dawn to its downfall *(p224)*.

Thessaloníki Archaeological Museum
Golden treasures from Macedonian tombs *(p226)*.

Tzistarákis mosque in Monastiráki square in the heart of Athens ↑

Triumphant Rome

Roman Imperial ruins clutter the heart of Athens. The Roman Agora *(p110)*, Temple of Olympian Zeus and Hadrian's Arch *(p118)* dominate the historic Pláka. The Odeon of Herodes Atticus *(p94)*, beneath the Acropolis, is still used for outdoor concerts. Travel a little further to explore Ancient Corinth *(p148)*, the greatest Roman city in Greece.

→

Hadrian's Arch in Athens, marking the entrance to the Roman city

Thousand-Year Byzantine Empire

Splendid churches and stern fortresses tell of the advent of Christianity and the long reign of the Byzantine Empire. Cruise around Mount Athos *(p232)* to see its great monasteries from the water, or visit the Metéora *(p196)* for a closer look at monastic life. The monastery churches of Daphni *(p128)* and Osios Loukás *(p198)* have wonderful mosaics and frescoes.

←

The skete of Agia Anna on holy Mount Athos, part of the Great Lavra monastery

Mighty Macedon

Voyage across northern Greece to follow the meteoric rise and fall of the kingdom of Macedon, from the royal tombs of Alexander the Great's ancestors at Vergína *(p242)* to the splendid mosaics of Pella and the Hellenistic, Roman and Byzantine ruins at Philippi *(p242)*.

Ottoman Era and the Eyes of Venice

Greece is full of vestiges of the Ottoman era, from mosques in Athens to Ioánnina's fortress *(p194)* and Thessaloníki's Bedestan *(p224)*. Dotted around the coasts are sea-castles built by the Venetians to guard the routes to their Aegean empire, such as those at Koróni *(p188)* and Methóni *(p189)*.

↑ Ruins of ancient Hellenistic columns at the site of Philippi in northern Greece

GODS, GODDESSES AND HEROES

The Greek myths that tell the stories of the gods, goddesses and heroes date back to the Bronze Age when they were told aloud by poets. They were first written down in the early 6th century BC and have lived on in Western literature. Myths were closely bound up with Greek religion and gave meaning to the unpredictable workings of the natural world. They tell the story of the creation and the "golden age" of gods and mortals, as well as the age of semi-mythical heroes, such as Theseus and Herakles, whose exploits were an inspiration to ordinary men and women. The gods and goddesses were affected by human desires and failings and were part of a divine family presided over by Zeus. He had many offspring, both legitimate and illegitimate, each with a mythical role.

The tale of Hades and Persephone is a story of love and abduction in Greek mythology. Hades, god of the Underworld, fell in love with Persephone, the daughter of Demeter, goddess of the harvest. With the help of his brother Zeus, Hades concocted a plan to abduct Persephone by causing the ground to split beneath her. She fell through the crack and Hades caught her and took her to the Underworld where he made her his wife. Demeter begged Hades to allow Persephone to come back to the world of the living. Hades consented to allow Persephone to return to her mother and live on earth for only eight months each year. The myth is associated with the coming of spring and winter. When Persephone returns to the earth it is spring and when she descends to Hades it is winter. Major festivals were held commemorating Hades and Persephone in ancient Greece, the most famous being the Eleusinian Mysteries *(p133)*.

↑ Persephone returning temporarily from Hades to earth, greeted by her mother Demeter

Zeus

The god of the sky and thunder and the king of all other gods, Zeus ruled over them and all mortals from Mount Olympos.

Hera

Sister and wife of Zeus, Hera was the goddess of marriage, family and childbirth and was famous for her jealousy.

Poseidon

The god of the sea was Zeus's brother – and sometimes his greatest rival. He married the sea-goddess Amphitrite. The trident is his symbol of power.

Artemis

The virgin goddess of the hunt was sister of Apollo. She can be identified by her bow and arrows, hounds and group of nymphs. She was the goddess of childbirth.

THE LABOURS OF HERAKLES

Herakles (Hercules to the Romans) was the greatest of the Greek heroes, and the son of Zeus and Alkmene, a mortal woman. With superhuman strength, he achieved success, and immortality, against seemingly impossible odds in the "Twelve Labours" set by Eurystheus, King of Tiryns.

For his first task, he killed the Nemean lion, and wore its hide ever after. Killing the Lernaean hydra was the second labour of Herakles. The many heads of this venomous monster, raised by Hera, grew back as soon as they were chopped off. As in all his tasks, Herakles was helped by Athena. The huge boar that ravaged Mount Erymanthos was captured next. Herakles brought it back alive to King Eurystheus who was so terrified that he hid in a storage jar. Destroying the Stymfalian birds was the sixth labour. Herakles rid Lake Stymfalía of these man-eating birds, which had brass beaks, by stoning them with a sling, having first frightened them off with a pair of bronze castanets. The seventh labour was to capture the Cretan Bull, father of the minotaur.

1 Herakles holds his baby son Telephos in this marble sculpture.

2 The first labour of Herakles is depicted on this vase - Herakles kills the Nemean lion to wear its skin.

3 Herakles is shown wrestling the wild Cretan Bull, his seventh task, in this relief.

Helios

The offspring of the titans Hyperion and Theia, the sun god Helios drove his four-horse chariot (the sun) daily across the sky.

Apollo

Son of Zeus and brother of Artemis, Apollo was god of healing, plague and music. He was also famous for his dazzling beauty.

Aphrodite

The temperamental goddess of love was born from the sea and had dozens of affairs.

Hermes

God of trade, thieves, travellers, and athletes, Hermes was also a guide to the Underworld and messenger of the gods.

The Athens Riviera

Sparklingly clear blue water and long stretches of sand are not far from the city centre. Those wishing to escape the bustle of Athens can relax on loungers, enjoy numerous watersports and sip a coffee at cafés lining the Athens Riviera, also known as the Attic Coast *(p139)*. The fun starts at Glyfáda, the closest beach to central Athens, while more upmarket beaches such as Kavouri and Astir can be found in the smart suburb of Vouliagméni.

←

Kavouri beach and its clear waters with the bustling city behind

ON THE COAST

With its long summer days, Greece is still the land of the sun god Helios, and modern sun worshippers will find plenty to thank him for on long sandy strands, secret coves and lively beaches next to big cities and around the immense coasts of mainland Greece.

Tropical Pílio

With lush green slopes rising from a turquoise sea, the seaside peak of Pílio looks truly tropical. Around its coasts you'll find secret white-pebble coves and sandy strands like Papá Neró and Pláka near the pleasantly low-key resort of Agios Ioánnis.

Azure waters hitting boulders and lush vegetation at the serene Pláka beach ↓

Revel in Relaxation

Miles of blessedly undeveloped sandy beaches stretch along the west coast of the Peloponnese, where it's easy to escape the crowds. For a truly relaxing experience, head to the shores of the Messinian Gulf between Kalamáta and Koróni to find a scattering of small, budget-friendly beach resort areas.

↑ The peaceful fishing village and tiny harbour on the coast of Koróni

Fun in the Sun

The beaches of Halkidikí's Kassándra peninsula are among Greece's finest, with seemingly endless white sands and sparkling blue seas. Head to Sani (www.sani-resort.com) to discover a sophisticated resort complex and marina with a splendid choice of water-sports and land-based activities.

←

Relaxing on the sand and swimming in the warm waters at a beach in the Halkidikí region

Thessaloníki's Seaside

Beautiful beaches are within easy reach of Greece's bustling second city. For an authentically Greek day at the seaside, join the locals at Perea, on the outskirts of Thessaloníki (p224), for a dip in the sea and a fish dinner along its esplanade.

↑ Walking along the jetty in Perea as the sun sets over the sea

Get Outside

Child-friendly outdoor spaces are few and far between in the mainland cities, but it's worth seeking out the gems that do exist. In the Athens neighbourhood of Kifisiá you'll find a playground decked out with slides, ropes and a play train at leafy Kefalari Park. After something a bit different? Let the kids run free and clamber over tiers of stone seats at ancient open-air theatres like those at Delphi *(p200)* and Olympia *(p152)*.

←

Exploring the vast ancient ruins at the Delphi archaeological site

FAMILY ADVENTURES

Greece offers adventurous families much more than just sun, sea and sand. Keep the kids entertained with explorations into secret grottoes and mystical caves, scenic train journeys of a lifetime and family-friendly ways to unearth and learn about Greece's ancient history.

GO ISLAND HOPPING

Island hopping makes for a fun and cultured day out for parents and kids alike. Take youngsters on a short boat trip that won't test their patience from Ioánnina *(p194)* to Nisí, in calm Lake Pamvotis. For a longer day trip, hop on a ferry or hydrofoil from Piraeus *(p130)* to Aegina or Hydra in the Argo-Saronic Gulf.

Hit the Beach

Most beaches on the mainland have gentle sands and calm waters where youngsters can safely play and paddle. Athens is full of family-friendly beaches, so hop on a tram to Glyfáda or Voula for cafés, changing rooms and water sports. On the Kassándra peninsula, the Sani complex *(www.sani-resort.com)* offers tennis coaching and a soccer youth academy, while the Costa Navarino resort *(www.costanavarion.com)* on the Ionian coast even has its own aquapark for the kids.

→

Families enjoying the seafront at a beach just outside Athens

All Aboard!
Take the kids on an adventure through Greece with a train ride. The little steam train that puffs its way from Ano Lechonia outside Vólos through the forests of Pílio to Milies makes a superb day out, while the Kalávryta-Diakoftó Railway (p182) inspires awe from sea level into the Peloponnese mountains. The Lycabettus funicular in Athens is a great city choice.

Riding through tracks dug into rocks on the Kalávryta-Diakoftó Railway

> 💬 INSIDER TIP
> **Family Folklore**
>
> For a day out with a difference, take the family to the captivating Spathario Museum of Shadow Theatre (www. karagiozismuseum.gr) in Athens's Kifisiá neighbourhood. Kids will enjoy the antics of the clownish Karagiozis character from folklore.

Discover the Past
With such a rich history, Greece is the perfect place for young time travellers to discover the history and mystery of the ancient world. Check out Kids Love Greece (www.kidslovegreece.com) and choose from a range of family adventures around the Acropolis and other Athens landmarks, including a pause at the parliament to see the *evzones* palace guards with their ceremonial and peculiar march.

→

Posing for a photograph next to a guard in front of the Athens parliament building

Go Underground
Below ground, Greece offers up otherworldly, enchanting landscapes. Stalactites drip from the roof above the underground lake at Pyrgos Dirou, while vibrant lights illuminate the Koutoúki Cave (p140) on Mount Ymittós and the vast labyrinth of the Pérama Caves (p195).

←

Walking through the caves of Pyrgos Dirou

RAISE A GLASS

Innovation meets tradition when it comes to alcohol here. Whether you're raising a glass in a traditional *ouzerí*, an Athenian cocktail bar or a winery where 21st-century skills meet cultivated varieties, say *Yamas* and enjoy!

New Wave Wines

Greek wines are much more varied and stylish than they used to be, with vintners across Greece rediscovering varietals such as Xinomavro, Sideritis, Aghiorgitiko and Atheri. Sample reds and rosés at Domaine Papagiannakos *(www.papagiannakos.com)* in the sunburnt plain of Attica, or head to the Boutari winery *(www.boutari.gr)* in the northern Naoussa region, famed for full-bodied reds. If you like sweet pudding wines, make a pilgrimage to Greece's oldest winery, Achaia Clauss *(www.achaiac lauss.gr)* near Patras, to sample sticky Mavrodaphne.

$\longrightarrow$

Tempting glasses of vivid red wine accompanied by strawberries

Raise Your Spirits

No visit to Greece is complete without washing down savoury morsels of cheese or olives with spirits distilled from the grape residue of wine-making. Ouzo, Greece's anise-flavoured signature spirit, is best served with a splash of water and a couple of ice cubes. To be really on trend, though, order a shot of Tsipouro. Less sticky-sweet than ouzo, it's traditionally unaged, but more distillers now mature it in oak casks for a richer taste.

← A glass of ouzo from the bottle (*inset*) served with a handful of appetizers

WINE AND PINE

The resin of the Aleppo pine, originally added as a preservative, gives Greece's best-known wine its very distinctive bouquet. Retsína may be less popular now than it was a generation ago – the vineyards of Attica, retsína's heartland, have shrunk by half since their 1960s heyday – but large brands such as Michali Georgiadi, Kourtakis and Malamatina still make retsína on an industrial scale. Connoisseurs say the best comes from the Mesogeia wine region.

💬 INSIDER TIP
Mix Up Your Retsína

Retsína too strong-flavoured for your taste? Do what some Greeks do and mix it with lemonade or cola.

Chic Cocktails

It's taken a while for urban Greeks to take 21st-century cocktail culture to their hearts, but you'll now find hip cocktail bars all over the cities. Watch mixologists create drinks that combine Greek spirits and fruit liqueurs with more exotic influences at MoMix Bar *(p112)*, or enjoy a relaxing tipple at 360 Cocktail Bar *(p112)* with an impressive view. You can even learn the art yourself at The Clumsies *(www.theclumsies.gr)* in Psyrri.

↑ Admiring the splendid view of the Acropolis in Athens with a fruity cocktail

Sunset Shows

Archaeological sites and rugged landscapes are even more magical against the setting sun. Watch nature's best show over the Aegean Sea from the ancient Temple of Poseidon *(p138)* at Sounion, or for something more civilized, grab a table on Thessaloníki's waterfront to see the sun set over distant Mount Olympos. The Ionian Sea is a canvas for even vaster panoramas from west coast spots like Párga.

→

Relaxing after watching the sunset from the Temple of Poseidon, and *(inset)* the view from Sounion

AFTER DARK

Life in Greece continues at full speed after dark, particularly in the hot summer months. Whether you're exploring the streetwise buzz of Thessaloníki, partying at exclusive beach clubs or savouring sophisticated performances at ancient theatres, you'll find plenty to entertain you.

GREAT VIEW
City Lights

For a great after-dark view of Athens, ride the funicular to the top of Lykavittós Hill. Once the sun goes down, the city turns into an endless sea of lights – a perfect setting for the superb floodlit columns of the Acropolis.

For One Night Only

The night of the August full moon is a special occasion at many ancient ruins and medieval castles in Athens and around mainland Greece. Iconic sites like the Acropolis, the Roman Agora at Delphi, Ancient Corinth and the Palamidi Fortress at Náfplio stay open until midnight, with free admission and jazz and classical music performances to enjoy.

←

The Acropolis lit up by floodlights at night

↑ Dancing near decks blasting music in a bustling club in Athens

Athenian Nights

No matter the time of year, Greece is a hive of nightclubs. Summer evenings see the Athenian beach suburbs of Glyfádha and Vouliagméni hot up, with top DJs playing the latest tunes at open-air clubs like Island *(www.islandclub restaurant.gr)* and Bolivar *(www.bolivar.gr)*. When summer ends, the party scene moves back to buzzy city-centre neighbourhoods.

DRINK

Rooftop bars are in abundance in Athens, and all promise stunning views to enjoy with superb drinks. Head to one of the following bars for an excellent night out.

Couleur Locale
🏠 Normanou 3
🌐 couleurlocale athens.com

GB Roof Garden
🏠 Vasileos Georgiou A 1
🌐 gbroofgarden.gr

Air Lounge
🏠 Sofokleous 26
🌐 freshhotel.gr

Hop To It

In Greece, entertainment means late-night dining in tavernas, followed by bar-hopping until dawn. Thessaloníki's waterfront is where this culture is at its best: start the evening with a stroll along Leoforos Nikis, then head for Ladadika, a former warehouse district filled with bars that start to rock late and continue into the small hours.

↑ Congregating and socializing with food and drinks at the Ladadika area in lively Thessaloníki

▷ Wonderful Walks

Greece is a paradise for walkers, particularly in the spring, when the countryside is at its greenest and the wildflowers are in bloom. The best location is the Víkos Gorge *(p218)*, and various companies offer guided and self-guided tours in and around the gorge. Mount Olympos *(p240)* is another one to tick off the bucket list, with a 160-km (100-mile) web of tough and easy-going trails to explore.

◁ On the Water

The turquoise waters along Greece's coastline beckon watersports lovers, with summer beach clubs offering an array of facilities. Top places for windsurfing include Várkiza on the Athens coast, Psakoudia in Halkidikí and Gialova in Messinía. Many companies also offer sea kayaking and sailing in the sheltered waters off the Kassándra and Sithonía peninsulas.

THE GREAT OUTDOORS

Beyond the urban buzz of Athens, a world of adventures awaits. Plunge into exhilarating whitewater, climb imposing cliffs while breathing in fresh mountain air or trek on centuries-old trails in Greece's vast playground.

▽ Where Eagles Dare

For an adrenaline rush like no other, explore Greece from above. Soar over Ancient Delphi for a bird's eye view of the ruins, the mountains behind and the olive-covered slopes below, stretching to the glittering Gulf of Corinth, with Paragliding Fun *(www.paraglidingfun. gr)*, which offers tandem flights with a pilot for novices as well as lessons for beginners.

△ Scale New Heights

Those with a head for heights are in for a serious treat in Greece. Head to Mount Olympos *(p240)* for a range of rock faces with an ascent that requires few mountaineering skills and an impeccable view as a reward. If you're looking for some technical challenges, though, you'll find them on almost 70 routes on the mountain's upper faces.

▷ Two Wheels

Whether you're looking for an adrenaline-pumping off-road adventure, a gentle morning ride beside the sea or a long-distance trip through green forests and mountain peaks, Greece offers cycling trails to suit all levels. Bikes can be rented with ease around the mainland; alternatively, take a bike tour – Cycle Greece *(www.cyclegreece.com)* offers excellent half-day and one-day tours in and around Athens as well as longer guided trips in the Peloponnese.

△ Run the Rapids

Thanks to winter rains feeding rivers in the Peloponnese and the northern and central mainland, Greece is a top destination for whitewater rafting. For the most thrilling trip, check out the Voidomatis, which flows through the Víkos Gorge, the Loúsios in the Peloponnese and other waterways.

Hot Summer Nights

Whether it's a mournful classical cello or a funky jazz concert, ancient open-air theatres are made for music. Marvel at the fine acoustics of the Herodes Atticus *(p97)* and the Epidaurus *(p168)* theatres during the Athens-Epidaurus Festival from June to early September, where fabulous sunsets accompany evening folk music and jazz concerts. Or head to Halkidikí for the multicultural Sáni Festival in July *(p55)*, a more modern celebration of jazz, Latin, Greek and world music.

$\longrightarrow$

The Greek National Opera rehearsing at the superb Herodes Atticus Theatre

MUSIC AND DANCE

Greeks love to dance to traditional rhythms and get *kefi* ("in the party mood"). Join them in dives where rebellious *rembetiko* provides a rousing soundtrack, watch a spectacular re-creation of folk dance and enjoy the magic of an evening of classical music under the stars in an ancient theatre.

Whirling Rhythms

Traditional Greek dances are not just reserved for festivals and Easter celebrations: deep-rooted folk dancing traditions live on in the mainland. Let yourself be hypnotized by elaborate costumes and classic rhythms at the Dóra Strátou Dance Theatre *(www.grdance.org)* on Filopáppou Hill in Athens, where a 75-strong company has been keeping Greek folk music and dance alive since 1953. You can catch a performance nightly in summer.

$\longleftarrow$

Outdoor performance of traditional Greek folk dancing in Athens

MUSICAL INSTRUMENTS

Bouzouki
The long-necked, six-stringed *bouzouki* is at the heart of traditional music ensembles.

Laouto
The *laouto* resembles the western European lute and is found all over mainland Greece.

Klarino
The melodious *klarino* or Greek clarinet is the main wind instrument in most folk groups.

Gaida
Played solo or with percussion accompaniment, the Greek version of the bagpipes is popular in the north.

Santouri
The *santouri* or hammer dulcimer is an ancient ancestor of the piano and is a key element of many folk music groups.

Country and Eastern

Wailing *rembetiko* may not sound much like country and western or the blues, but its lyrics, imported to Central Greece by refugees from the Greek diaspora in the 1920s, evoke the same themes of hard luck and troubled times. *Rembetiko* is a fundamental part of Greek culture and can be heard in bars, cafés taverns and concert halls throughout Greece.

A band playing *rembetiko* in a café ↓

Classical Music

The music scene in Greece isn't all about age-old traditions and rural roots. Lovers of classical music and ballet will find both in a majestic setting amid superlative acoustics at the Mégaron Mousikís Concert Hall *(www.megaron.gr)*, Athens's main venue for highbrow musical performances since 1991.

←

Israel Philharmonic Orchestra performing in the Mégaron Mousikís Concert Hall

Gods and Heroes

Immerse yourself in the artistic glories of ancient Greece at temples where colossal images of gods and goddesses once stood. The Parthenon *(p98)* is the big one, but Ancient Corinth *(p148)* and Olympia *(p152)* are also worth journeying to. Find statuary from these sites at the National Archaeological Museum *(p74)* in Athens and at Thessaloníki *(p226)*.

←

Roman-era statues at the National Archaeological Museum in Athens

ART LOVERS

Greece's deep artistic heritage spans millennia, but it's not all about marble friezes of Olympian deities, painted pottery and bronze statues. With self-taught painters, village embroiderers and 21st-century street artists all playing their part, Greece's art scene has treasures for every taste.

By the People, For the People

Impressive textiles housed at folk art museums across Greece testify to the immense skill of Greek weavers and embroiderers. Discover these charming works of art in Athens, Náfplio, Pílio and Thessaloníki, where collections include elaborate embroidery work and lively paintings of village festivities, battle scenes, ships and seascapes.

→

Traditional costumes on display at the Benáki Museum, Athens

Saints and Sinners

Early Christian mosaics and frescoes depicting Old Testament scenes abound in monastery churches. However, nothing beats watching icon-painters applying age-old skills in studios around Plateía Mitropóleos (p114) – you can even commission an image of your chosen saint.

St Charalambos fresco in the Monastery of Agios Stefanos, Metéora ↓

TOP 4 IMPRESSIVE ART GALLERIES

National Gallery of Art, Athens
A large number of works by Greek and other European artists (p85).

Ghikas Gallery, Athens
Twentieth-century art in the home of one of Greece's greatest painters (p87).

Peloponnesian Folklore Foundation, Náfplio
Textiles and regional costumes displayed across two floors (p172).

Macedonian Museum of Contemporary Art, Thessaloníki
Avant-garde modern and contemporary art (www.momus.gr).

Modern Masters

Greek art thoroughly evolved in the 19th and 20th centuries following Independence, which led the way for more secular works. Painters that helped to shape this period have pride of place at the National Gallery of Art (p85) in Athens. Be sure to seek out quirky paintings by the eccentric self-taught mural painter Theophilos Hatzimihail.

←

Panais Koutalianos by Theophilos Hatzimihail, inspired by folk culture in Greece

On the Street

Impressive street art has an increasing presence in the Greek capital. You'll find an ever-changing portfolio of huge, vivid murals by hip young artists covering the walls of buildings in neighbourhoods like Psyrri and Gazi. Or opt for a tour with Alternative Athens (www. alternativeathens.com).

→

Psychedelic graffiti in Athens's Psirri neighbourhood

GREEK WRITERS AND PHILOSOPHERS

The literature of Greece began with long epic poems, accounts of war and adventure, which established the relationship of the ancient Greeks to their gods. The tragedy and comedy, history and philosophical dialogues of the 5th and 4th centuries BC became the basis of Western literary culture. Much of our knowledge of the Greek world is derived from Greek literature.

EPIC POETRY

As far back as the 2nd millennium BC, poets were reciting the stories of the Greek heroes and gods. Passed on from generation to generation, these poems, called *rhapsodes*, were never written down but were embellished by successive poets. The oral tradition culminated in the *Iliad* and *Odyssey (p164)*, composed around 700 BC. Both works are ascribed to the poet Homer, of whose life nothing reliable is known. Hesiod, whose most famous poems include

the *Theogony*, a history of the gods, and the *Works and Days*, on how to live an honest life, also lived around 700 BC.

PASSIONATE POETRY

For private occasions, and to entertain guests at the cultivated drinking parties known as *symposia*, shorter poetic forms were developed. These poems were often full of passion, whether love or hatred, and could be personal or, often, highly political. Much of this poetry, by writers such as Archilochus, Alcaeus, Alcman, Hipponax and Sappho, survives only in quotations by later writers or on scraps of papyrus from libraries in Hellenistic and Roman Egypt. Since

←

Aristotle (384–322 BC), a student of Plato and teacher of Alexander the Great

The School of Athens ↑ showing leading Greek philosophers by Raphael

Herodotus's account of the great war between Greece and Persia (490–479 BC). Herodotus attempted to record objectively what people said about the past. In his account of the long years of the Peloponnesian War between Athens and Sparta (431–404 BC), Thucydides concentrated on the political history, and his aim was to work out the "truth" that lay behind the events of the war.

↑ Statue of Plato (428–348 BC), the pupil of Socrates, in front of the Athens Academy

symposia were an almost exclusively male domain, there is a strong element of misogyny in much of this poetry. In contrast, the fragments of poems by the author Sappho are exceptional for showing a woman competing in a literary area in the male-dominated society of ancient Greece, and for describing with intensity her passions for other women.

HISTORY
Until the 5th century BC, little Greek literature was composed in prose – even early philosophy was in verse. In the latter part of the 5th century, a new tradition of lengthy prose histories was established with

ORATORY
Public debate was basic to Greek political life. From the late 5th century BC some orators, such as Lysias and Demosthenes, began to publish their speeches. These texts give insights into Athenian politics and private life. The verbal attacks on Philip of Macedon by Demosthenes became models for Roman politicians seeking to defeat their opponents.

DRAMA
Almost all the surviving tragedies come from the hands of the three great 5th-century BC Athenians: Aeschylus, Sophokles and Euripides. The latter two playwrights had an interest in individual psychology. While 5th-century comedy is full of dirty jokes and direct references to contemporary life, the comedy developed in the 4th century BC is essentially situation comedy employing character types.

GREEK PHILOSOPHERS
The Athenian Socrates was recognized in the late 5th century BC as a moral arbiter. He wrote nothing himself but we know of his views through the "Socratic dialogues", written by his pupil, Plato, examining the concepts of justice, courage and virtue. Plato set up his academy in the suburbs of Athens. His pupil, Aristotle, founded the Lyceum, to teach subjects from biology to ethics, and helped to turn Athens into one of the first university cities. In 1508–11, Raphael painted the vision of Athens shown left in the Vatican.

A YEAR IN
GREECE

JANUARY

Agios Vasileios (1 Jan). New Year's Day gifts and greetings of "Kali Chronia" are exchanged.

△ **Theofania** (6 Jan). Youths plunge into harbours, lakes and rivers to recover crosses thrown into the water by priests at an Epiphany ceremony.

FEBRUARY

Ypapanti (2 Feb). Candlemas is celebrated with religious processions and Orthodox services at churches throughout Greece.

△ **Karnavali** (3rd Sun before Lent). Three weeks of pre-Lenten celebrations begin all over the country.

MAY

△ **Protomagia** (1 May). Greeks adorn homes and vehicles with wreaths of poppies and garlic to ward off evil spirits; also proclaimed Labour Day.

Analipsi (40 days after Easter). Ascension is celebrated across Greece, marked by some northern villages with fire-walking ceremonies.

JUNE

Athens Pride (1st week in Jun). Social, cultural and political events culminating in a flamboyant parade through the heart of the city.

△ **Athens Festival** (mid-Jun–early-Sep). Performances take place across the city for a cultural festival of music, drama and ballet.

SEPTEMBER

Drama International Film Festival (mid-Sep). Drama, in northern Greece, hosts this festival for aficionados of short film.

△ **Aeschylia** (Aug–mid-Sep). Works by Aeschylus and other Classical playwrights are performed at this festival of ancient drama, held at Eleusis.

OCTOBER

△ **Agios Dimitrios** (26 Oct). Thessaloníki celebrates its patron saint and the city's reconquest by Greece in 1912 with a parade and an elaborate mass in Greece's largest church.

Ochi Day (28 Oct). Military parades throughout towns and cities commemorate Greece's entry into World War II.

MARCH

Apokries *(1st Sun before Lent).* Pátra's carnival season climaxes with lively parades.

△ **Independence Day/Evangelismos** *(25 Mar).* Military parades celebrate the start of the War of Independence, proclaimed in 1821.

APRIL

△ **Megali Evdomada** *(varies, mid-Apr).* Holy Week, Greece's most important religious festival, peaks at midnight on Easter Saturday with candlelit parades and fireworks. Easter Sunday is a day of feasting.

Agios Georgios *(23 Apr).* St George, patron saint of shepherds, is celebrated with dancing, feasting and parades throughout Greece, especially at Arachova.

JULY

Sani Festival *(Jul–Aug).* World-class talents meet in Chalkidiki for an all-summer music fest.

Olympus Festival *(Jul–Aug).* A huge cultural festival held in the shadow of Mount Olympus.

△ **Kalamata International Dance Festival** *(mid–late Jul).* Contemporary choreographers from all over the world perform in Kalamáta.

AUGUST

Epirotika Festival *(mid-Aug).* Performances of music, dance and drama take place in and around the lakeside citadel at Ioánnina.

△ **Koimisis tis Theotokou** *(15 Aug).* Athenians and other urbanites return to their ancestral villages for the feast of the Dormition of the Virgin, celebrated with all-night *panegyria* that feature traditional music, dancing and communal feasting.

NOVEMBER

Athens Marathon *(mid-Nov).* Runners race the city's gruelling course, from the ancient battlefield to the Olympic Stadium.

△ **Thessaloníki International Film Festival** *(early–mid-Nov).* The city hosts one of Europe's main cinematic events, with workshops, lectures and screenings of both new and classic films.

DECEMBER

Agios Nikolaos *(6 Dec).* St Nicholas, patron saint of seafarers and travellers, is celebrated in churches at harbour communities around the coasts of mainland Greece.

△ **Christougenna** *(25 Dec).* Christmas is an important religious holiday in Greece, although less significant than Easter.

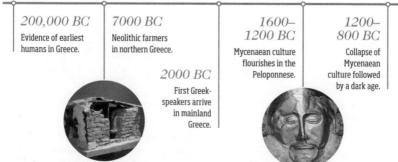

A BRIEF
HISTORY

Home to Europe's first civilizations and its oldest living language; birthplace of philosophy, drama and democracy, Greece has seen the rise and fall of empires over millennia. From its earliest days, the country's history is bound up with an indomitable struggle for independence and ancient freedoms.

From Stone Age to Bronze Age

Early humans roamed Greece 200,000 or more years ago, and there are traces of Neolithic farming on the northern mainland from as far back as 7000 BC. Bronze-wielding Greek-speakers arrived around 2000 BC and a culture evolved around fortified palaces at Mycenae, Tiryns and Pylos. Their civilization collapsed about 1200 BC and a centuries-long "dark age" followed. By the end of this period, in around 800 BC, city-states had appeared, and Greek adventurers subsequently spread their culture to colonies around the shores of the Mediterranean and the Black Sea.

1 Map of ancient Greece, first published in 1570.

2 A depiction of Darius I, King of Persia.

3 Phoenician sailors building a pontoon bridge to aid a Persian invasion.

4 Titus Quinctius Flamininus, a Roman leader born c 229 BC.

Timeline of events

200,000 BC
Evidence of earliest humans in Greece.

7000 BC
Neolithic farmers in northern Greece.

2000 BC
First Greek-speakers arrive in mainland Greece.

1600–1200 BC
Mycenaean culture flourishes in the Peloponnese.

1200–800 BC
Collapse of Mycenaean culture followed by a dark age.

DARIVS.

Classical Greece and the Great Wars

The Classical period was a golden age, when Athens and other city-states fostered great thinkers and artists, and created the world's first democracies. However, it was also an era of devious politics, warfare and bloodshed. Cities flourished in southern Greece and the islands, while much of the northern mainland remained a realm of bandits. Persians threatened invasion from 490 BC, but in 479 BC the Greek cities allied to defeat their army at Plataea, near Thebes. This victory was followed by a decades-long struggle known as the Peloponnesian War as Athens, Sparta and Thebes grappled for power, only to be ultimately defeated by Philip II of Macedon in 338 BC, who became ruler of Greece.

Hellenistic Hegemony

Philip II's son Alexander the Great went on to conquer Persia and create an empire that stretched from Egypt to India. After his death in 323 BC, his generals divided the empire among themselves, creating a Hellenistic realm that spread Greek language and culture across the ancient world and lasted until the Roman conquest of Greece.

DEMOCRACY

Athenian democracy was not truly democratic. Only property-owning, free men born in the city could vote. Women, non-natives, and enslaved people were excluded, so only a tiny fraction of the population might take part in the political life of the city. Still, Athens was more free than its great rival Sparta, where a dual monarchy and a tiny warrior elite ruled with an iron fist.

800 BC
Beginning of city-state era.

776 BC
First Olympic Games held in Olympia.

490 BC
Athens defeats Persians at Marathon.

431–404 BC
Peloponnesian War between Athens and Sparta.

480 BC
Second Persian invasion delayed by Spartans at Thermopylae. Persian fleet destroyed at Salamis.

Enter the Romans

After the Romans gained final control of Greece with the sack of Corinth in 146 BC, Greece became the Roman Empire's cultural hub. Corinth was gloriously rebuilt under Julius Caesar, and become a great provincial capital. Sacred sites such as Delphi and Dodona drew Roman tourists, and trade flourished.

The Glory of Byzantium

In AD 323 Emperor Constantine moved the imperial capital to the city of Byzantium, renaming it Constantinople. A recent convert, he also made Christianity the official state religion. Constantine's successors built great churches and monasteries, but they also extinguished the last flickers of ancient Greek culture, religion and philosophy. The Byzantine Empire ruled Greece until Constantinople fell to the Crusaders in 1204. These Frankish marauders and their Venetian allies divided the Greek mainland and islands between them, creating an assortment of petty kingdoms and principalities. The Empire recovered Constantinople and took back most of mainland Greece after defeating the Frankish princes at Pelagonia in 1259.

1 A depiction of the Roman invasion in 146 BC.

2 An authentic Byzantine icon of St Elijah, now housed in a museum.

3 Woodcut of a 1571 defeat of the Turkish fleet.

Did You Know?

Greek author Pausanias (110–180 AD) wrote the first ever travel guide, aimed at Roman visitors.

Timeline of events

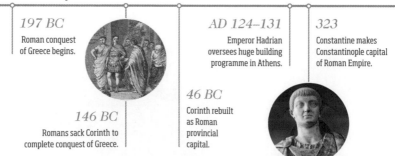

197 BC
Roman conquest of Greece begins.

146 BC
Romans sack Corinth to complete conquest of Greece.

46 BC
Corinth rebuilt as Roman provincial capital.

AD 124–131
Emperor Hadrian oversees huge building programme in Athens.

323
Constantine makes Constantinople capital of Roman Empire.

Ottoman and Venetian Greece

In the 13th century, a new threat from the east began to grow. The Ottoman Turks captured Thessaloníki in 1430, and thirteen years later their momentous 1453 conquest of Constantinople itself ended the Byzantine Empire. Athens fell in 1456, and Mystrás – the last Byzantine redoubt – in 1460. Under the Ottomans, rebellion and dissent were savagely punished. Turkish rule was not always oppressive, but Athens and much of mainland Greece became a depopulated, impoverished backwater.

The mighty Venetian Republic contested Ottoman control of mainland Greece for almost 300 years. The Venetians built fortresses around the shores of the Peloponnese to safeguard sea-routes to their island possessions in Crete and the Cyclades, and supported rebel Greeks against the Turkish occupiers. In 1571 the Venetians and their Spanish allies destroyed an Ottoman fleet at Lepanto in the Gulf of Corinth, and in the late 18th century Venice came close to ousting the Ottomans from Athens and the Peloponnese. Venice was finally defeated in 1715, although it retained Corfu and the Ionian Islands.

↑ A portion of the well-preserved Byzantine walls of Thessaloníki

529
Emperor Justinian closes schools of philosophy in Athens.

393
Emperor Theodosius I bans all non-Christian practices, including the Olympic Games.

1204
Frankish crusaders conquer Constantinople; Venetians seize Crete and the Cyclades islands.

1430
Ottoman Turks conquer Thessaloníki.

1259
Byzantine Empire recovers Constantinople and mainland Greece following Battle of Pelagonia.

1

2

Age of Rebellion

The Greeks never gave up hope of throwing off the Turkish yoke. Remote regions such as the Máni and the mountains of central Greece were never totally controlled by the Ottomans, and Russian-backed revolt broke out in the Peloponnese in 1770. It was quickly crushed, but Greeks continued to plan rebellion. They launched their final offensive in 1821, raising the rebel flag in the Máni and at Kalavryta in the Peloponnese. War stuttered across the mainland and the Greek islands for the next seven years. The Ottomans seemed close to gaining the upper hand until France, Russia and Britain intervened, sinking the Ottoman fleet at Navarino. In 1821 the Ottomans were forced to grant independence to the new Greek Republic, although Turkey kept most of the western, central and northern mainland.

Birth of a Kingdom

Kapodistrias, the republic's first president, was assassinated in 1831, and the regime collapsed. The Great Powers imposed Otto, a Bavarian prince, as King of the Hellenes. He moved his capital to Athens and began rebuilding the city in grand Neo-Classical

1 An artist's depiction of the Battle of Navarino, during the Greek War of Independence.

2 A watercolour showing the procession of King Otto through Greece in 1833.

3 Greek troops in 1912, during the Balkan Wars.

4 Greek soldiers at an Athens artillery post during World War I.

Timeline of events

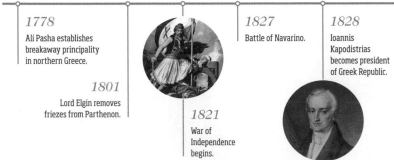

1778
Ali Pasha establishes breakaway principality in northern Greece.

1801
Lord Elgin removes friezes from Parthenon.

1821
War of Independence begins.

1827
Battle of Navarino.

1828
Ioannis Kapodistrias becomes president of Greek Republic.

style, but was ousted by liberal officers and politicians in 1863. The Great Powers parachuted in another princeling: Danish-born George I, who founded Greece's first constitutional monarchy.

Making Modern Greece

Modernization gathered pace in the second half of the 19th century. Steamships began to supplant sailing ships, and the first railway opened in 1869 between Athens and Piraeus. For Greek politicians, however, the goal was liberation of land still in Ottoman hands. Military offensives in 1854 and 1897 failed, but in the Balkan Wars of 1912–13 Greece acquired mainland territory up to its present-day frontiers, including Thessaloníki.

The Great Idea

Pro-German King Constantine I was ousted by liberal officers in 1917, when Greece formally entered World War I on the side of the Entente. Backers of the Megali Idea ("Great Idea") wanted Greece to seize parts of Turkey with large ethnic Greek populations, and even dreamed of reconquering Constantinople. However, a Greek invasion of Asia Minor ended in grim defeat.

↑ King Constantine I of Greece, c 1913

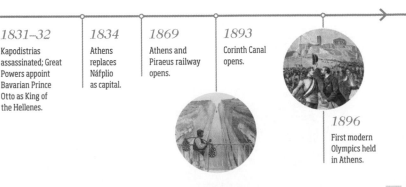

1831–32
Kapodistrias assassinated; Great Powers appoint Bavarian Prince Otto as King of the Hellenes.

1834
Athens replaces Náfplio as capital.

1869
Athens and Piraeus railway opens.

1893
Corinth Canal opens.

1896
First modern Olympics held in Athens.

Between the Wars

Destitute Greek refugees flooded into Athens and Thessaloníki from Turkey in 1923, and the 1920s and 1930s were a time of poverty, deprivation and political chaos. In 1936, General Ioannis Metaxas established an authoritarian regime that brought some stability, at the expense of democratic freedom.

Occupation and Resistance

Greece successfully resisted an Italian invasion during World War II in 1940 but was defeated and occupied by German, Italian and Bulgarian troops in 1941. Greek partisans, sometimes aided by British commandos, resisted, and in October 1944 British and Free Greek forces liberated Athens.

The Civil War

The new royalist government and its British backers soon fell out with their former allies in the Communist-dominated resistance movement. Three years of civil war followed before the last Communist fighters were driven out of Northern Greece. The war left Greece poverty-stricken, unstable and divided.

Did You Know?

During his rule, Metaxas banned anything he felt was Eastern-inspired, including decorative palm trees.

Timeline of events

1923–36

Years of political chaos culminate with authoritarian regime of Ioannis Metaxas.

1940

Greece enters World War II; Italian invasion of western Greece defeated.

1947–49

Civil war between royalist government and Communist forces.

1967

Right-wing officers seize power, forcing King Constantine II into exile.

1974

Junta forced to resign; referendum affirms creation of Greek Republic.

3

The Junta Years

In 1967 a group of army officers overthrew the government and established a military junta, ousting King Constantine II. The dictatorship's backing for a coup against the Cypriot government led to Turkish invasion and partition of the island, and forced the junta to quit. Konstantinos Karamanlis became prime minister of the new Greek Republic.

Modern Greece

Greece joined the European Community (now the European Union) in 1981, and subsequent funding aided massive improvement to the country's infrastructure. Package tourism also soared, and the 1990s were boom years. In 2010, however, years of irresponsible borrowing led to the near-collapse of the economy. The government was forced to beg its creditors for a financial bailout and cut public spending, causing social unrest; but after a decade of austerity the economy has begun to show signs of recovery. However, Greece remains indomitably Greek: proud of its past, fiercely independent and still looking to a vibrant future.

① Greek and Armenian child refugees gathered in Athens in the 1920s. ↑

② Georgios Papadopoulos, a Greek officer and politician, dancing with members of the Royal Guard on the anniversary of the 1967 revolution.

③ Hellenic Parliament, pictured on 20 August 2018, the day that Greece finally ended its bailout programme after eight years of austerity measures.

1981
Greece joins European Community.

2004
Athens hosts Olympic Games.

2015
Refugees arrive on Greek shores, placing Greece at the centre of a migrant crisis.

2010
Economic crisis forces Greece to accept austerity programme in return for international financial aid.

2019
Right-wing New Democracy party regains power.

EXPERIENCE
ATHENS

Monastiráki Square, with the Acropolis in the background, Athens

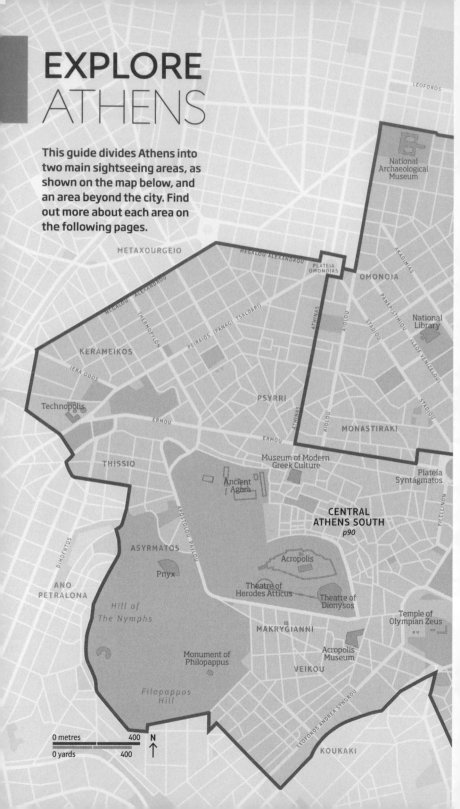

EXPLORE
ATHENS

This guide divides Athens into two main sightseeing areas, as shown on the map below, and an area beyond the city. Find out more about each area on the following pages.

LEOFOROS

National Archaeological Museum

METAXOURGEIO

MEGALOU ALEXANDROU

PLATEÍA OMONOÍAS

OMONOIA

AKADIMIAS

MEGALOU ALEXANDROU

THERMOPILON

PEIRAIOS (PANAGI TSALDARI)

ATHINAS

AIOLOU

STADIOU

PANEPISTIMIOU

ELEFT. VENIZELOU

National Library

KERAMEIKOS

IERA ODOS

PSYRRI

Technopolis

ERMOU

ATHINAS

AIOLOU

STADIOU

MONASTIRAKI

ERMOU

THISSIO

Museum of Modern Greek Culture

Plateía Syntágmatos

Ancient Agora

FILELLINON

CENTRAL ATHENS SOUTH
p90

DIMOFONTOS

APOSTOLOU PAVLOU

ASYRMATOS

Pnyx

Acropolis

ANO PETRALONA

Hill of The Nymphs

Theatre of Herodes Atticus

Theatre of Dionysos

Temple of Olympian Zeus

MAKRYGIANNI

Monument of Philopappus

Acropolis Museum

VEIKOU

Filopappos Hill

LEOFOROS ANDREA SYNGROU

0 metres 400
0 yards 400

N ↑

KOUKAKI

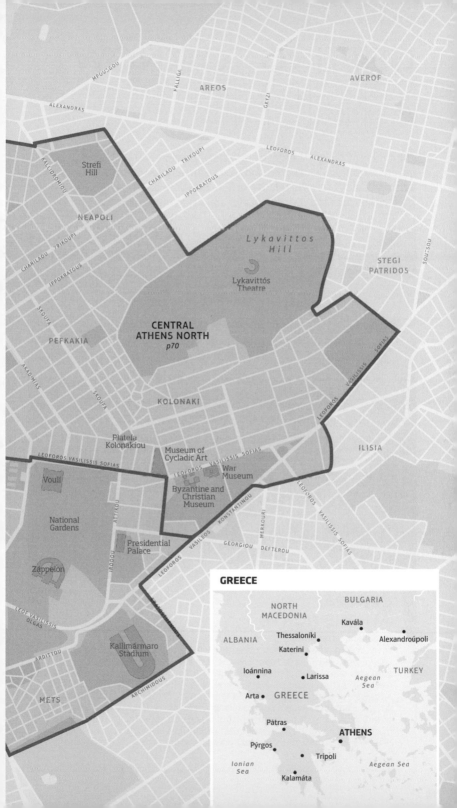

GETTING TO KNOW
ATHENS

The glories of ancient Greece; world-class museums and contemporary art galleries; traditional tavernas and hip fusion restaurants; old-school ouzo bars and classy cocktail spots: if the non-stop buzz of Athens is overpowering, tranquil beaches and clear blue water are just minutes from the centre.

PAGE 70

CENTRAL ATHENS NORTH

Broad 19th-century avenues link the varied neighbourhoods of the northern part of the city centre. With its upscale shops and cafés, chic Kolonáki is the place to see and be seen. A younger crowd hangs out in the dive bars of gritty Exárcheia, close to the National Archaeological Museum – a great treasury of ancient art, and in bohemian Psyrrí. Along the southern edge, on Leoforos Vassilis Sofías, is a parade of fascinating museums and, overlooking the entire area, Lykavittós Hill offers a spectacular view of the city from its summit.

Best for
Museums, café society, urban buzz

Home to
National Archaeological Museum, Museum of Cycladic Art, Benáki Museum

Experience
Sunset on Lykavittós Hill

CENTRAL ATHENS SOUTH

PAGE 90

With its narrow traffic-free streets, clusters of ancient ruins, dozens of tavernas and hidden squares crammed with café tables, the Pláka area sums up Athens. Beneath the mighty crag of the Acropolis and in and around the ruins of the Ancient Agora, this oldest part of the city is a delight for history buffs, bar-hoppers and shoppers. Monastiráki is the social hub, with its tavernas and labyrinthine flea market. Connecting the southern and northern halves of central Athens, palm-shaded Platteía Syntágmatos sees *evzones* in their kilts guard Greece's parliament.

Best for
Ancient sites, shopping, eating and drinking

Home to
Acropolis, Ancient Agora, Mikri Mitropóli

Experience
An open-air concert at the ancient Theatre of Herodes Atticus

AROUND ATHENS

PAGE 126

Glittering seas, bustling beach resorts, quiet rocky coves and wild mountains lie just minutes from central Athens. High above the city, thickly forested hills covered in the dense foliage of dark pines and bare mountains contrast with urban sprawl and the fields and vineyards of Attica. Ancient, mysterious temples stand near great Byzantine churches and historic battlefields where the fate of Greek civilization was decided. Crowning the Attica peninsula, at southernmost Cape Sounion, is the Temple of Poseidon, sparkling like a beacon over the Aegean.

Best for
Ancient sites, mountain views, glorious beaches

Home to
Monastery of Daphni, Piraeus, Ancient Eleusis, Ancient Brauron

Experience
Watching the sunset over Cape Sounion

CENTRAL ATHENS NORTH

The northern half of the city centre has grown since the 1830s, when King Otto imported architects to design a new capital fit for his kingdom. The royal architects laid out broad avenues and lined them with grand Neo-Classical public buildings, such as the National Theatre, National Library and Athens Academy, and gracious mansions including the Ilíou Melathron, designed for the great archaeologist Heinrich Schliemann, and the building that now houses the Benáki Museum. Within half a century, they had created a modern city of elegant administrative buildings, squares and tree-lined avenues.

Kolonáki, around Plateia Filiki Eterias, became the area's upmarket social hub, filled with chic cafés and expensive boutiques that are still favoured by the city's upper crust. The palatial National Archaeological Museum, completed in 1889, set the tone for the Exárcheia neighbourhood, which became a fashionable area of grand homes. Many of these survive today, but Exárcheia has become better known as a hotbed of student unrest and bohemian nightlife. Meanwhile, the Psyrri neighbourhood – where the romantic poet Lord Byron stayed on his first visit to Greece in the early 19th century – still retains some of its Belle Epoque charm and has become once again a fashionable residential and entertainment hub.

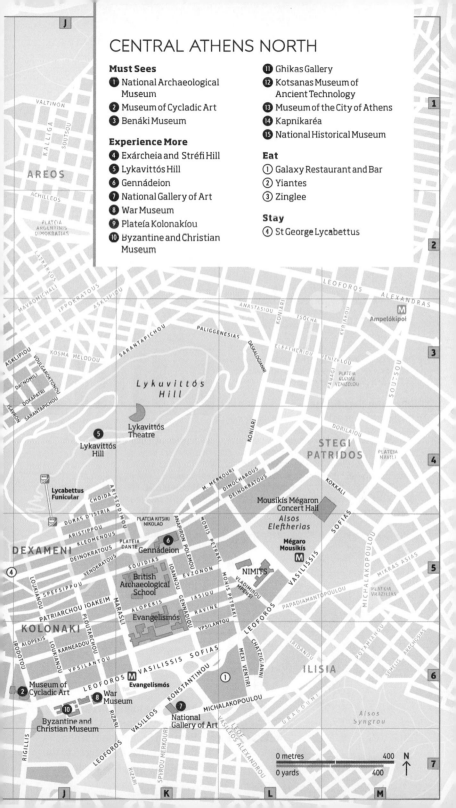

CENTRAL ATHENS NORTH

Must Sees

1. National Archaeological Museum
2. Museum of Cycladic Art
3. Benáki Museum

Experience More

4. Exárcheia and Stréfi Hill
5. Lykavittós Hill
6. Gennádeion
7. National Gallery of Art
8. War Museum
9. Plateía Kolonakíou
10. Byzantine and Christian Museum
11. Ghikas Gallery
12. Kotsanas Museum of Ancient Technology
13. Museum of the City of Athens
14. Kapnikaréa
15. National Historical Museum

Eat

1. Galaxy Restaurant and Bar
2. Yiantes
3. Zinglee

Stay

4. St George Lycabettus

① ⊘ Ⓜ ▭ ⌂

NATIONAL ARCHAEOLOGICAL MUSEUM

ΕΘΝΙΚΟ ΑΡΧΑΙΟΛΟΓΙΚΟ ΜΟΥΣΕΙΟ

📍F2 🚶44 Patissíon, Exárcheia Ⓜ Omónoia 🕐 Apr-Oct: 1-8pm Tue, 8am-8pm Wed-Mon; Nov-Apr: 1-8pm Tue, 9am-4pm Wed-Mon 🌐 namuseum.gr

With unique exhibits that include fabulous Mycenaean gold, along with an unrivalled quantity of sculpture, pottery and jewellery on display, this is without doubt one of the world's finest museums.

Opened in 1891, this superb museum brought together a collection that had previously been stored all over the city. Additional wings were added in 1939. The priceless collection was then dispersed and buried during World War II to protect it from possible damage. The museum reopened in 1946, but it took a further 65 years of renovation and reorganization finally to do justice to its formidable collection.

Museum Highlights

On the ground floor, Mycenaean, Neolithic and Cycladic finds are followed by Geometric, Archaic, Classical, Roman and Hellenistic sculpture. Egyptian artifacts, an important jewellery collection and the Karapános collection are also on the ground floor. The first floor houses pottery, glassware, jewellery and finds from ancient Thera (on Santorini).

Among the highlights are a gold death mask found at Mycenae by Heinrich Schliemann, originally thought to have belonged to the

↑ Neo-Classical façade of the National Archaeological Museum

legendary king Agamemnon. It dates from the mid-1600s BC. The huge *Dípylon Amphora*, a geometric vase found by the Dípylon Gate in the Kerameikos *(p112)*, was used to mark an 8th-century BC woman's burial and shows the dead body surrounded by mourning women. Cycladic sculpture, such as the *Harp Player*, flourished in the 3rd millennium BC and originated in the Cyclades. The simple lines and bold forms of the marble figurines influenced many early 20th-century artists, including the British sculptor Henry Moore. The *Ephebe of Antikythera* is a fine Hellenistic bronze statue discovered off the island of Antikýthira in 1900. Larger than life, it stands around 2 m (7 ft) tall. A marble sculpture of Aphrodite, Eros and the goat-footed Pan was found on Delos and dates from c 100 BC.

> Among the highlights are a gold death mask found at Mycenae by Heinrich Schliemann, originally thought to have belonged to the legendary king Agamemnon.

↑ Following the development of sculpture through the galleries

Did You Know?

If the Artemision Bronze was Poseidon, it would have held a trident; if Zeus, a thunderbolt.

The *Artemision Bronze*, a 5th-century BC statue representing Poseidon or Zeus ↑

EXPLORING THE NATIONAL ARCHAEOLOGICAL MUSEUM'S COLLECTION

Neolithic and Cycladic Art

The dawning of Greek civilization (3500–2900 BC) saw primitive decorative vases, terracotta figurines, jewellery and a selection of weapons. Vibrant fertility gods and goddesses, such as the *kourotróphos* (nursing mother) with child, are particularly well preserved. Of exceptional importance are

↑ Geometric vase depicting a funerary procession, c 750 BC

the largest known Cycladic marble figurine, from Amorgós, and the earliest known figures of musicians – the *Flute Player* and *Harp Player*, both from Kéros. Later finds from Mílos, such as the painted vase with fishermen, reveal changes in pot shapes and colour that took place in the late Cycladic Bronze Age.

Mycenaean Art

It is easy to understand the allure of the museum's most popular attraction, the Hall of Mycenaean Antiquities, with its dazzling array of 16th-century BC gold treasures. From the famous shaft graves (*p162*) came daggers, cups, seals and rings as well as a number of regal death masks, including the justly famous *Mask of Agamemnon*. Two superb *rhytons*, or wine jugs, are also on display: one in the shape of a bull's head, made in silver with gold horns, and the other gold shaped like a lion's head. Equally rich finds from sites other than Mycenae include two gold bull cups found at Vafeió, in Crete, a gold phial entwined with

dolphins and octopuses (excavated from a royal tomb at Déntra), clay tablets with the early Linear B script from Nestor's Palace (*p188*) and a magnificent sword from the Tomb of Staphylos on the island of Skópelos.

Geometric and Archaic Art

Famed for its monumental burial vases, such as the *Dípylon Amphora*, the Geometric period developed a more ornate style in the 7th century BC with the introduction of mythological and plant and animal motifs. By the 6th century BC, the full artistry of the black-figure vases had developed. Two rare examples from this period are a *lekythos* depicting Peleus, Achilles and the centaur Cheiron, and the sculpted heads known as *aryballoi*.

Classical Sculpture

The collection of Classical sculpture contains both fine statues and a selection of grave monuments, mostly from the Kerameikos. These

← Learning more about the context of the exhibits via interactive displays

some excellent pieces on display. These include the famous bronzes *Poseidon* and the *Horse with the Little Jockey*, both found on Evvoia at Cape Artemísion, and the *Ephebe of Antikythera*, found in the sea off that island. Another of the best-known sculptures is the *Marathon Boy* (340 BC).

Other Collections

The museum also houses several smaller collections, many donated by private individuals. Among these is the glittering Eléni Stathátou jewellery collection, which covers the Bronze Age through to the Byzantine period. The Karapános collection, which is composed mainly from discoveries made at the site at Ancient Dodona (p210), contains many fine bronzes, including *Zeus Hurling a Thunderbolt*. Also on display are small decorative and votive pieces, together with strips of lead inscribed with questions for the oracle at Dodona.

Other collections include the Egyptian collection and the Bronze collection, which comprises many small

include the beautiful stele of Hegeso (c 410 BC). Classical votive sculpture on display includes parts of a statue of the goddess Hera, from the Argive Heraion in the Peloponnese, and many majestic statues of the goddess Athena, including the Roman *Varvakeion Athena*, a reduced copy of the original ivory and gold statue from the Parthenon (p98).

Roman and Hellenistic Sculpture

Although many Greek bronzes were lost in antiquity, as metal was melted down in times of emergency for making weapons, the museum has

pieces of statuary and decorative items discovered on the Acropolis.

Thera Frescoes

Two of the famous frescoes discovered at Akrotíri on the island of ancient Thera (today Santoríni) in 1967, and originally thought to be from the mythical city of Atlantis, are displayed in the museum. Dating from 1500 BC, they confirm the sophistication of late Minoan civilization. The colourful, restored images depict boxer boys, and animals and flowers symbolizing spring time.

Pottery Collection

The strength of this vast collection lies not only in its size, but in the quality of specific works, representing the flowering of Greek ceramic art. The real gems belong to the 5th century BC when red-figure vases and white-ground *lekythoi* became the established style and were produced in vast numbers. Expressive painting styles and new designs characterize this period. The most poignant pieces are by the "Bosanquet Painter" and the "Achilles Painter" who portrayed young men by their graves.

THE DEVELOPMENT OF GREEK SCULPTURE

Sculpture was one of the most sophisticated forms of Greek art. We are able to trace its development from the early *koúroi* – highly stylized, rigid figures owing much to Egyptian art - to the superbly naturalistic works of named sculptors such as Pheidias and Praxiteles in Classical times. Portraiture only began in the 5th century BC; even then, most Greek sculptures were of gods and goddesses, heroes and athletes and idealized men and women. These have had an enduring impact on Western art down the centuries. The works of great Renaissance sculptors such as Donatello and Michelangelo clearly display the influence of Classical "heroic nudes" such as the *Marathon Boy* (right). The dreamy expression and easy pose of this bronze figure (who would originally have been leaning against a pillar) are characteristic of the works of Praxiteles, the leading late Classical sculptor.

VASES AND VASE PAINTING

The history of Greek vase painting continued without a break from 1000 BC to Hellenistic times. The main centre of production was Athens, which was so successful that by the early 6th century BC it was sending its high-quality black- and red-figure wares to every part of the Greek world. The Athenian potters' quarter of Kerameikos can still be visited today (p112). Beautiful works of art in their own right, the painted vases are the closest we can get to the vanished paintings with which ancient Greeks decorated the walls of their houses. A huge number of vases still survive intact or in reassembled pieces.

THE DEVELOPMENT OF PAINTING STYLES

Vase painting reached its peak in 6th- and 5th-century BC Athens. In the potter's workshop, a fired vase would be passed to a painter to be decorated. Archaeologists have been able to identify the varying styles of many individual painters of both black-figure and red-figure ware.

Geometric style characterizes the earliest Greek vases, from around 1000 to 700 BC, in which the decoration is in bands of figures and geometric patterns.

Black-figure style was first used in Athens around 630 BC. The figures were painted in black liquid clay onto the iron-rich clay of the vase, which turned orange when fired. Red-figure style was introduced in c 530 BC. The figures were created in the original red-orange colour of the clay, silhouetted against a black glaze.

> **Archaeologists have been able to identify the varying styles of many individual painters of both black-figure and red-figure ware.**

THE SYMPOSION

A significant part of ancient Greek culture from the 7th century BC, the symposion was a social gathering held in a private Greek home. These episodes of mostly male feasting, drinking, conversing and singing were also occasions for playing the skilled game of kottabos (flinging wine sediment at targets). This detail of the exterior of a 5th-century BC kylix shows a man holding a kylix during a symposion, ready to flick out the dregs. The thrower was expected to retain the reclining posture usual at feasts while taking aim.

Vase Shapes

Krater

▽ This krater with curled handles or "volutes" is a wide-mouthed vase in which the Greeks mixed water with their wine before drinking it.

Amphora

△ The amphora was a two-handled vessel used to store wine, olive oil and foods preserved in liquid such as olives. It also held dried foods.

Hydria

△ The hydria was used to carry water from the fountain. Of the three handles, one was vertical for holding and pouring, two horizontal for lifting.

Great detail could be shown in red-figure painting as lines were drawn onto the pottery instead of scraped out. It also allowed for perspective, and the figures were portrayed in more dimensions than the postures of black-figure painting, which were almost always in profile. Red-figure pottery grew in popularity and quickly surpassed black-figure pottery.

Distinguished by pairs of eyes under arched brows painted on the external surface, eye cups were drinking vessels usually in the shape of a *kylix*. They were given an almost magical power by the painted eyes, which were considered to avert evil. The handles of the cups looked like ears and the square base resembled feet.

The white-ground lekythos was developed in the 5th century BC as an oil flask and was used especially for grave offerings. These flasks were usually decorated with funeral scenes and used the white-ground technique of painting in which figures appear on a white background, making the surface too fragile for ordinary, everyday use.

The rhyton was a roughly conical drinking vessel used in ancient Greece for watered-down wine. It was typically formed in the shape of an animal's head, such as a ram.

1 Detail of black-figure painting of Spartan warriors in ancient Greece.

2 Black-figure eye cup, attributed to Nikosthenes, a potter active between 540 and 510 BC in Athens.

3 Ram-head rhyton, c 480-470 BC by Brygos, an ancient Greek vase painter.

Lekythos

▽ The lekythos could vary in height from 3 cm (1 in) to nearly 1 m (3 ft). It was used to hold oil, both in the home and as a funerary gift to the dead.

Kylix

▽ The kylix, a two-handled drinking cup, was one shape that could take interior decoration.

Oinochoe

△ The oinochoe, the standard wine jug, had a round or trefoil mouth for pouring, and just one handle.

2 ⬙ ⬙ ⬙ ⬙

MUSEUM OF CYCLADIC ART
ΜΟΥΣΕΙΟ ΚΥΚΛΑΔΙΚΗΣ ΤΕΧΝΗΣ

📍J6 🏠Neofýtou Doúka 4, Kolonáki (entrance to Stathátos Mansion at Irodótou 1) 🚌3, 7 🕐10am–5pm Mon, Wed, Fri & Sat; 10am–8pm Thu; 11am–5pm Sun 🚫Main public hols 🌐cycladic.gr

This museum houses one of the world's finest collections of Cycladic art. The elegant carvings, unlike anything found in contemporary civilizations, are remnants of an ancient culture that flourished in the Cyclades.

The collection was initially assembled by Nikolaos and Dolly Goulandrís, members of Greece's greatest shipping dynasty, and has expanded with donations from other Greek collectors.Dating from the 3rd millennium BC, the Cycladic marble sculptures depicting women and men have a haunting simplicity that inspired many 20th-century artists and sculptors, including Picasso, Henry Moore and Modigliani. The museum also has an excellent selection of ancient Greek and Cypriot art, the earliest from about 5,000 years ago. In the main building, the Cycladic collection is on the first floor. Ancient Greek art is on the second, and the third shows Ancient Cypriot art. The fourth floor houses objects from everyday life in antiquity. The adjoining Neo-Classical Stathátos Mansion, designed by Bavarian architect Ernst Ziller in 1895, hosts temporary exhibitions, receptions and lectures.

The Cycladic marble sculptures have a haunting simplicity that inspired many 20th-century artists.

←

Beyond Death and Afterlife in Ancient Greece gallery; Cycladic "Folded Arm" marble figurine of a woman *(inset)*

THE CYCLADIC CIVILIZATION

A Bronze Age culture, the Cycladic civilization flourished from about 3,200 to 1,000 BC. The Cycladic islands were a homogenous unit. As well as the pristine white marble found on Paros and Naxos, other islands were rich in mineral deposits, including gold, silver and copper. The result was a thriving industry in many arts and crafts, especially sculpture, metallurgy and jewellery-making. Items were traded throughout the rest of Greece and with Asia Minor (modern-day Turkey). The marble figurines are mostly female forms – perhaps symbolic companions for the deceased.

1 The porch of the Stathátos Mansion has typical Neo-Classical features.

2 A gallery narrates the history and development of Cycladic art.

3 The main entrance doorway of the Stathátos Mansion. The mansion and main part of the museum are interconnected.

3 ⓐ ⓜ ⓓ

BENÁKI MUSEUM

ΜΟΥΣΕΙΟ ΜΠΕΝΑΚΗ

📍H6 🏛Corner of Koumpári & Vasilísis Sofías, Sýntagma ⓂSýntagma
🚌3, 7, 8, 13 🕐10am–6pm Mon, Wed, Fri & Sat; 10am–midnight Thu; 10am–4pm Sun
🚫Tue & main public hols 🌐benaki.org

This vast museum gives a panoramic view of Greek history from the Stone Age to the 20th century by way of Classical Greece and the Byzantine and Ottoman empires. Over 20,000 objects show the evolution of Greek painting, sculpture and handicrafts.

↑ The main entrance of the Benáki Museum of Greek Culture

Founded in 1931 by Antónis Benákis, the museum is housed in an elegant Neoclassical mansion of 1867 that was once the home of the Benákis family. The outstanding collection contains a diverse array of Greek arts and crafts, paintings and jewellery, local costumes and political memorabilia that spans over 5,000 years, from the Neolithic era (7,000 BC) to the 20th century.

The ground floor collection is arranged into different periods and ranges from prehistoricto late Byzantine art and Cretan icon painting. The first floor exhibits are organized geographically and are from Asia Minor, mainland Greece and the Greek islands. There is also a collection of ecclesiastical silverware and jewellery. The second floor has artifacts relating to Greek spiritual, economic

↑ Gallery of paintings; detail of a 17th–18th-century gold-embroidered bridal cushion from Lefkádia *(inset)*

and social life, and the third floor concentrates on the Greek War of Independence *(p60)* and modern political and cultural life, as well as having a wing for temporary exhibitions.

Museum Highlights

The stunning display of Thessaly treasure – Hellenistic gold jewellery from the 3rd–2nd centuries BC – employs filigree and granulation (beads of gold soldered onto metal) to produce minutely crafted earrings, necklaces, bracelets and diadems.

Reconstructions of two mid-18th-century and mid-19th-century reception rooms from Macedonian mansions, furnished with wooden panels, carved wooden ceilings, rugs, cushions and wrought-iron tables, recall times when these crafts flourished locally.

The displays of Greek Independence memorabilia include finely decorated swords, sabres and rifles, paintings and flags.

THE BENÁKIS FAMILY

Antónis Benákis (1873–1954) was born in Egypt to an immensely wealthy merchant, Emmanuel Benákis, who later became Mayor of Athens. Antónis began collecting Islamic art and went on to collect Byzantine art and Greek folk art once in Athens. He donated the entire collection to the Greek state in 1931 and continued to be involved in enriching the museum's holdings until his death. His sister, Penelope Delta (1874–1941), was an author of much-loved children's books.

The Athens cityscape seen from the top of tranquil Stréfi Hill ↑

EXPERIENCE MORE

❹
Exárcheia and Stréfi Hill
Εξάρχεια Λόφος Στρέφη

📍F3 & H2 Ⓜ Omónoia

Until recently, the area around Plateía Exarcheíon was notorious as a hotbed of anarchist activity. Today, although parts are still rather run down, gentrification has brought many fashionable cafés, bars and *ouzerí* to the area. Themistokléous, which leads off the square down to Omónoia, is pleasant to wander along. Its local food stores and small boutiques make a refreshing change from the noisy cafés in the square, which are especially lively at night.

Every year, a demonstration takes place on 17 November, the date in 1973 when many students were killed by the Junta *(p63)* during a sit-in.

The nearby park of Stréfi Hill, with its intriguing maze of paths, is quiet and peaceful by day but comes to life at night when tavernas in the vicinity fill up. Stréfi Hill is one of the many green areas in Athens that provide welcome relief from the noise and grime of the city, particularly in the oppressive heat of summer.

---

❺
Lykavittós Hill
Λόφος Λυκαβηττού

📍J4 🚠From Ploutárchou; 9am-2:30am daily

The peak of Lykavittós (also known as Lycabettus) reaches 277 m (910 ft) above Athens, and is its highest hill. There are panoramic views of the city from the observation decks that rim the summit. The hill can be climbed on foot by various paths or by the easier, albeit vertiginous, ride in the funicular from the top of Ploutárchou. On foot, it should take about 45 minutes. The hill may derive its name from a combination of the words *lýki* and *vaino*, meaning "path of light". The ancient belief was that this was the gigantic rock once destined to be the Acropolis citadel, accidentally dropped by the city's patron goddess, Athena. The small whitewashed chapel of Agios Geórgios crowns the top of the hill. It was built in the 19th century on the site of an older Byzantine church, dedicated to Profítis Ilías (the Prophet Elijah). Both saints associated with the site are celebrated here on their name days (20 July and 23 April respectively). On the eve of Easter Sunday, a spectacular candlelit procession winds down the peak's wooded slopes.

The hill has a summit restaurant and café and the stunning open-air Lykavittós Theatre, which has hosted a number of concerts for years.

> 💬 INSIDER TIP
> ### Food with a View
>
> For panoramic views extending from the Acropolis to the port of Piraeus while dining on fine Mediterranean cuisine, book a table at Orizontes Restaurant at the top of Lykavittós Hill (www.orizontesly cabettus.gr).

over 70,000 rare books and manuscripts, but selected exhibits are on show, and books, posters and postcards are for sale at the souvenir stall. Exhibits in the main reading room include 192 Edward Lear sketches purchased in 1929. There is also an eclectic mix of Byron memorabilia, including the last known portrait of the poet made before his death in Greece in 1824 (p139).

---

7 ♿

National Gallery of Art
Εθνική Πινακοθήκη

Q K6 **A** Vasiléos Konstantínou 50, Ilísia **M** Evangelismós **🚌** 3, 13 **C** 10am-6pm Mon & Thu-Sun, 10am-9pm Wed **W** nationalgallery.gr

The National Gallery of Art has undergone an eight-year extension and refurbishment project, which was completed in spring 2021. The museum's collection focuses on Greek paintings from the 18th to the 20th century. The 19th century is represented mainly by depictions of the War of Independence and seascapes, enlivened by portraits such as Nikólaos Gýzis's *The Loser of the Bet* (1878), *Waiting* (1900) by Nikifóros Lýtras and *The Straw Hat* (1925) by Nikólaos

Lýtras. There are many fine works by major Greek artists including Theophilos, Móralis, Hadjikyriakos-Ghikas, Kontoglou and Tsaroúchis.

The more minor collection of non-Greek European art comprises studies, engravings and paintings by Rembrandt, Dürer, Brueghel, Van Dyck, Watteau, Utrillo, Cézanne and Braque, among others. These include Caravaggio's *Singer* (1620), Eugène Delacroix's *Greek Warrior* (1856) and Picasso's Cubist period *Woman in a White Dress* (1939). As part of the renovation a new space has been created for temporary exhibitions, an amphitheatre and a rooftop café-restaurant.

Did You Know?

The climb up Stréfi Hill is shorter than to the top of Lykavittós and the views are comparable.

6

Gennádeion
Γεννάδειον

Q K5 **A** American School of Classical Studies, Souidías 54, Kolonáki **M** Evangelismós **🚌** 3, 7, 8, 13 **C** 9:30am-5pm Mon-Wed & Fri, 9:30am-8pm Thu, 9:30am-2pm Sat **C** Aug, main public hols **W** ascsa.edu.gr

The Greek diplomat and bibliophile Ioánnis Gennádios (1844–1932) spent a lifetime accumulating rare first editions and illuminated manuscripts. In 1923, he donated his collection to the American School of Classical Studies. The Gennádeion building, named after him, was designed and built between 1923 and 1925 by a New York firm to house the collection. Above the façade of Ionic columns is an inscription which translates as "They are called Greeks who share in our culture" – from Gennádios's dedication speech at the opening in 1926.

Researchers need special permission to gain access to

↑ Paintings by Colombian artist Fernando Botero on display at the National Gallery of Art, Athens

EAT

Galaxy Restaurant and Bar

Gourmet fare and fine wines are served at this upmarket retreat with Acropolis views.

📍L6 🏠Hilton Hotel, Vasilíssis Sofías 46
🌐hiltonathens.gr

€€€

Yiantes

Creative Greek taverna fare served in a colourful courtyard garden in the hip neighbourhood of Exarhia.

📍F3 🏠Valtetsíou 44, Exárcheia ☎21033 01369

€€€

Zinglee

Casual bistro/bar serving breakfast, brunch and full meals including a magnificent moussaka. Great choice of wines by the glass.

📍H6 🏠Tsakalov 2
🌐zinglee.gr

€€€

↑ The War Museum, which charts the history of conflict in Greece from antiquity to the present

 8

War Museum
Πολεμικό Μουσείο

📍J6 🏠Corner of Vasilíssis Sofías & Rizári, Ilísia
Ⓜ Evangelismós 🚌3, 7, 8, 13 ⏰9am-7pm daily
🚫Main public hols
🌐warmuseum.gr

The War Museum opened in 1975 after the fall of the military dictatorship (p63). The main galleries are chronologically ordered, and contain battle scenes, plans, armour and weapons from ancient Mycenaean times through to the German occupation of 1941. There are fine paintings and prints of leaders from the Greek War of Independence, such as General Theódoros Kolokotrónis (1770–1843). His death mask is also here. Oils and sketches by Flora-Karavía vividly capture the hardships of the two world wars.

9

Plateía Kolonakíou
Πλατεία Κολωνακίου

📍H6 🏠Kolonáki
🚌3, 7, 8, 13

Kolonáki Square and its side-streets form a chic enclave often missed by those who stick to the ancient

sites and the flea markets of Monastiráki. The square is named after a small ancient column (kolonáki) found in the area. Celebrated for its designer boutiques and fashionable bars and cafés, smart antique shops and art galleries and sumptuous pastry shops, it revels in its status as the city's most fashionable quarter.

10

Byzantine and Christian Museum
Βυζαντινό και Χριστιανικό Μουσείο

📍J6 🏠Vasilíssis Sofías 22, Plateía Rigílis, Kolonáki
Ⓜ Evangelismós 🚌3, 8, 7, 13 ⏰8am-8pm Mon & Wed-Sun, 1-8pm Tue
🚫Main public hols
🌐byzantinemuseum.gr

Originally called the Villa Ilissia, this elegant Florentine-style mansion was built in the 1840s for the Duchesse de Plaisance (1785–1854), a key figure in Athens society in the mid-19th century and a dedicated philhellene. Collector Geórgios Sotiríou converted the house into a museum in the 1930s,

↑ Icons and stone carvings
in the Byzantine and
Christian Museum

transforming the entrance into a monastic court with a copy of a fountain from a 4th-century mosaic in Daphni (p128). A modern, open-plan, split-level exhibition space has been built underground, below the courtyard.

The collection is organized into five main themes (including the role of women, burial practices and gold artifacts), divided into two sections. Section one, From the Ancient World to Byzantium, is dominated by fragments of ornamental stone carvings and mosaics taken from basilicas, sarcophagi, and early religious sculpture such as the *Shepherd Carrying a Lamb* and *Orpheus Playing a Lyre*, which illustrate the way in which the Christian church absorbed and adapted pagan symbols. Section two, The Byzantine World, presents an array of icons, frescoes and precious ecclesiastical artifacts. Fine pieces include the Treasury of Mytilene (a hoard of 7th-century gold and silver jewellery, coins and goblets), and magnificent frescoes rescued from the Church of the Episkopi.

In summer, there are often concerts in the courtyard.

11

Ghikas Gallery
Πινακοθήκη Γκίκα

📍G6 🏠Kriezótou 3 📞210
361 5702 Ⓜ Syntagma 🚌3,
8, 13 🕐10am–6pm Fri & Sat
🔒Aug, main public hols
🌐benaki.org

This annexe of the Benáki Museum (p82) is somewhat misnamed. It is situated in the former home of the great painter Nikos Hadjikyriakos-Ghikas, with his top-floor residence and atelier preserved as when he lived and worked here, but most of its many galleries highlight just about everybody who has had an influence on 20th-century Greek cultural life. Such figures include archaeologist-architect Athanasios Orlandos, designer-architects Dimitris Pikionis and Aris Konstantinidis, photographers Nelly's, Takis Tloupas and Spyros Meletzis, the cartoonist Bost, and painters Yiannis Moralis and Yorgos Manousakis. Allow plenty of time for a pleasant survey of the shaping of modern Greece.

ICONS IN THE ORTHODOX CHURCH
The word icon simply means "image" and has come to signify a holy image through association with its religious use. Subjects range from popular saints to lesser-known martyrs, prophets and archangels. The image of the Virgin and Child is easily the most popular and exalted. A prominent feature in the Greek Orthodox religion, icons appear in many areas of Greek life: on public transport and in restaurants, homes and churches. An icon can be a painting on wooden boards or metal, or a fresco or mosaic.

12

Kotsanas Museum of Ancient Technology
Μουσείο Αρχαίας Ελληνικής
Τεχνολογίας Κώστα Κοτσανά

📍G5 🏠Pindarou 6,
Kolonáki Ⓜ Syntagma
🚌3, 7, 8, 13 🕐10am–6pm
daily 🌐kotsanas.com

The artistic achievements of the ancient world are well known, but this museum reveals its technological genius. Discover the stories behind astonishing Greek and Roman inventions such as the world's first working robot and the Antikythera mechanism, the earliest mechanical computer.

⑬ 🖊️ 🖥️ 🛍️

Museum of the City of Athens

Μουσείο της Πόλεως των Αθηνών

📍 F5 🏠 Paparrigopoúlou 7, Plateía Klafthmónos, Sýntagma Ⓜ Panepistímio 🚌 1, 2, 4, 5, 9, 11, 12, 15, 18 🕙 9am–4pm Mon & Wed-Fri, 10am–3pm Sat & Sun 🚫 Main public hols 🌐 athenscitymuseum.gr

King Otto, the first king of Greece and Queen Amalía lived here from 1831 until their new palace, today's Voulí parliament building in Plateía Syntágmatos *(p119)*, was completed in 1838. It was joined to the neighbouring house to create what was known as the Old Palace.

The palace was restored in 1980 as a museum devoted to royal memorabilia, furniture and family portraits, maps and prints. It offers a look at life during the early years of King Otto's reign. Exhibits include the manuscript of the 1843 Constitution, coats of arms from the Frankish (1205–1311) and Catalan (1311–88) rulers of Athens, and a scale model of the city as it was in 1842, made by architect Giánnis Travlós (1908–85).

The museum also has a fine art collection, including

Did You Know?

King Otto, a Bavarian prince, introduced beer to Greece.

Nikólaos Gýzis's *The Carnival in Athens* (1892) and a selection of watercolours by the English artists Edward Dodwell (1767–1832), Edward Lear (1812–88) and Thomas Hartley Cromek (1809–73).

---

⑭

Kapnikaréa

Καπνικαρέα

📍 E6 🏠 Corner of Ermoú & Kalamiótou, Monastiráki Ⓜ Monastiráki 🕙 9am–2pm Mon-Sun 🚫 Main public hols

This charming 11th-century Byzantine church was destined for demolition in 1834 as part of Otto I's new city plans for Athens but was saved thanks to the timely intervention of King Ludwig of Bavaria. Stranded in the middle of a square between Ermoú and Kapnikaréa streets, it is surrounded by the modern office blocks and shops of Athens' busy garment district.

Traditionally called the Church of the Princess, its foundation is attributed to Empress Irene, who ruled the Byzantine Empire from AD 797 to 802. She is revered as a saint in the Greek Orthodox church for her efforts in restoring icons to the Empire's churches.

The true origins of the name "Kapnikaréa" are unknown, although according to some sources, the church was named after its founder, a "hearth tax gatherer" *(kapnikaréas)*. Hearth tax was imposed on buildings by the Byzantines.

Restored in the 1950s, the dome of the church is supported by four Roman columns. Frescoes by Phótis Kóntoglou (1895–1965) were painted during the restoration, including one of the Virgin and Child. Some of Kóntoglou's work is also on display in the National Gallery of Art *(p85)*.

ATHENIAN NEO-CLASSICAL ARCHITECTURE

Neo-Classicism flourished in the 19th century, when the architects who were commissioned by King Otto to build the capital in the 1830s turned to this style. Among those commissioned were the Danish Hansen brothers, Christian and Theophil, as well as Ernst Ziller. In its early days, Neo-Classicism had imitated the grace of the buildings of ancient Greece, using marble columns, sculptures and decorative detailing. In later years, it evolved into an original Greek style.

KEY NEO-CLASSICAL BUILDINGS

Grand Neo-Classical architecture is seen at its best in the public buildings along Panepistimíou; its domestic adapation can be seen in the houses of Pláka.

The National Theatre (Agiou Konstantinou 22-24), built between 1882 and 1890 by Ernst Ziller, has a Renaissance-style exterior with arches and Doric columns.

The University of Athens fine building (Panepistimíou 30) was designed by Christian Hansen. Completed in 1864, it has an Ionic colonnade and a portico frieze depicting the resurgence of arts and sciences under the reign of King Otto. Statues on the façade include Sphinx (a symbol of wisdom), and Patriarch Gregory V, a martyr of the War of Independence.

Near the university, also on Panepistimíou, the Athens Academy was designed by Theophil Hansen and built between 1859 and 1887. Statues of Apollo, Athena, Socrates and Plato convey a Classical style, as do the Ionic capitals and columns.

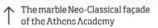

↑ The marble Neo-Classical façade of the Athens Academy

15

National Historical Museum
Εθνικό Ιστορικό Μουσείο

📍F6 🏛Stadíou 13, Sýntagma Ⓜ Sýntagma 🚌1, 2, 4, 5, 9, 10, 11, 18 🕐8:30am-2:30pm Tue-Sun 🚫Main public hols 🌐nhmuseum.gr

Designed by French architect François Boulanger (1807–75), this museum was originally built as the first home of the Greek parliament. Queen Amalía laid the foundation stone in 1858, but only 13 years later did it become the first permanent site of the Greek parliament. The country's most famous early prime ministers have sat in the

←

The diminutive church of Kapnikaréa in the middle of a busy street

Imposing chamber of the Old Parliament of the Hellenes, including Chárilaos Trikoúpis and Theódoros Deligiánnis, who was assassinated on the steps in front of the building in 1905. The parliament moved to its present-day site in the Voulí building on Plateía Syntágmatos (p119) after the Voulí was renovated in 1935.

In 1961, the building opened as the National Historical Museum, owned by the Historical and Ethnological Society of Greece. Founded in 1882, the society's aim is to collect objects that illuminate the history of modern Greece. The museum covers the major events of Greek history from the Byzantine period to the 20th century. Venetian armour, regional costumes and figure-heads from the warships used during the 1821 Revolution are some of the exhibits on show.

The collection also focuses on major parliamentary figures, philhellenes and leaders in the War of Independence, displaying such items as Byron's sword, the weapons of Theódoros Kolokotrónis (1770–1843), King Otto's throne and the pen used by Elefthérios Venizélos to sign the Treaty of Sèvres in 1920. Among the paintings on view is a fine rare woodcut of the *Battle of Lepanto* (1571), the work of Bonastro.

Outside is a copy of Lázaros Sóchos's equestrian statue of Kolokotrónis, made in 1900, the original of which is in Náfplio (p166), the former capital of Greece. A dedication on the statue reads (in Greek): "Theódoros Kolokotrónis 1821. Ride on, noble commander, through the centuries, showing the nations how slaves may become free men." The Greek Communist Party used to have its headquarters across the street. A running joke stated that Kolokotrónis's finger pointed that way to indicate his indignation.

CENTRAL ATHENS SOUTH

People lived on the Acropolis as early as 3,000 BC, while finds from the Kerameikos cemetery show that south central Athens has been inhabited since the 12th century BC. From around 600 BC the Ancient Agora, where demagogues declaimed and philosophers debated, was the heart of Athens.

Razed by the Persians in 480 BC, Athens was avenged when its navy destroyed the Persian fleet at Salamis. Perikles inspired Athenians to rebuild, and magnificent temples that still symbolise the city rose on the Acropolis. Conquered by Rome in the 2nd century BC, Athens enjoyed peace and prosperity. The Roman legacy can be seen everywhere in the area. The Emperor Hadrian funded completion of the Temple of Olympian Zeus, the Arch of Hadrian and the Library of Hadrian next to the Roman Agora. The Tower of the Winds and Theatre of Herodes Atticus are also relics of the Roman era.

Byzantine rule, which succeeded the Eastern Roman Empire, left a legacy of Byzantine churches in Pláka and Monastiráki. Athens declined under the Ottomans; derelict mosques and bathhouses are scattered around the area. The Acropolis was besieged by the Venetians in 1687, and the Parthenon was wrecked by cannon fire.

As part of the rebuilding programme in 1834, Plateía Syntágma, a grand new square, became the hub of the reconstructed city. From the 1960s, tourism began to change the face of Pláka as visitors flocked here. Hosting the 2004 Olympic Games breathed new life into the area, as did the opening of the new Acropolis Museum in 2008.

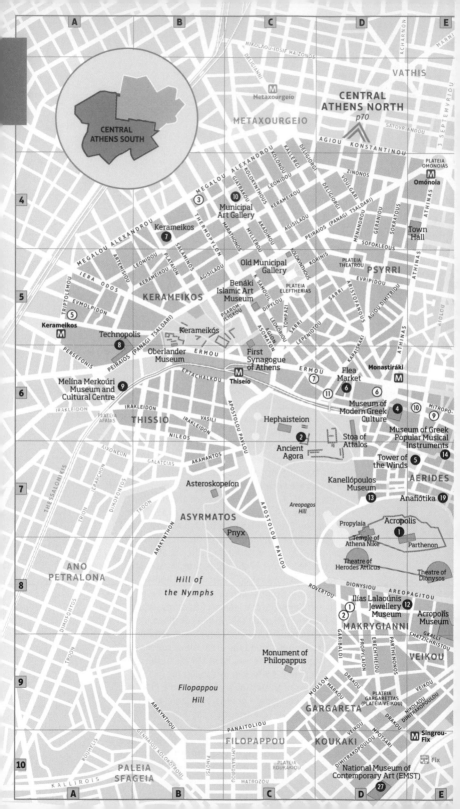

CENTRAL ATHENS SOUTH

Must Sees
1. Acropolis
2. Ancient Agora
3. Mikrí Mitrópoli

Experience More
4. Museum of Modern Greek Culture
5. Tower of the Winds
6. Flea Market
7. Kerameikos
8. Technopolis
9. Melína Merkoúri Museum and Cultural Centre
10. Municipal Art Gallery
11. Mitrópoli
12. Ilías Lalaoúnis Jewellery Museum
13. Kanellópoulos Museum
14. Museum of Greek Popular Musical Instruments
15. Benizelos Mansion
16. Agios Nikólaos Ragkavás
17. Plateía Lysikrátous
18. Frissiras Museum
19. Anafiótika
20. Russian Church of the Holy Trinity
21. Temple of Olympian Zeus
22. Jewish Museum of Greece
23. Plateía Syntágmatos
24. First Cemetery of Athens
25. National Gardens
26. Presidential Palace
27. National Museum of Contemporary Art (EMST)
28. Kallimármaro Stadium

Eat
1. Strofi
2. GH Attikos
3. Aleria
4. Scholarhio

Drink
5. MoMix Bar
6. 360 Cocktail Bar
7. K8 Point

Stay
8. Athens Gate Hotel

Shop
9. Orpheus Icon Gallery
10. Centre for Hellenic Tradition
11. Olgianna Melissinos Sandals

❶ ⓐⓑ

ACROPOLIS
ΑΚΡΟΠΟΛΗ

📍**D7** 🚇**Dionysíou Areopagítou (main entrance), Pláka** Ⓜ**Akrópoli**
🚌**230, X80** 🕐**Apr–Oct: 8am–7pm daily; Nov–Mar: 8:30am–3pm daily**
📅**1 Jan, 25 Mar, Easter Sun, 1 May, 25 & 26 Dec** 🌐**odysseus.culture.gr**

One of the most famous archaeological sites in the world, the Acropolis and its breathtaking temples stand as a monument to the political and cultural achievements of Greece. The Acropolis overlooks the city from a plateau that has been in use for 5,000 years.

First settled in Neolithic times, the Acropolis began to take on the form of a city when it was fortified by the Mycenaeans in about 1400 BC. In 510 BC the Delphic Oracle declared it to be a holy place of the gods, banning habitation by mortals. After all the buildings were destroyed by the Persians in 480 BC Perikles began his grand programme of rebuilding, sparking a new golden age. Athens's leading architects, sculptors and painters transformed the Acropolis with three temples and a monumental gateway, the Propylaia.

Since 1975, visitors have not been allowed to enter the temples. It is a miracle that anything remains at all, as the ravages of war, the removal of temple treasures and pollution have all taken their toll on the Acropolis.

The south porch of the Erechtheion has statues of women in place of columns. The originals have been replaced by casts.

An olive tree grows where Athena is said to have first planted her tree in a competition against Poseidon.

④

The Propylaia was built in 437–432 BC to form a new entrance to the Acropolis (p96).

This temple of Athena Nike is on the west side of the Propylaia. It was built in 426–421 BC (p96).

③

②

The Beulé Gate was the first entrance to the Acropolis (p96).

①

Pathway to Acropolis from ticket office

⑤

↑ Caryatids supporting the roof of the porch of the Erechtheion

The Odeon of Herodes Atticus was originally built in AD 161. It was restored in 1955 and is used today for outdoor concerts (p97).

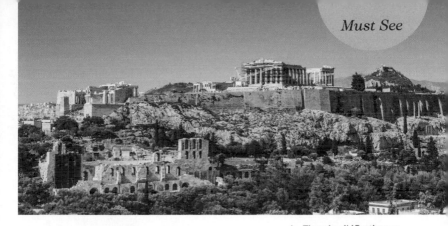

↑ The splendid Parthenon on the Acropolis, with restoration underway

The most famous temple on the Acropolis, the massive Parthenon, is dedicated to the city's patron goddess, Athena (p98).

Two Corinthian columns are the remains of choregic monuments erected by sponsors of successful dramatic performances (p97).

Panagía i Spiliótissa is a chapel set up in a cave in the Acropolis rock (p97).

The Theatre of Dionysos visible today was built by Lykourgos in 342–326 BC (p97).

Sanctuary of Asklepios

Stoa of Eumenes

As the highest part of the city, the Acropolis rock was an easily defended site.

↑ Illustration of the Acropolis rock as it looks today

> **INSIDER TIP**
> **Ticket Saver**
>
> Entry to the Acropolis is free on the first Sunday of every month from November to March. A combined ticket gives you entry to the Acropolis and six other archaeological sites in Athens within five days.

① Beulé Gate

The first entrance to the Acropolis, the Beulé Gate is named after the French archaeologist Ernest Beulé who discovered it in 1852. It was built in AD 267 after the raid of the Heruli, a Germanic people, as part of the fortifications of the Roman Acropolis.

② Temple of Athena Nike

This small temple was built in 426–421 BC to commemorate the Athenians' victories over the Persians. The temple frieze has representative scenes from the Battle of Plataea (479 BC). Designed by Kallikrates, the temple has been used as both observation post and an ancient shrine to the goddess of Victory, Athena Nike, of whom there is a remarkable sculpture on the balustrade. Legend records the temple site as the place where King Aegeus stood waiting for his son Theseus to return from his mission to Crete to slay the Minotaur. Theseus had promised to swap his ships' black sails for white on his return, but he forgot his promise. When the

king saw the black sails, he presumed his son to be dead and threw himself into the sea, which now bears his name (Aegean). Built of Pentelic marble, the temple has four Ionic columns at each portico end. It was reconstructed in 1834–8, after being destroyed in 1686 by the Ottomans. On the point of collapse in 1935, it was again dismantled and reconstructed according to information resulting from more recent research.

③ Propylaia

Work began on this enormous entrance to the Acropolis in 437 BC. Although the outbreak of the Peloponnesian War in 432 BC curtailed its completion, its architect Mnesikles created a building admired throughout the ancient world. It comprises a rectangular central building divided by a wall into two porticoes. These were punctuated by five entrance doors, rows of Ionic and Doric columns and a vestibule with a blue-coffered ceiling decorated with gold stars. During its chequered history – later as archbishop's resi-dence, Frankish palace, and Turkish fortress and armoury – parts of the building have been accidentally destroyed.

The Odeon of Herodes Atticus, now used for summer festivals

④ Erechtheion

Built between 421 and 406 BC, the Erechtheion is situated on the most sacred site of the Acropolis. It is said to be where Poseidon left his trident marks in a rock, and Athena's olive tree sprouted, in their battle for patronage of the city. Named after Erechtheus, one of the mythical kings of Athens, the temple was a sanctuary to both Athena Polias and Erechtheus-Poseidon.

Famed for its elegant and highly ornate Ionic archi-tecture and caryatid columns in the shape of women, this extraordinary monument is built on different levels. The large rectangular cella was divided into three rooms. One contained the holy olive-wood statue of Athena Polias. The cella was bounded by north, east and south porticoes. The south portico is the Porch of the Caryatids, which are now in the Acropolis Museum.

The Erechtheion complex has been used for a range of purposes, including a harem

The Propylaia, the monumental gateway that serves as the main entrance to the Acropolis

for the wives of the Ottoman commander in 1463. It was almost completely destroyed by a Turkish shell in 1827 during the War of Independence (p60). Restoration work has caused heated disputes: holes have been filled with new marble, and copies have been made to replace original features that have been removed to the safety of the museum.

⑤
Odeon of Herodes Atticus (Iródio)

Herodes Atticus (101–177 AD) was a wealthy Athenian scholar and Roman consul who endowed the giant odeon (building for musical peformances) that bears his name, completed in 161 AD, to the city of Athens. The orchestra area would have been roofed in cedar, though

seating was apparently open to the sky, as no supports for an extended roof have been found. Extending to three storeys in places, the odeon is immensely tall. Restored during the 20th century, it is now one of the main venues for the summer Athens Festival (p54).

⑥ ✎
Theatre of Dionysos

🚇 D Areopagitou, Makrygiánni 📞 210 322 4625 🕐 Apr-Oct: 8am-7pm daily; Nov-Mar: 8:30am-3pm daily

Cut into the southern cliff face of the Acropolis, the Theatre of Dionysos is the birthplace of Greek tragedy, and was the first theatre built of stone. Aeschylus, Sophokles, Euripides and Aristophanes

all had their plays performed here, during the dramatic contests of the annual Dionysia festival, when it was little more than a humble wood-and-earth affair. The theatre was rebuilt in stone by the Athenian statesman Lykourgos in 342–326 BC, but the ruins that can be seen today are in part those of a much bigger structure, built by the Romans, which could seat 17,000. They used it as a gladiatorial arena and added a marble balustrade with metal railings to protect spectators. Above the theatre, there is a cave sacred to the goddess Artemis. This was converted into a chapel in the Byzantine era, dedicated to Panagía i Spiliótissa (Our Lady of the Cave) and was the place where mothers brought their sick children. Two large Corinthian columns nearby are the remains of *choregic* monuments erected to celebrate the benefactor's team winning a drama festival. The Sanctuary of Asklepios to the west, founded in 420 BC, was dedicated to the god of healing.

The Erechtheion is said to be where Poseidon left his trident marks in a rock, and Athena's olive tree sprouted, in their battle for patronage of the city.

THE PARTHENON
Ο ΠΑΡΘΕΝΩΝΑΣ

One of the world's most famous buildings, the Parthenon is the epitome of ancient Greek Classical art. Built as an expression of ancient Athens's glory, it remains the city's emblem to this day.

Work began on the Parthenon in 447 BC, when, under the direction of the sculptor Pheidias, the architects Kallikrates and Iktinos started building a magnificent new Doric temple to Athena, the patron goddess of the city. It was designed primarily to house the Parthenos, Pheidias's impressive 12-m- (39-ft-) high cult statue of Athena covered in ivory and gold. Taking nine years to complete, the temple was dedicated to the goddess in 438 BC. Over the centuries it has been used as a church, a mosque and an arsenal and has suffered severe damage.

Akroterion

The west cella was used as a treasury.

The external frieze consisted of triglyphs and metopes.

The Parthenon frieze, designed by Pheidias, ran around the inner wall of the Parthenon. The metopes (sections of the frieze) depicted the Great Panathenaia festival, which took place every four years on Athena's birthday.

Marble walls concealed the cellas, or inner rooms.

THE ILLUSION OF PERFECTION

Every aspect of the Parthenon was built on a 9:4 ratio to make the temple completely symmetrical. The sculptors also used visual trickery to counteract the laws of perspective. The illustration below is exaggerated to show the techniques they employed.

The Parthenon Marbles (p100) were taken largely from the internal frieze.

Each column was constructed from fluted drums of marble. The fluting was added once the columns were in place.

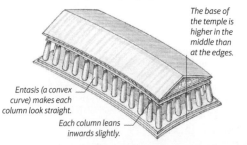

The base of the temple is higher in the middle than at the edges.

Entasis (a convex curve) makes each column look straight.

Each column leans inwards slightly.

Reconstruction, from the southeast, showing the Parthenon as it was in the 5th century BC ↑

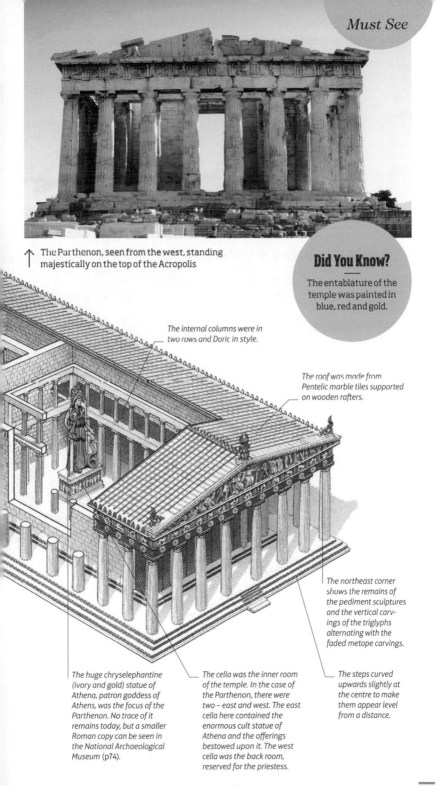

↑ The Parthenon, seen from the west, standing majestically on the top of the Acropolis

Did You Know?

The entablature of the temple was painted in blue, red and gold.

The internal columns were in two rows and Doric in style.

The roof was made from Pentelic marble tiles supported on wooden rafters.

The northeast corner shows the remains of the pediment sculptures and the vertical carvings of the triglyphs alternating with the faded metope carvings.

The huge chryselephantine (ivory and gold) statue of Athena, patron goddess of Athens, was the focus of the Parthenon. No trace of it remains today, but a smaller Roman copy can be seen in the National Archaeological Museum (p74).

The cella was the inner room of the temple. In the case of the Parthenon, there were two – east and west. The east cella here contained the enormous cult statue of Athena and the offerings bestowed upon it. The west cella was the back room, reserved for the priestess.

The steps curved upwards slightly at the centre to make them appear level from a distance.

Sculptures that once adorned the ↑
pediments of the Parthenon
in the Parthenon Gallery

⑧ 🖌 🍴 ☕

ACROPOLIS MUSEUM

ΜΟΥΣΕΙΟ ΑΚΡΟΠΟΛΗΣ

🏛 Dionysiou Areopagitou 15, Akrópoli Ⓜ Akrópoli Ⓒ Apr-Oct: 8am-8pm
daily (to 4pm Mon, to 10pm Fri); Nov-Mar: 9am-5pm daily (to 10pm Fri, to
8pm Sat & Sun) 🚫 Major public hols 🌐 theacropolismuseum.gr

**This glittering all-glass museum contains the stunning ancient
treasures found in and around the Acropolis, and provides a
fascinating insight into what daily life was like in ancient Athens.**

The museum opened in 2008 southeast of the Acropolis. It had been planned since the late 1970s to replace the old Acropolis Museum next to the Parthenon, which was thought too small and dilapidated to do justice to the sculptures and architectural pieces. Today, the multi-storey modern showpiece designed by Bernard Tschumi is undoubtably a more fitting home for the Acropolis hill's treasures. Tschumi had the challenge of constructing the building over excavations of an early Christian settlement. Concrete pillars and a glass walkway allow the building to hover over the ruins, which are on view as you approach the entrance.

The collection is installed in chronological order and begins with finds from the slopes of the Acropolis, including statues and reliefs from the Sanctuary of Asklepios. The Archaic Collection is set out in a magnificent double-height gallery. Fragments of painted pedimental statues include mythological scenes of Herakles grappling with monsters. On the level below, the post-Parthenon Collection comprises sculptures from the Temple of Athena Nike, and architectural features from the Propylaia and the Erechtheion, including five of the original six caryatids from the south porch; the sixth is in the British Museum.

THE PARTHENON MARBLES

Between 1800 and 1803 the seventh Earl of Elgin removed two-thirds of the sculptures of gods, men and monsters adorning the Parthenon and took them to England. Most were sold to the British Museum, which refuses to return them, saying that the sculptures are integral to its role in narrating human cultural achievement. The Acropolis Museum has answered previous criticism that Athens could not display them adequately or safely, as a special room awaits their return. Greece hopes that when thousands of international visitors see the sparkling but empty showcase, it will increase the pressure on Britain, forcing a much-anticipated return of the marbles.

Museum Highlights

The Parthenon Marbles

The sky-lit Parthenon Gallery is on the top floor. Here, arranged around an indoor court and looking out onto the Parthenon, the remaining original parts of the Parthenon frieze still in Greece are displayed in the order in which they would have graced the Parthenon (plaster casts occupy the spaces of those held in London). The sculptures depict the Panathenaic procession, including the chariot and apobates (slaves riding chariot horses) and a sacrificial cow being led by youths.

The Caryatids

◁ The original statued pillars that supported the Erechteion's porch have been brought inside. Their arms are broken now, but initially they held libation bowls.

The Calf-Bearer

▷ This joyous Archaic sculpture shows a bearded man carrying a calf, to be offered as a sacrifice to Athena. The statue itself was a votive offering and dates to 570 BC.

The Peplos Core

▽ This is one of the most exquisite of the Archaic votive statues. The gown, called a peplos, was painted with decorative colours. Traces of paint are still visible on her eyes, lips and curly hair.

Pediment of the Ancient Temple

Part of the pediment of an ancient temple to Athena, built before the Parthenon and later destroyed, shows Athena fighting against a Titan. It dates to 520 BC.

The Kritios Boy

This sculpture of a young male athlete dating to 480 BC marks the transition from Archaic to early Classical sculpture, with the introduction of a naturalistic pose.

Frieze on the Temple of Athena Nike

▷ The small but dynamically sculpted frieze shows scenes of battle, with gods, Persians and Greeks all stepping into the fray.

HILLS NEAR THE ACROPOLIS

⑨ Areopagos Hill

There is little left to see on this low hill today, apart from the rough-hewn, slippery steps and what are thought to be seats on its summit. The Areopagos was used by the Persians and Turks during their attacks on the Acropolis citadel, and played an important role as the home of the Supreme Judicial Court in the Classical period. It takes its name, meaning the "Hill of Ares", from a mythological trial that took place here when the god Ares was acquitted of murdering the son of Poseidon. The hill achieved renown in AD 51, when St Paul delivered his sermon "On an Unknown God" and gained his first convert, Dionysios the Areopagite, who became the patron saint of Athens.

Locator Map
For more detail see p92

> **PICTURE PERFECT**
> **Stunning Vistas**
>
> The summit of the Areopagos Hill offers some of the best views of the Ancient Agora, the whole city and the mountains of the Attica Basin. You can take plenty of iconic photos from this rocky outcrop.

⑩ Pnyx Hill

If Athens is the cradle of democracy, Pnyx Hill is its exact birthplace. During the 4th and 5th centuries BC, the Ekklesia (citizens' assembly) met here to discuss and vote upon all but the most important matters of state, until it lost its powers during Roman rule. In its heyday, 6,000 Athenians gathered here 40 times a year to listen to speeches and take vital political decisions. Themistokles, Perikles and Demosthenes all spoke from the bema (speaker's platform) that is still visible today. Carved out of the rock face, it formed

↑ Climbing to the top of Areopagus Hill, with the Athens cityscape beyond

↑ The Acropolis and southern Athens seen from the summit of Filopáppou Hill

the top step of a platform that doubled as a primitive altar to the god Zeus. There are also the remains of the huge retaining wall which was built to support the semicircular terraces that placed citizens on a level with the speakers. This completely surrounded the auditorium, which was 110 m (358 ft) high.

⑪
Filopáppou Hill

The highest summit in the south of Athens, at 147 m (482 ft), offers spectacular views of the Acropolis. It has always played a decisive defensive role in Athens' history – the general Demetrios Poliorketes built an important fort here overlooking the strategic Piraeus road in 294 BC, and the Venetians bombarded the Acropolis from here in 1687.

Built between AD 114 –16, the Monument of Philopappus on the summit, after which the hill was named, was raised by the Athenians in honour of Caius Julius Antiochus Philopappus, a Roman consul and philhellene. Its unusual concave marble façade, 12 m (40 ft) high, contains niches with statues of Philopappus and his grandfather, Antiochus IV. A frieze around the monument depicts the arrival of Philopappus by chariot for his inauguration as Roman consul in AD 100.

Located on the hill is the pretty Byzantine church of Agíos Dimítrios Lombardiaris, named after an incident that took place in 1656. The Ottoman commander at the time, Yusuf Aga, laid plans to fire a huge cannon called Loumpárda, situated by the Propylaia (p96), at worshippers in the church as they celebrated the feast day of Agios Dimítrios. However, the night before the feast, lightning struck the Propylaia, miraculously killing the commander and his family.

⑫
Hill of the Nymphs

This 103-m- (340-ft-) high tree-clad hill takes its name from dedications found carved on rocks in today's Observatory Garden. The Asteroskopeíon (Observatory) was built in 1842 by the Danish architect Theophil Hansen. It occupies the site of a sanctuary to nymphs associated with childbirth. The modern church of Agía Marína nearby has similar associations of child-birth; pregnant women used to slide effortlessly down a smooth rock near the church in the hope of an equally easy labour.

TEMPLE ARCHITECTURE

Temples were the most important public buildings in ancient Greece, largely because religion was a central part of everyday life. Often placed in prominent positions, temples were also statements about political and divine power. The earliest temples, in the 8th century BC, were built of wood and sun-dried bricks. Many of their features were copied in marble buildings from the 6th century BC onwards.

THE DEVELOPMENT OF TEMPLE ARCHITECTURE

Greek temple architecture is divided into three styles, which evolved chronologically, and are most easily distinguished by the shape and decoration of the column capitals.

Doric temples were surrounded by sturdy columns with plain capitals and no bases. As the earliest style of stone buildings, they recall wooden prototypes. Ionic temples differed from Doric in their tendency to have more columns, of a different form. The capital has a pair of volutes, like rams' horns, front and back. Corinthian temples in Greece were built in Athens and Corinth under the Romans. They feature slender columns with elaborate capitals decorated with acanthus leaves.

The triangular pediment often held relief sculpture.

The cella, or inner sanctum, housed the cult statue.

The cult statue was of the god or goddess to whom the temple was dedicated.

A ramp led up to the temple entrance.

The stepped platform was built on a stone foundation.

The column drums were initially carved with bosses for lifting them into place.

CARYATIDS

Caryatids, sculpted figures of women, served as architectural supports in the place of columns or pillars. They were used instead of columns in the Erechtheion *(p96)* at Athens' Acropolis. In Athens' Agora *(p106)*, tritons (half-fish, half-human creatures) were used.

The gable ends of the roof were surmounted by statues, known as akroteria, in this case of a Nike or "Winged Victory". Almost no upper portions of Greek temples survive.

The roof was supported on wooden beams and covered in rows of terracotta tiles, each ending in an upright akroterion.

Stone blocks were smoothly fitted together and held by metal clamps and dowels: no mortar was used in the temple's construction.

Fluting on the columns was carved in situ, guided by that on the top and bottom drums.

The ground plan was derived from the megaron of the Mycenaean house: a rectangular hall with a front porch supported by columns.

↑ Drawing of an idealized Doric temple, showing how it was built and used

Evolution of the Temple

700 BC
▶ First temple of Poseidon, Ancient Isthmia (Archaic; *p182*) and first Temple of Apollo, Corinth (Archaic; *p148*)

c 600
Temple of Hera, Olympia (Doric; *p152*)

550
Second temple of Apollo, Corinth (Doric; *p148*)

520
▽ Temple of Olympian Zeus, Athens, begun (Doric; completed Corinthian 2nd century AD; *p118*)

460
Temple of Zeus, Olympia (Doric; *p152*)

447–405
Temples of the Acropolis, Athens: Athena Nike (Ionic), Parthenon (Doric), Erechtheion (Ionic) *(pp94-9)*

445–425
Temple of Apollo, Bassae (Doric with Ionic; *p185*)

440–430
Temple of Poseidon, Sounion (Doric; *p138*)

425–415
▶ Temple of Artemis, Ancient Brauron (Doric; *p134*)

4th century
Temple of Apollo, Delphi (Doric; *p200*); Temple of Athena Aléa, Tegea (Doric and 1st Corinthian capital; *p185*)

ANCIENT AGORA
ΑΡΧΑΙΑ ΑΓΟΡΑ

📍C6 🏛Main entrance at Adrianoú 24, Monastiráki Ⓜ Thiseío,
Monastiráki ⏰ Apr–Oct: 8am–7pm daily; Nov–Mar: 8am–5pm daily
🚫 1 Jan, 25 Mar, Easter Sun, 1 May, 25 & 26 Dec 🌐 odysseus.culture.gr

The Agora, or marketplace, formed the political heart of
ancient Athens from 600 BC. Here, in the council buildings,
the law courts and the streets, democracy took shape.

The American School of Classical Studies began excavations of
the Ancient Agora in the 1930s, and since then, the vast remains
of a complex array of public buildings, temples, altars and
statuary have been revealed. Theatres, schools and stoas –
roofed arcades filled with shops – also made this the centre of
social and commercial life. Here too was the state prison, where
in 399 BC Socrates was indicted and executed, together with
the city mint that produced Athens' silver coins.

Treasures from the Excavations

An impressive two-storey stoa founded by King Attalos of
Pergamon (ruled 159–138 BC), rebuilt in the 1950s using the
original foundations and ancient materials, now houses the site's
museum. Its exhibits and artifacts reveal the great diversity and
sophistication of ancient life: rules from the 2nd-century
AD Library of Pantainos, the text of a law against
tyranny from 336 BC, and bronze and stone
lots used for voting. *Ostraka* (voting tablets
on which names were inscribed) bear
such famous names as Themistokles
and Aristeides the Just, the latter
banished, or "ostracized", in 482 BC.
More everyday items – terracotta
toys, portable ovens and hobnails
and sandals found in a shoemaker's
shop, are equally fascinating.

Library of Pantainos

*The colonnaded Stoa
of Attalos dominated
the eastern quarter
of the Agora until it
was burned down
by raiding Germanic
Heruli in AD 267.*

*Monopteros
temple*

*The Panathenaic
Way, linking the
Acropolis and the
Kerameikos, runs
straight through
the Agora*

*Altar of the
twelve gods*

← Statue of a triton, half-
man, half-fish, now
in the museum

Temple of Ares

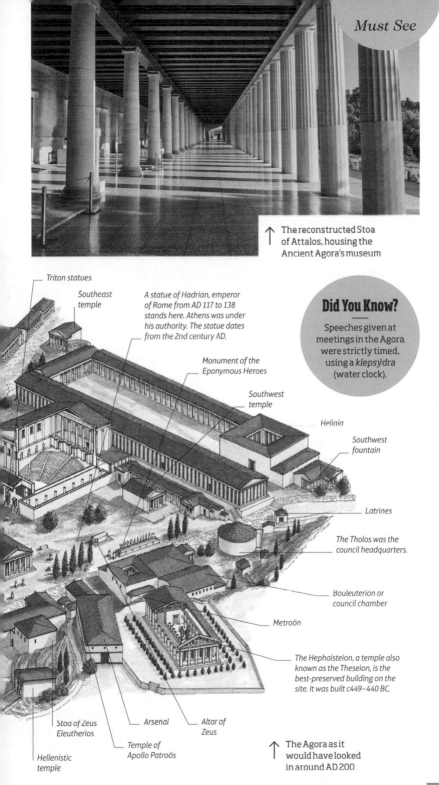

The reconstructed Stoa of Attalos, housing the Ancient Agora's museum

Triton statues

Southeast temple

A statue of Hadrian, emperor of Rome from AD 117 to 138 stands here. Athens was under his authority. The statue dates from the 2nd century AD.

Monument of the Eponymous Heroes

Southwest temple

Heliaia

Southwest fountain

Did You Know?

Speeches given at meetings in the Agora were strictly timed, using a *klepsýdra* (water clock).

Latrines

The Tholos was the council headquarters.

Bouleuterion or council chamber

Metroön

The Hephaisteion, a temple also known as the Theseion, is the best-preserved building on the site. It was built c449–440 BC.

Stoa of Zeus Eleutherios

Arsenal

Altar of Zeus

Temple of Apollo Patroös

Hellenistic temple

The Agora as it would have looked in around AD 200

③

MIKRÍ MITRÓPOLI

ΜΙΚΡΗ ΜΗΤΡΟΠΟΛΗ

📍E6 🅰Plateía Mitropóleos, Pláka Ⓜ Monastiráki
🕐7am-7pm daily

Nestling in the shadow of the gigantic 19th-century Mitrópoli cathedral *(p114)* is the dimunitive but lovely Mikrí Mitrópoli, or "little cathedral". Built in the 12th century, when Athens was just a village, it measures only 7.5 m (25 ft) long by 12 m (40 ft) wide.

PICTURE PERFECT
Old and New
One of the delights of Athens is finding ancient churches among its modern buildings. For a photo capturing the contrast, stand with your back to the main cathedral near the front or rear corner of the Mikrí Mitrópoli.

This domed cruciform church is dedicated to Panagía Gorgoepíkoös (the Madonna who Swiftly Hears) and Agios Elefthérios (the saint who protects women in childbirth) . It is built entirely from Pentelic marble, now weathered to a rich corn-coloured hue. What makes the architecture so intriguing is that a great proportion of the building materials used were recycled from earlier buildings, and many of these stones had already been carved and sculpted. The result is a church in Byzantine style, but incorporating decorative elements such as friezes and bas-reliefs that date back to more ancient Classical times.

A pair of 12th-century bas-reliefs depicting allegorical animals ornament the west façade.

↑ Mary Panagía, the only surviving fresco in Mikrí Mitrópoli

The lintel frieze depicting personifications of the months of the year, and their accompanying festivals, dates from the 4th century BC.

Main entrance

Fragments of Classical buildings made from Pentelic marble were combined with Byzantine sections in the style of a Classical frieze.

↑ The exterior of the small church; detail of a marble relief on the façade *(inset)*

Four brick pillars replaced the original marble ones in 1834.

The floor is lower than ground level by about 30 cm (12 in).

↑ The cross-in-square plan of Mikrí Mitrópoli, typical of Byzantine-era churches

SHOP

Orpheus Icon Gallery

This family-run shop has been near Mikrí Mitrópoli in the Monastiráki market area since the 1980s. It stocks exquisite replicas of original Byzantine icons that are handmade by a workshop of icon painters. It also has some replicas of ancient Greek bronze and marble artifacts.

📍 F8 🏛 Pandrosou 28
📞 210 324 5034

EXPERIENCE MORE

4

Museum of Modern Greek Culture

Μουσείο Νεότερου Ελληνικού Πολιτισμού

⚲ D6 🏛 Areos 10 Ⓜ Monastiraki ⌚ Annexes only; check website for updates on main building 🌐 mnep.gr

Formerly the Museum of Greek Folk Art, the Museum of Modern Greek Culture is being expanded to create a multi-centre portfolio of fascinating collections, housed at locations within walking distance of each other on the outskirts of the Roman Agora. The core collection includes displays of Greek folk arts and crafts ranging from embroidery and lace-making to elaborate wedding dresses and costumes worn for dances and festivals. It is housed in a modern main building between Areos and Vrysakiou in Monastiraki, opposite the Roman Forum.

The 18th–19th-century renaissance of decorative crafts such as weaving, woodcarving and metalwork is also well represented. Among the gems are vividly coloured ceramics, including everyday items such as terracotta jugs and dishes, decorative plates and pottery figures drawn from legends and folk tales.

While the new building is completed, two annexes are open to visitors. Built in the Ottoman era, the **Bath House of the Winds** with its domed steam rooms was one of the old city's public baths. The beautifully restored hammam offers a glimpse into an easily missed part of the city's heritage. **Panos 22** houses a fascinating exhibition, "Men and Tools". With its collection of old farming equipment and artisans' tools – some in use within living memory – it reveals how vastly working life for many Greeks has changed within a few generations.

Bath House of the Winds

Ⓐ 🏛 Kyristou 8 📞 210 324 5957 ⌚ 9am-4pm Wed-Mon 🚫 Tue, main public hols

Did You Know?

Athenians enjoyed the bathing facilities at the Bath House of the Winds right up until 1956.

Panos 22

Ⓐ 🏛 Panos 22 📞 210 324 5957 ⌚ 9am-4pm Wed-Mon 🚫 Main public hols

---

5

Tower of the Winds

Αέρηδες

⚲ E7 🏛 Within Roman Agora ruins, Pláka 📞 210 324 5220 Ⓜ Monastiráki ⌚ 8am-3pm Mon-Fri, 8am-5pm Sat & Sun 🚫 Main public hols

The remarkable Tower of the Winds is set within the ruins of the Roman Agora. Constructed from marble in the 2nd or 1st century BC by the Syrian astronomer

Browsing the covered stalls at the large Monastiráki flea market

Andrónikos Kyrrestes, it was designed as a combined weather vane and water clock. The name comes from the external friezes, personifying the prevailing wind on each of the eight sides. Sundials are etched into the walls beneath each relief and a weather vane stood on the roof, making this the world's first meteorological station.

The tower is well preserved, standing today at over 12 m (40 ft) high with a diameter of 8 m (26 ft). Still simply called Aérides ("the winds") by Greeks today, in the Middle Ages it was thought to be either the school or prison of Socrates, or even the tomb of Philip II of Macedon (p59). It was at last correctly identified as the Horologion (water clock) of Andrónikos in the 17th century. All that remains today of its elaborate water clock are the origins of a complex system of water pipes and a circular channel cut into the floor, which can be seen inside the tower.

The Tower of the Winds in the old Roman Agora, catching the rays of the rising sun

6

Flea Market
Πιουσουρουμι

📍 D6 🚶 From Plateía Monastirakíou to Plateía Avyssinías, Monastiráki 🚇 Monastiráki 🕐 8am–2pm Sun

Plunge into the famous flea market off the southwest corner of Plateia Monastiráki to discover a maze of alleys either side of Odos Ifestou, crammed with shops selling everything from genuine antiques and worthless junk to street fashion, army surplus and camping gear, antiquarian books and maps. The market is liveliest on Sunday morning, when traders set out their wares on stalls and on the pavement. Plateia Avyssinías is the heart of the original market and offers a selection of open-air cafés and tavernas.

The "New Flea Market" runs along Odos Pandrossou, from the southeast corner of Monastiraki, and offers a rather more upmarket range of small shops selling gold and silver jewellery, attractive linen clothes and hand-made sandals as well as tackier tourist trinkets.

SHOP

Centre for Hellenic Tradition
A range of high-quality traditional handicrafts, ceramics and sculptures, made by artisans from all over Greece, are for sale at this cultural centre of Greek folk art, a short walk from Monastiráki Flea Market.

📍 E6 🏠 Pandrossou 36 📞 210 321 3023

Olgianna Melissinos Sandals
This shop is known for its hand-made leather sandals, but it stocks much more than footwear. If you are looking for a backpack, a belt or a beautiful leather handbag, you'll find it here too.

📍 D6 🏠 16 Tzireon St 📞 210 331 1925

⑦ Kerameikos

Κεραμεικός

📍B4 🚪Ermoú 148, Thiseío 📞210 346 3552 🚇Kerameikos 🕐Apr-Oct: 8am-7pm daily; Nov-Mar: 8:30am-4pm daily 🚫Main public hols

This ancient cemetery has been a burial ground since the 12th century BC. The Sacred Way led from Eleusis (p132) to Kerameikos, and the Panathenaic Way ran from the Dípylon Gate here to the Acropolis (p94). Most of the graves remaining today are along the Street of the Tombs. Largely dating from the 4th century BC, they vary in style, from lavish *stelae* (relief sculptures) to simple *kioniskoi*

Did You Know?

Kerameikos was once the potters' quarter; the word "ceramics" derives from *kéramos*, potter's clay.

(small columns). Several depict scenes from the lives of the deceased: the Stele of Dexilious shows the young soldier bravely slaying an enemy before being killed in the Corinthian War. Others are more domestic – the vase-like monument to Loutrophoros of Hegetaor portrays a simple farewell scene, while on the Stele of Hegeso the wife of Koroibos of Melite admires her jewels with a servant.

Most of these monuments are plaster copies; the originals are in the National Museum, or in the small museum within the cemetery. Now the Kerameikos Museum, it was formerly named after Gustav Oberlander (1867–1936), a German-American industrialist whose donations enabled the museum to open in 1937. In Gallery 1, some large fragments from grave stelae found incorporated into the Dípylon and Sacred Gates are exhibited. These include a marble sphinx (c 550 BC) that once crowned a grave stele. Galleries 2 and 3 offer an array of huge Proto-Geometric and Geometric amphorae and black-figure *lekythoi* (funerary vases). The most moving

exhibits come from children's graves and include pottery toy horses and terracotta dolls. There are also examples of some of the 7,000 *ostraka* (voting tablets) found in the river Eridanos. Among the painted pottery, there is a red-

← Peaceful Kerameikos cemetery, a resting place for Athenians for millennia

figure *hydria* (water vase) of Helen of Troy and a *lekythos* of Dionysos with satyrs.

Technopolis
Τεχνόπολη

⚲ A5 ⌂ Pireos 100
Ⓜ Kerameikos or Thiseio
⊙ Times vary with events and exhibitions, check website Ⓦ athens-technopolis.gr

Housed on the site of a former gas works, this large cultural centre hosts cutting-edge art exhibitions and theatre and music performances. Retaining some of the original industrial buildings, including one of the gas holders, the complex has a retro feel. Warehouses and former machine workshops have been transformed into unique events venues including a 300-seat amphitheatre. Take a theatrical walking tour with an actor and experience the stories of people who worked on the gas production line from 1850 to the present day.

Part of the complex includes the Industrial Gas Museum, which relates the city's

industrial heritage and features the work of contemporary industrial designers. Another small museum is devoted to the opera singer Maria Callas, who lived in this area of Athens for several years.

Melína Merkoúri Museum and Cultural Centre
Πολιτιστικό Κέντρο Μελίνα

⚲ A6 ⌂ Iraklidon 66
Ⓜ Thiseio ⊙ 10am-8pm Tue-Sat, 10am-2pm Sun

This testament to the legacy of Athens-born actress, singer and politician Melína Merkoúri (1920–1994) is housed in a former hat factory that was built in 1886. Merkoúri first achieved fame as an actress, receiving many awards and an Oscar nomination for her role in the classic Greek film *Never on Sunday* (1960). She was equally distinguished when she went into politics and became the first woman to hold the role of Minister of Culture and Sports in 1981. She came up with the idea of having an annual European City of Culture, a tradition which continues to this day. She was also the first to lobby for the return to Greece of the Parthenon marbles from London's British Museum.

The museum and cultural centre has two permanent exhibitions focusing on issues that Merkoúri felt passionately about. "Athens Journey" depicts what various Athens neighbourhoods were like in the early 20th century when Melína Merkoúri was growing up. The Haridimos Shadow Puppet Museum is centred on this much-loved art form in Greece. There are also temporary exhibitions and frequent events.

---

⑩

Municipal Art Gallery
Δημοτική Πινακοθήκη

⚲ C4 ⌂ Pireos 52 ☏ 210 324 3022 Ⓜ Metaxourgeíou ⊙ 9am-1pm & 5-9pm Mon-Fri; 9am-1pm Sun

This little-visited building has one of the finest archive collections of modern Greek art. Designed by the architect Christian Hansen originally as a silk workshop, since 2010 it has sheltered this art gallery. The Municipality of Athens has been amassing the collection since 1923. It now offers a fine introduction to the diverse styles of modern Greek artists. Many paintings are passionate reflections on the Greek landscape, such as Dímos Mpraésas's (1878–1967) landscapes of the Cyclades or the works of Konstantínos Parthénis (1882–1964) depicting olive and cypress trees.

There are also portraits by Giánnis Mitarákis and still lifes by Theófrastos Triantafyllídis. Paintings such as Níkolaos Kartsonákis's *Street Market* (1939) also reveal the folk roots that are at the heart of much modern Greek art.

↑ Geometric painting by Opy Zouni (1941-2008), Municipal Art Gallery

⑪ Mitrópoli
Μητρόπολη

⚲E6 ⌂Plateía Mitropóleos, Pláka 📞210 322 1308 Ⓜ Monastiráki ⏰7am–7pm daily

Work began in 1840 on this huge cathedral, using marble from 72 demolished churches for its walls. The cornerstone was laid in a ceremony by King Otto and Queen Amalía on Christmas Day 1842. It took another 20 years to finish the building, using three different architects (François Boulanger, Theophil Hansen and Dimítrios Zézos), which may account for its slightly ungainly appearance. On 21 May 1862, it was formally dedicated to Evangelismós Theotókou (the Annunciation

---

---

of the Virgin) by the king and queen. At 40 m (130 ft) long, 20 m (65 ft) wide and 24 m (80 ft) high, it is the largest church in Athens.

The cathedral is the official seat of the Bishop of Athens, and remains a popular city landmark that has been used for ceremonial events from the coronations of kings to the weddings and funerals of the rich and famous.

Inside, there are the tombs of two saints murdered by the Ottoman Turks: Agía Filothéi and Gregory V. The bones of Agía Filothéi, who died in 1589, are still visible in a silver reliquary. Her charitable works included the ransoming of Greek women enslaved in Turkish harems. Gregory V, Patriarch of Constantinople, was hanged and thrown into the Bosphorus in 1821. His body was rescued by Greek sailors and taken to Odessa. It was eventually returned to Athens by Black Sea (Pontic) Greeks 50 years later.

← The sumptuous chancel of the Mitrópoli and the twin-towered exterior of the cathedral *(inset)*

↑ Stringed folk instruments at the Museum of Greek Popular Musical Instruments

⑫
Ilías Lalaoúnis Jewellery Museum
Μουσείο Κοσμήματος Ηλία Λαλαούνη

📍E8 **🏛Karyatidon & P Kallisperi 12, Akrópoli** **Ⓜ Akrópoli** **🕐10am-2pm daily** **⏰Main public hols** **🌐lalaounis-jewelry museum.gr**

Situated just below the Theatre of Dionysos, this small museum is a delight for anyone interested in decorative arts. The permanent collection comprises over 4,000 pieces spanning 60 years of jewellery-making by designer Ilías Lalaoúnis, who is credited with the revival of the Greek practice of the art in the 1950s. There is a studio in which young and visiting metalsmiths can be seen at work; more extended tours are also available that include hands-on workshops.

---

⑬
Kanellópoulos Museum
Μουσείο Κανελλοπούλου

📍D7 **🏛Corner of Theorías & Pános 12, Pláka** **Ⓜ Monastiráki** **🕐8:30am-4pm Wed-Mon** **⏰Main public hols** **🌐pacf.gr**

In an immaculately restored Neo-Classical town house, this museum has a varied collection of artifacts from all over the Hellenistic world. These include 6th-century BC helmets, 5th-century BC gold Persian jewellery and Attic vases, as well as Cycladic figurines, some unusual terracotta figures of actors in their Classical theatrical masks and a fine El Faiyûm portrait of a woman dating to the 2nd century AD.

A huge block of stone that fell from the walls of the Acropolis can still be seen as an exhibit on the ground floor.

⑭
Museum of Greek Popular Musical Instruments
Μουσείο Ελληνικών Λαϊκών Μουσικών Οργάνων

📍E7 **🏛Diogénous 1-3, Pláka** **📞210 325 0198** **Ⓜ Monastiráki** **🕐10am-2pm Tue & Thu-Sun, noon-6pm Wed**

Cretan musicologist Phoivos Anogianákis (1915–2003) donated his collection of over 1,200 musical instruments to the Greek state in 1978. In 1992, this study centre and museum was opened, devoted to the history of Greek folk and popular music, including Anogianákis's collection. The museum traces the development of different styles of island music and the arrival of *rempétika* (Greek "blues") from Smyrna in 1922.

Instruments from all over Greece are displayed; next to many of the exhibits are headphones which you can use to hear recordings of the instruments being played. The differences between regional musical and playing styles are also demonstrated.

The basement contains church and livestock bells, as well as water whistles, wooden clappers and flutes. Elsewhere there are wind instruments including *tsampoúna* (bagpipes made from goatskin) and string instruments such as the Cretan *lýra*.

⑮
Benizelos Mansion
Αρχοντικό Μπενιζέλου

📍E7 **🏛Adrianou 96** **Ⓜ Monastiraki** **🕐10am-1pm Tue-Thu, 11am-4pm Sun** **🌐archontiko-mpenizelon.gr**

This 17th-century Ottoman-style mansion, also known as the House of St Philothei, is the oldest surviving house in Athens. It is a fine example of a *konaki*, an urban aristocratic house that was a feature of Ottoman cities. The *konaki* has been renovated and its rooms reconstructed and furnished to show what life was like in a wealthy 17th-century Athenian household.

Interactive digital displays narrate the story of the Benizelos family and their daughter, who chose a monastic philanthropic life and was canonized as St Philothei. There is also a delightful garden with views over Athens.

💬 INSIDER TIP
Summer Sounds

If you're visiting Athens in summer, check out whether the Museum of Greek Popular Musical Instruments is holding one of its evening concerts in the garden. It's a lovely setting for some authentic music.

16

Agios Nikólaos Ragkavás

Άγιος Νικόλαος ο Ραγκαβάς

📍 E7 📍 Corner of Tripodon & Prytaneíou 1, Pláka
📞 210 322 8193
Ⓜ Monastiráki 🚌 1, 2, 4, 5, 10, 11 🕐 8am–noon, 5–8pm daily

Once part of the Rangavas family estate, this typical 11th-century Byzantine church, rebuilt in the 18th century and restored to some of its former glory in the late 1970s, incorporates marble columns and other remains of ancient buildings in its external walls. It is one of the favourite parish churches of Pláka, frequently used for colourful Greek weddings which spill out onto the street at weekends. It was the first church in Athens to have a bell after the War of Independence (1821), and this bell was the

EAT

Aleria

Housed in a Neo-Classical building with a romantic courtyard, Aleria serves contemporary gourmet cuisine (dinner-only).

📍 B4 📍 Megalou Alexandrou 57, Metaxourgeíou
🅦 aleria.gr

€€€

Scholarhio

Choose from a large variety of delicious home-made meze at this family-run traditional restaurant.

📍 E7 📍 Tripodon 14
🅦 scholarhio.gr

€€€

Choregic **monuments were built to commemorate the victors at the annual choral and dramatic festival at the Theatre of Dionysos.**

first to ring out after the city's liberation from the Germans on 12 October 1944.

17

Plateía Lysikrátous

Πλατεία Λυσικράτους

📍 F8 📍 Lysikrátous, Sélley & Epimenídou, Pláka 🚌 1, 5, 15

Situated in the east of the Pláka district, this square is named after the monument of Lysikrates that dominates it. Despite Lord Elgin's vain attempts to remove it to England, the elegant structure is the city's only intact *choregic* monument. These monuments were built to commemorate the victors at the annual choral and dramatic festival at the Theatre of Dionysos (*p97*). They take their name from the rich sponsor (*choregos*) who produced the winning team. Built in 334 BC, this is the earliest known example where Corinthian capitals

are used externally. Six columns rise in a circle to a marble dome, decorated with an elegant finial of acanthus leaves which supported the winner's bronze trophy. The dome bears the inscription "Lysikrates of Kikynna, son of Lysitheides, was choregos; the tribe of Akamantis won the victory with a chorus of boys; Theon played the flute; Lysiades, an Athenian, trained the chorus; Evainetos was archon". The Athenians elected nine magistrates known as archons each year, and referred to the year by the name of one of them, the "eponymous archon".

A frieze above this inscription depicts a battle between Dionysos, the god of theatre, and Tyrrhenian pirates. Surrounded by satyrs, the god transforms the pirates into dolphins and their ship's mast into a sea serpent.

Capuchin friars converted the monument into a library. Grand tour travellers, such as

↑ The choregic monument to artistic triumph in Plateía Lysikrátous

A slice of Greek island life in the city: the whitewashed Anafiótika neighbourhood

Chateaubriand (1768–1848) and Byron (*p139*), stayed at their convent, which was founded on the site in 1669. Byron was inspired while staying there and wrote some of his famous poem *Childe Harold's Pilgrimage* while sitting in the monument during his final visit to Athens in 1810.

Not far from the monument is the beautifully restored 11th-century Byzantine church of Agía Aikateríni (St Catherine). In 1767, it was given to the monastery of St Catherine of Mount Sinai. It was renovated, but in 1882, the monastery was forced to exchange it for land elsewhere and it became a local parish church.

---

18 🏛️

Frissiras Museum
Μουσείο Φρυσίρα

📍**F7** 🏛️**Monís Asteríou 3 & 7** Ⓜ️**Sýntagma and Akrópoli** 🚌**2, 4, 9, 10, 11, 12, 15** 🔒**For renovation** 🌐**frissirasmuseum.com**

Vlassis Frissiras started collecting modern Greek art in 1978 but, in the 1990s, he expanded his collection to include art from all over Europe. His acquisitions centre on the human form and its representation.

The Frissiras is split over two buildings on the same street. At no 7, in a Neo-Classical edifice designed by the German architect Ernst Ziller, the permanent collection includes 3,500 excellent holdings of modern and contemporary European paitings and sculptures. Familiar names here include the likes of Paula Rego, R B Kitaj and David Hockney. The premises at no 3 are devoted to hosting rotating

temporary exhibits, which sometimes include up-and-coming Greek artists.

19

Anafiótika
Αναφιώτικα

📍**E7** Ⓜ️**Akrópoli**

Nestling below the northern slopes of the Acropolis, this area is one of the oldest settlements in Athens. Today, its whitewashed houses, cramped streets, lazy cats and pots of basil on windowsills still give it the atmosphere of a typical Cycladic village. Its first residents were refugees from the Peloponnesian War (*p57*). By 1841 it had been colonized by workmen from the island of Anáfi, in the Cyclades, which eventually

gave the area its name. Part of the influx of island craftsmen who helped to construct the new city following Independence, they ignored an 1834 decree declaring the area an archaeological zone, and completed their houses overnight, installing their families by morning. By Ottoman law, this meant the authorities were powerless to knock the new houses down. In the 20th century the Greek government reasserted the illegality of the dwellings and some have been demolished.

The area is bounded by two 17th-century churches: Agios Geórgios tou Vráchou to the east, which has a tiny courtyard filled with flowers, and Agios Symeón to the west, which contains a copy of a miraculous icon, originally brought from Anáfi.

13,000

The number of people of Russian origin living in Athens.

20

Russian Church of the Holy Trinity

Ρωσική εκκλησία Αγίας Τριάδας

📍F7 🏠Souri 1, Pláka
Ⓜ️Sýntagma 🚌1, 2, 4, 5, 9, 10, 11, 12, 15, 18
🕐7–11am Sat & Sun
🚫Main public hols

Still in use by the Russian community, this was once the largest church in the city. Built in 1031 by the Lykodímou family (also called Nikodímou), it was ruined by an earthquake in 1701. In 1780, the Turkish governor, Hadji Ali Haseki, partly demolished the church to use its materials for the defensive wall that he built around the city. During the siege of the city in 1827, it received more damage from Greek shells

↓ The Temple of Olympian Zeus, breathtaking in its massive scale

fired from the Acropolis. The church remained derelict until the Russian government restored it 20 years later. It was then reconsecrated as the Church of the Holy Trinity.

A large cruciform building, its most unusual feature is a wide dome, 10 m (33 ft) in diameter. Its interior was decorated by the Bavarian painter Ludwig Thiersch. The separate bell tower also dates from the 19th century, its bell a gift from Tsar Alexander II.

---

21 🅿️

Temple of Olympian Zeus

Ναός του Ολυμπίου Διός

📍F8 🏠Corner of Amalías & Vasilíssis Olgas, Pláka
📞210 922 6330 Ⓜ️Akrópoli
🚌2, 4, 11 🕐8am–7pm daily (Nov–Mar: to 3pm) 🚫Main public hols

Awe-inspiring even in ruins, the Athenian temple of Olympian Zeus is the largest in Greece, exceeding even the Parthenon in size. Work began on this vast edifice in the 6th century BC, in the reign of the tyrant Peisistratos, who allegedly initiated the building work to gain public favour. Although there were several attempts over many years

to finish the temple, it was not completed until 650 years later.

The Roman emperor Hadrian dedicated the temple to Zeus Olympios during the Panhellenic festival of AD 132, on his second visit to Athens. He also set up a gold and ivory inlaid statue of the god inside the temple, a copy of the original by Pheidias at Olympia (p152). Next to it, he placed a huge statue of himself. Both these statues have since been lost.

Only 15 of the original 104 Corinthian columns remain, each 17 m (56 ft) high – but enough to give a sense of the enormous size of this temple, which would have been approximately 96 m (315 ft) long and 40 m (130 ft) wide. Corinthian capitals were added to the simple Doric columns by a Roman architect in AD 174.

The temple is situated next to Hadrian's Arch, built in AD 131. It was positioned deliberately to mark the boundary between the ancient city and the new Athens of Hadrian.

INSIDER TIP
Changing of the Guard

The best time to watch the Changing of the Guard in front of the Greek parliament is 11am on Sunday when crowds gather to watch the extra-elaborate official ceremony.

22

Jewish Museum of Greece

Εβραϊκό Μουσείο της Ελλάδας

F7 **Níkis 39, Sýntagma** **Sýntagma** **1, 2, 4, 5, 10, 11, 15** **9am–2:30pm Mon–Fri, 10am–2pm Sun** **Main public hols & Jewish festivals** **jewishmuseum.gr**

This small museum traces the history of Greece's Jewish communities, which date back to the 3rd century BC. The exhibits present a revealing portrait of both Romaniot Jews, who had always lived in Greece, and Sephardic Jews, who fled Spain and Portugal in the 15th century and settled throughout Greece during the religiously tolerant years of the Ottoman Empire.

Weekday Changing of the Guard in Plateía Syntágmatos ↑

Among the fine examples of traditional costumes, jewellery and religious ceremonial instruments on display, one item of particular interest is the reconstruction of the *ehal*. This is the ark containing the Torah from the Pátra synagogue, which dates from the 1920s. It was rescued by Nikólaos Stavroulákis, founder of the museum, who has also written several books about the Greek Jews. These are on sale in the museum bookshop.

Moving displays of documentation record the German occupation of Greece during World War II, when 87 per cent of the Jewish population here was wiped out. More than 45,000 Greeks from Thessaloníki alone were sent to the concentration camp at Auschwitz during a period of five months in 1943. Others were deported as late as summer 1944.

Less than one-third of the museum's collection is permanently on display, so it hosts regular temporary exhibitions to showcase the remaining artifacts.

23

Plateía Syntágmatos

F6 **Sýntagma** **Sýntagma** **1, 4, 5, 11, 12, 13, 15**

Sýntagma Square is home to the Greek parliament, in the Voulí building, and the Tomb of the Unknown Soldier, decorated with an evocative relief depicting a dying Greek hoplite warrior. Unveiled on 25 March 1932 (Independence Day), the tomb is flanked by texts from the famous funeral oration by Perikles. The other walls that enclose the space are covered in bronze shields celebrating military victories since 1821.

The National Guard (*évzones*) are on continuous patrol in front of the tomb, and change guard hourly on every hour, with a colourful, synchronzied high-stepping routine, dressed in their famous uniform of kilt and pom-pom clogs.

24

First Cemetery of Athens

Πρώτο Νεκροταφείο Αθηνών

📍 G10 🚪 Entrance from Anapáfseos, Méts 📞 210 923 6118 🚌 2, 4, 10 🕖 7am–dusk daily

Athens' municipal cemetery, which is not to be confused with the Kerameikos, the ancient cemetery (p112), is a peaceful place, filled with pine and olive trees and the scent of incense burning at the well-kept tombs.

Fine examples of 19th-century funerary art range from the flamboyance of some of the marble mausoleums to the simplicity of the Belle Epoque *Oraía Koimoméni* or *Sleeping Beauty*. Created by Tiniot artist Giannoúlis Chalepás, this beautiful tomb is found to the right of the main cemetery avenue where many of Greece's foremost families are buried.

Among the notable 19th- and 20th-century figures with tombs here are Theódoros Kolokotrónis (p89), British philhellene historian George Finlay (1799–1875), German archaeologist Heinrich Schliemann (p163), the Nobel Prize-winning poet Giórgos Seféris (1900–71) and the actress and politician Melína Merkoúri (1920–94; p113).

In addition to the large number of tombs for famous people who are buried here, the cemetery contains a moving, single memorial to the 40,000 Athenians who perished through starvation during World War II.

↑ Avenue of fan palms planted by Queen Amalía in the National Gardens

25

National Gardens

Εθνικός Κήπος

📍 G7 🚪 Borders Vasilíssis Sofías, Iródou Attikoú, Vasilíssis Olgas & Vasilíssis Amalías, Sýntagma Ⓜ Sýntagma 🚌 1, 3, 5, 7, 8, 10, 13, 18 🕖 Dawn–dusk

Behind the Voulí parliament building, this 16-ha (40-acre) park, cherished by all Athenians and formerly known as the "Royal Gardens", was renamed the National Gardens by decree in 1923. Queen Amalía ordered the creation of the park in the 1840s; she even used the fledgling Greek navy to bring 15,000 seedlings from around the world. The gardens were landscaped by the Prussian

Sleeping Beauty by Giannoúlis Chalepás at the First Cemetery

horticulturalist Friedrich Schmidt, who travelled the globe in search of rare plants. Queen Amalía herself planted the striking avenue of Washingtonia fan palms, which are native to the southwestern United States.

Although the gardens have lost much of their original grandeur, they remain one of the most peaceful spots in the city. Shady paths meander past small squares, park benches, and ponds filled with koi. Remains of Roman mosaics excavated in the park and an old aqueduct add atmosphere. Modern sculptures of writers, such as Dionýsios Solomós, Aristotélis Valaorítis and Jean Moreas, can be found throughout the park. South of the park lies the Záppeion exhibition hall, an impressive building in use today as a conference centre. It was donated by Evángelos and Konstantínos Záppas, cousins who made their fortunes in Romania. Built by Theophil Hansen, architect of the Athens Academy (p89), between 1874 and 1888, it also has its own gardens. The elegant café next door to the Záppeion is a pleasant place to relax and take refreshment after a walk around these charming, peaceful gardens.

26

Presidential Palace

⊙H7 ⚑Iródou Attikoú, Sýntagma Ⓜ Sýntagma ⊞3, 7, 8, 13 ⚑To the public

This former royal palace was designed by Ernst Ziller *(p89)* in c 1878. It was occupied by the Greek Royal Family from 1890 until the deposition of King Constantine in 1967. It is still guarded by *évzones* whose barracks are at the top of the street *(p119)*. After the abolition of the monarchy, the palace became the official residence of the President of Greece, and is now mostly used to receive foreign visitors. For security reasons, it is forbidden to approach the palace perimeter on foot or stop nearby in a car.

27

National Museum of Contemporary Art (EMST)

Εθνικό Μουσείο Σύγχρονης Τέχνης

⊙D10 ⚑Leoforos Kallirrois/Amrovsiou Frantzi Ⓜ Syngrou Fix ⊙11am-7pm Tue-Sun (to 10pm Thu) ⚑emst.gr

Originally opened in 2000 in a striking building that was formerly a brewery, this museum has had a chequered history, closing a few years later during the Greek financial crisis. It reopened in 2016 and has been slowly acquiring artworks in a variety of media, especially video. Much of the artwork comments on modern Greek politics and the impact of the economic recession but there are also temporary exhibitions of works by international artists.

---

28 ⊘

Kallimármaro Stadium

Καλλιμάρμαρο Στάδιο

⊙H8 ⚑Vasileos Konstantinou Avenue ☎210 752 2985 ⊞3, 4, 10, 11 ⊙8am-7pm daily (Nov-Feb: to 5pm)

This huge marble structure in a small valley by Ardittós Hill occupies the exact site of the original Panathenaic Stadium built by Lykourgos in 330–329 BC. It was first reconstructed for gladiatorial contests during Hadrian's reign (AD 117–138), and then rebuilt in white marble for the Panathenaic Games in AD 144. Its marble was then quarried for use in buildings.

In 1895, Geórgios Avéroff funded the restoration of the stadium in time for the first modern Olympic Games on 5 April 1896. Designed by

Anastásios Metaxás, the present structure is a replica of Herodes Atticus's stadium, as described in the 2nd-century *Guide to Greece* by Pausanias. Built in white Pentelic marble, it is 204 m (669 ft) long and 83 m (272 ft) wide and seats up to 60,000. Between 1869 and 1879, Ernst Ziller excavated the site. His finds included a double-headed statue of Apollo and Dionysos, one of many used to divide the running track down its length. The statue is on show in the National Archaeological Museum *(p74)*. Today the stadium is the finishing point for the annual Athens marathon.

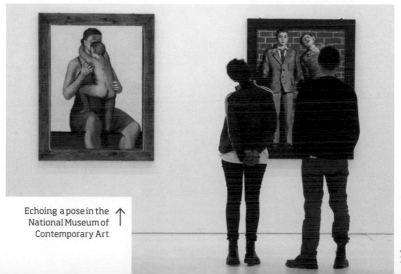

↑ Echoing a pose in the National Museum of Contemporary Art

A SHORT WALK
MONASTIRÁKI

Distance 1.5 km (1 mile) **Time** 20 minutes
Nearest metro Monastiráki

This old area of the city takes its name from the little sunken monastery in Plateía Monastirakíou of which only the Pantánassa church remains today. The former heart of Ottoman Athens, Monastiráki is still home to a bazaar and market stalls selling everything from junk to jewellery. The Fethiye and Tzistarákis mosques stand as reminders of the area's Ottoman past. Roman influences are also strong. The area borders the Roman Agora and includes the remains of Emperor Hadrian's library and the unique Tower of the Winds, a Hellenistic water clock. Wander around this neighbourhood and soak up the atmospheric surroundings of ancient ruins before bargaining in the bazaar.

Plateía Avissynías *is the heart of the flea market (p111), which extends through the surrounding streets. It is particularly busy at weekends.*

```
0 metres        50   N
0 yards         50   ↑
```

Ifaístou Street *is named after Hephaistos, the god of fire and metal craftsmanship. Areos is named after Ares, the war god.*

START

POIKILIS

↑ Clothing and trinket stalls at the famous Monastiráki Flea Market

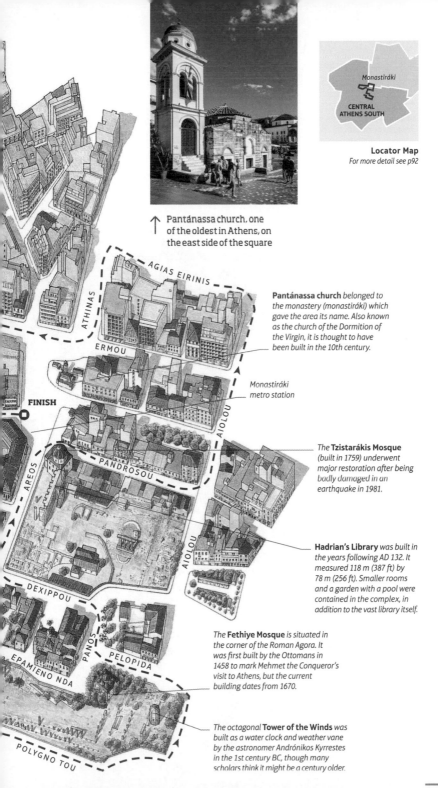

↑ Pantánassa church, one
of the oldest in Athens, on
the east side of the square

AGIAS EIRINIS

ATHINAS

ERMOU

Monastiráki
metro station

FINISH

AIOLOU

PANDROSOU

AREOS

AIOLOU

DEXIPPOU

PANOS

PELOPIDA

EPAMEINO NDA

POLYGNO TOU

Pantánassa church *belonged to
the monastery (monastiráki) which
gave the area its name. Also known
as the church of the Dormition of
the Virgin, it is thought to have
been built in the 10th century.*

The **Tzistarákis Mosque**
*(built in 1759) underwent
major restoration after being
badly damaged in an
earthquake in 1981.*

Hadrian's Library *was built in
the years following AD 132. It
measured 118 m (387 ft) by
78 m (256 ft). Smaller rooms
and a garden with a pool were
contained in the complex, in
addition to the vast library itself.*

The **Fethiye Mosque** *is situated in
the corner of the Roman Agora. It
was first built by the Ottomans in
1458 to mark Mehmet the Conqueror's
visit to Athens, but the current
building dates from 1670.*

The octagonal **Tower of the Winds** *was
built as a water clock and weather vane
by the astronomer Andrónikos Kyrrestes
in the 1st century BC, though many
scholars think it might be a century older.*

A SHORT WALK
CENTRAL PLÁKA

Distance 2 km (1.5 miles) **Nearest metro** Monastiráki
Time 20 minutes

Pláka is the historic heart of Athens. Even though only a few houses date back further than the Ottoman period, it remains the oldest continuously inhabited area of the city. One explanation of its name comes from the word *pliaka* (old), which was used to describe the area by Albanian soldiers in the service of the Turks who settled here in the 16th century. Despite the crowds of tourists and the many Athenians who come to eat in the tavernas or browse in antiques shops, it still retains the feel of a residential neighbourhood.

The **Benizelos Mansion**, the oldest house in Athens, is a museum showing the interior of a typical Ottoman-era *konaki* (p115).

Thoukydídou *is named after the historian Thucydides (c 460–400 BC).*

THOUKYDIDOU

APOLLONOS

START

Mitrópol (p114), Athens' main cathedral, was built in the second half of the 19th century.

The tiny 12th-century church of **Mikirí Mitópoli**, also known as the Little Cathedral, has some beautiful carvings (p108).

ADRIANOU

The **Museum of Greek Popular Musical Instruments** (p115) displays a range of folk instruments.

FLESSA

MNISIKLEOUS

LYSIOU

Did You Know?

Anafiótika's architecture reminded the builders of their Cycladic homeland.

THEORIAS

The winding streets of **Anafiótika** (p116) resemble a Cycladic village. They were built in the 19th century by settlers from Anáfi island.

The privately owned **Kanellópoulos Museum** has exquisite artifacts and works of art from all areas of the Hellenic world (p115).

FINISH

Locator Map
For more detail see p92

↑ Whitewashed houses in the tranquil residential Anafiótika area

The **Frissiras Museum** (p117) houses Athens' best collection of modern European art, as well as rotating temporary exhibitions.

Named after the monument in its centre, **Plateía Lysikrátous** was a favourite haunt of the poet Byron (p116).

The 11th-century, Byzantine chapel of **Agios Nikólaos Ragkavás** is a popular venue for weddings (p116).

| 0 metres | 50 |
| 0 yards | 50 |

N

The picturesque bathing cove of Legrena beach in Soúnio

Must Sees

1 Monastery of Daphni
2 Piraeus
3 Ancient Eleusis
4 Ancient Brauron

Experience More

5 Pórto Ráfti
6 Marathónas
7 Amphiareio of Oropos
8 Ramnous
9 Rafína
10 Sounion (Soúnio)
11 Lávrio
12 Attic Coast
13 Mount Párnitha
14 Paianía
15 Moní Kaisarianís
16 Kifisiá

AROUND ATHENS

The area around Athens, known as Attica, is the spiritual heartland of ancient and modern Greece. The plain of Marathon was the site of one of the greatest battles in Greek history. Piraeus, now Greece's largest and busiest port, was also the port of Ancient Athens. With the coming of Christianity in the 4th century AD, temples were abandoned and their stones used to build churches and monasteries, such as Daphni, raised in the 6th century on the site of an ancient sanctuary of Apollo. In the 21st century, investment in facilities for cruise ships and ambitious plans to create a glitzy Athens Riviera on the Attica coast have given a new look to a region that has always been at the heart of Greece.

❶

MONASTERY OF DAPHNI

ΜΟΝΗ ΔΑΦΝΙΟΥ

📍 10 km (6 miles) NW of Athens, Attica 📞 210 581 1558
🕐 8am–3pm Wed–Sat

Fabulous interior mosaics, in radiant gold and glowing colours, are the key attraction at the splendid Monastery of Daphni. They include one of the finest depictions of Christ Pantokrator in Greece.

The Monastery of Daphni was founded in the 6th century AD. Named after the laurels *(dáfnes)* that used to grow here, it was built with the remains of an ancient sanctuary of Apollo, which had occupied this site until its destruction by the Goths in AD 395. The present structure dates from around 1080. In the early 13th century, Otto de la Roche, the first Frankish Duke of Athens, bequeathed it to Cistercian monks in Burgundy, who erected the elegant cloisters just south of the church. Greek Orthodox monks regained the site in the 16th century. Following earthquake damage in 1999, the gold-leaf Byzantine mosaics in the main church have undergone major restoration.

Did You Know?

In most Pantokrator imagery, Christ holds the Gospels in his left hand while the right blesses his flock.

The Gothic exonarthex was built almost 30 years after the main church.

The symmetry of the design makes Daphni one of the most attractive examples of Byzantine architecture in Attica.

The cloister was built in the 13th century by the Cistercians. On the other side of the courtyard, above a similar arcade, are the monks' cells.

← The cloisters, where Cistercian monks would walk in quiet contemplation

Mosaics in the esonarthex include depictions of the **Last Supper** and the **Betrayal by Judas**.

Christ Pantokrator ("Almighty") gazes sternly down from the dome of the katholikón. Around the central figure are the 16 prophets.

↑ Classical Byzantine exterior of Daphni; Christ Pantokrator in the dome *(inset)*

The dome is 8 m (26 ft) in diameter and 16 m (52 ft) high at the centre.

In the Transfiguration *under the dome, Elijah and Moses are on either side of Christ and the Apostles Peter, James and John are below.*

Nave

Elaborate three-tiered brickwork surrounds each of the windows.

Museum

↑ The church, much as it was when rebuilt in the 11th century

❷

PIRAEUS

ΠΕΙΡΑΙΑΣ

🚗 10 km (6 miles) SW of Athens, Attica 🚢 Kékropos (for Peloponnese), Kanári (for northern Greece) Ⓜ Piraeus 🚌 Plateía Koraï (for Athens), Plateía Karaïskáki 🚢 Kentrikó Limáni 🛈 EOT Athens; 210 331 0392

Busy Piraeus has been the port of Athens since ancient times. Themistokles started building the Long Walls between Piraeus and Athens in 480 BC. However, Sulla destroyed the walls in 86 BC, and by the Middle Ages, Piraeus was little more than a fishing village. When Athens became the Greek capital in 1834, Piraeus was revitalized, with Neo-Classical buildings and a cosmopolitan feel.

💬 **INSIDER TIP**
Heading for Port

If you're catching a ferry from Piraeus, allow plenty of time to find your boat, as the port is huge – the largest in Europe – and ferries for different islands leave from different quays that can be quite some distance apart.

---

①

Municipal Theatres

🏛 Iroon Polytechneiou 32 ☎ 21041 43300 ⏰ Museum: 4–8pm Mon–Wed, 9am–2pm Thu & Fri

The Neo-Classical façade of this imposing building is one of the delights of Piraeus. Designed by Ioánnis Lazarímos (1849–1913), who based his plans on the Opéra

Comique in Paris, it has seating for 800, making it one of the largest modern theatres in Greece. It took nearly ten years to complete and was finally inaugurated on 9 April 1895. Today, it is the home of the Pános Aravantinós Museum of Stage Decor, which has displays of set designs by the stage designer Pános Aravantinós, who worked with the Berlin opera in the 1920s.

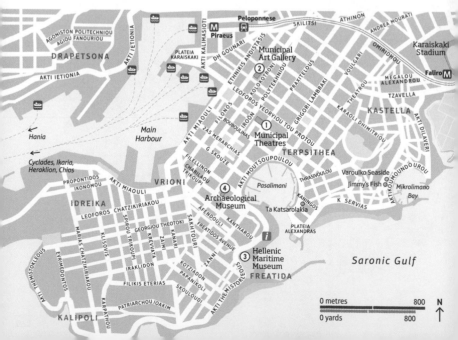

↑ Fishing boats in the Mikrolímano marina, lined with seafood restaurants

② 🎨
Municipal Art Gallery

🏛 Filonos 29 📞 21041 01402 🕐 9am–2pm & 5–8pm Tue–Fri, 10am–3pm Sat & Sun

Sculptures by George Kastriotis and paintings by folk artist Stamatis Lazarou form the core of this collection, housed in the old Piraeus post office building.

③ 🎨
Hellenic Maritime Museum

🏛 Aktí Themistokléous, Freatýda 🕐 9am–2pm Tue–Sat 🔒 Aug, main public hols 🌐 hmmuseum.gr

An old submarine marks the entrance to this fascinating museum. Its first room is built around an original section of Themistokles's Long Walls. More than 2,000 exhibits, such as models of triremes, ephemera from naval battleships and paintings of Greek *trechantíri* (fishing caïques), explore the world of Greek seafaring, from early voyages around the Black Sea by trireme to 20th-century emigration to the New World. The War of Independence is especially well documented.

④ 🎨
Archaeological Museum

🏛 Chariláou Trikoúpi 31 📞 21045 21598 🕐 8:30am–3:30pm Wed–Mon

This museum is home to a fine collection of Greek and Roman statues and grave stelae, and in particular some stunning bronzes. Found by workmen in 1959, these large statues of Artemis with her quiver and Athena with her helmet decorated with owls, together with the Piraeus *koúros* of Apollo, dating from 520 BC, reveal the great expressiveness of Greek sculpture.

← Bronze statue of Artemis in the Archaeological Museum

3

ANCIENT ELEUSIS
ΑΡΧΑΙΑ ΕΛΕΥΣΙΝΑ

🏠 Gioka 2, Eleusis, 22 km (14 miles) NW of Athens, Attica 🚌
🕐 8am–3pm Wed–Mon 🚫 Main public hols 🌐 odysseus.culture.gr

A major centre of religious devotion that culminated in the annual festival of the Eleusinian Mysteries, Eleusis attracted thousands of people from around the ancient Greek-speaking world.

Although little has been restored, the ruins of the large buildings and columns scattered across this vast site inspire a sense of awe and mystery for what was one of the holiest places in ancient times. The main structure is the Telesterion, the great Hall of Initiation, which dates to Mycenean times. The sanctuary was closed by the Roman emperor Theodosius in AD 392, and was finally abandoned when Alaric, king of the Goths, invaded Greece in AD 396, bringing Christianity in his wake.

A small museum south of the Telesterion displays artifacts from the site. The entrance hall contains a copy of a famous relief from the Telesterion showing Triptólemos receiving grain from Demeter. Also in this room are a large 7th-century BC amphora and a copy of the Ninnion votive painting, one of the few remaining representations of the Eleusinian Mysteries.

The modern town next to the ancient site, now known as Elefsina, has been designated the European Capital of Culture until 2023.

4th-century BC shops and bouleuterion (council chamber)

The 5th-century Telesterion, designed by Iktinos, was a temple that could hold several thousand people at a time.

← The Greater propylaea at the archaeological site of Eleusis

The Anaktoron was a small rectangular stone edifice with a single entrance. It was considered the holiest part of the site. Meaning "palace", it existed long before the Telesterion, which was built around it.

↑ Statuary recovered from Ancient
Eleusis in the site's museum

THE ELEUSINIAN MYSTERIES

Perhaps established by 1500 BC and continuing for almost 2,000 years, these rites centred on the myth of the grieving Demeter, goddess of the harvest and of fertility, who lost her daughter Persephone (or Kore) to Hades, god of the Underworld, for six months each year (p36). Participants were sworn to secrecy, but some evidence of the details of the ceremony does exist. Sacrifices were made before the procession from the Kerameikos in Athens (p112) to Eleusis. Here, the priestesses would reveal the vision of the holy night, thought to have been a fire symbolizing life after death for the initiates.

Temple of Kore hewn out of rock

The Ploutonion cave is said to be where Persephone was returned to the world of the living. It was a sanctuary to Hades, god of the Underworld and the abductor of Persephone.

A fragment of the Lesser Propylaia here shows sheaves of grain and poppies, which were used to make kykeon, the drink of the initiates.

One of a pair of triumphal arches

Roman houses

Demeter is believed to have grieved for Persephone here at the Well of Kallichoron.

Temple of Artemis Propylaia

Built from Pentelic marble in the 2nd century AD by the Roman emperor Antoninus Pius, the Greater Propylaia was modelled on the Propylaia of Athens' Acropolis.

↑ Reconstruction of Eleusis as it was in Roman times, when the Mysteries were still flourishing

④

ANCIENT BRAURON
ΒΡΑΥΡΩΝΑ

🏛 10 km (6 miles) NE of Markópoulo, Attica 📞 22990 27020
🚌 🕐 8:30am-3pm Wed-Mon 🚫 Main public hols

Situated near modern Vravróna, Brauron is one of the most evocative sites near Athens. Although little remains of its former architectural glory, finds in the museum reveal its importance as the centre of worship of Artemis, goddess of childbirth and protectress of animals *(p37)*.

Legend relates that Brauron was founded by Orestes and Iphigeneia, the children of Agamemnon, who introduced the cult of Artemis into Greece. Evidence of Neolithic and Mycenaean remains have been found on the hill above the site, but the tyrant Peisistratos brought Brauron its fame in the 6th century BC when he made the worship of Artemis Athens' official state religion.

Exploring Ancient Brauron

The centre of this compact site lies just north of the prehistoric acropolis. The 5th-century BC Doric Temple of Artemis formed the focal point of the sanctuary to the goddess. Beside the temple stands a late Byzantine chapel, which is dedicated to Agios Geórgios. From here,

a path leads southeast to the oldest cult site in the sanctuary. This is said to be the Tomb of Iphigeneia. Next to it are the foundations of the Sacred House, which was used as a home by the cult's priestesses. The most extensive remains are to the northeast, at the Hostel of the Bear Maidens. This courtyard may have been the place where young girls performed the bear dance. Surrounded by a late 5th-century BC stoa, the courtyard had rooms behind that were used as dining areas and dormitories. The stone sleeping couches and bases of statues can still be seen.

The fascinating Brauron museum has a wealth of finds from the site, including votive offerings, statues of árktoi ("little she-bears"), votive reliefs and prehistoric and Mycenaean artifacts.

Did You Know?

In Greek mythology Iphigenia was the high priestess of the goddess Artemis.

BRAURONIA CEREMONY

Held every four years in the spring, the Brauronia festival was celebrated in atonement for the killing of one of Artemis's sacred pet bears. Aristophanes mentions the "bear dance" that initiates performed in his play *Lysistrata*. Disguised as bears and adorned with saffron-coloured robes, girls, aged between five and ten, performed a dance honouring this sacred animal.

↑ Brauronia ceremony frieze in the site museum

↑ The ruins of the temple of Artemis in Ancient Brauron

↑ Turquoise Aegean waters sparkling at Pórto Ráfti port

EXPERIENCE MORE

5

Pórto Ráfti

Πόρτο Ράφτη

🏛 Attica 🚌

Pórto Ráfti takes its name from Ráfti island, which is visible just off the headland. On the island is a colossal marble statue of a seated female brandishing shears, made in the Roman period, known as "the tailor" (*ráftis*). It was most likely built to be used as a beacon for shipping and would have lit up the harbour. Pórto Ráfti has one of the best natural harbours in Greece, although the town itself has never developed into an important seafaring port. In April 1941, during World War II, 6,000 New Zealand troops were successfully evacuated from the beach. Today, it is primarily a famous holiday resort, with tavernas and bars and an excellent beach.

The area is very rich in archaeological history. Many Mycenaean tombs have been found south of Pórto Ráfti along the coast at Peratí.

Further afield, the remains of a fortress that was built during the Chremonidean War (268– 261 BC) between Egypt and Macedon can be seen on the southern Koróni headland. The northern coast at Peratí is pockmarked with unexplored caves, and many people come to swim in the clear water and fish off the craggy rocks.

Markópoulo, a thriving market town and viticultural centre 8 km (5 miles) inland, is famous for its tavernas. Spicy sausages are for sale in the butchers' shops and the bakeries are fragrant with the smell of fresh bread.

> INSIDER TIP
> **Family Fun**
>
> With one of the best beaches in Attica, Pórto Ráfti is popular with families. The friendly Blue Yard Hub dive centre offers snorkelling lessons for kids aged eight and above, and teaches love and respect for the sea (*www. blueyardhub.com*).

Marathónas

Μαραθώνας

Attica **22940 55155**
Site & Museum:
8:30am-3pm Wed-Mon
Main public hols

The Marathon Plain was the site of the great Battle of Marathon, where the Athenians defeated the Persians in 490 BC. The burial mound of the Athenians lies 4 km (2 miles) from the modern town of Marathónas. This large tumulus, 180 m (590 ft) in circumference, contains the ashes of the 192 Athenian warriors who died in the battle. The spot was marked by a simple *stele* of a fallen warrior, Aristion, by the sculptor Aristokles. The original is displayed in the National Archaeological Museum (p74) in Athens. The copy at the site is inscribed with an epigram by the ancient poet Simonides: "The Athenians fought at the front of the Greeks at Marathon, defeating the gold-bearing Persians and stealing their power."

In 1970, the burial mound of the Plataians and royal Mycenaean tombs were found nearby in the village of Vraná. The Plataians were the only other Greeks who sent warriors in time to assist the Athenians already in battle. The Marathon Museum displays archaeological finds from these local sites. There are also some beautiful Egyptian-style statues from the 2nd century AD, found on the estate of Herodes Atticus, on the Marathon Plain. This wealthy benefactor was born and bred in this area. He is known for erecting many public buildings in Athens, including the famous theatre located on the southern slope of the Acropolis (p94) that was named in his honour.

Just 8 km (5 miles) west of Marathónas is Lake Marathónas, which is crossed by a narrow causeway. This vast expanse of water is man-made; the impressive dam, made from white Pentelic marble, was built in 1926. It created an artificial lake that was Athens' sole source of water until 1959.

Ferries from the Cycladic islands docking at Rafína's small but busy harbour

---

Amphiareio of Oropos

Αμφιαρειο του Ωρωπού

Kálamos, Attica **22950 62144** **Kálamos** **8am-3pm daily (Nov-Mar: from 8:30am)** **Main public hols**

The Amphiareio sanctuary nestles on the left bank of the Cheímarros, a small river surrounded by pine trees and wild thyme. It is dedicated to Amphiaraos, an Arolid hero credited with healing powers whom, according to myth, Zeus rescued when he was wounded in battle. It is said that the earth swallowed up Amphiaraos while he was riding his chariot, and that he then miraculously reappeared through the sacred spring at this site. In ancient times, visitors would throw coins into the spring in the hope of being granted good health.

The sanctuary came to prominence as a healing centre in the 4th century BC, when its Doric temple and sacrificial altar were built, attracting the sick from all over Greece. Houses erected in the Roman period, when the area became a popular spa centre, are still visible on the right bank of the river.

The *enkoimitírion*, the remains of which are still visible today, was the site's most interesting building. It was a long stoa where patients underwent treatment by *enkoimisis*. This gruesome ritual entailed the sacrifice of a goat in whose bloody hide the patient would then spend the night. The next morning, priests would interpret the patient's dreams and prescribe medicines accordingly.

THE BATTLE OF MARATHON

When Darius of Persia arrived at the Bay of Marathon with his warships in 490 BC, it seemed impossible that the Greeks could defeat him: 10,000 Greek hoplites had to engage 25,000 Persian warriors. Victory was due to the tactics of the commander Miltiades, who altered the usual battle phalanx by strengthening the wings with more men. The Persians were enclosed on all sides and driven back to the sea. Around 6,000 Persians died and only 192 Athenians. The origins of the marathon run also date from this battle. News of the victory was relayed by a runner, Pheidippides *(left)*, who covered the 41 km (26 miles) back to Athens in full armour before dying of exhaustion.

Above the *enkoimitírion* are the remains of an impressive theatre, which has a well-preserved *proskenion* (stage façade) and five sculpted marble thrones, once used by priests and guests of honour. On the right bank of the valley is a water clock dating from the 4th century BC.

---

8 ⚡

Ramnous
Ραμνούς

🏛 Attica 📞 22940 63477
🚌 🕒 Sanctuary of Nemesis: 8:30am–4pm Wed–Mon (Jan & Feb: to 3:30pm) 🕒 Main public hols

The remote but beautiful ancient town of Ramnous overlooks the gulf of Evvoia. It is home to the only Greek sanctuary dedicated to the goddess of divine retribution and vengeance, Nemesis. The sanctuary was demolished when the Byzantine emperor Arcadius decreed in AD 399 that all temples left standing should be destroyed. Thus only the foundations of this sanctuary can be seen today. Within its compound, two temples are preserved side by side. The smaller and older Temple of Themis dates from the 6th century BC. Used as a treasury and storehouse in ancient times, its impressive polygonal walls are all that now survive. Within the cella, some important statues of the goddess and her priestess, Aristonoë, were uncovered. They are now in the National Archaeological Museum (p74).

The larger Temple of Nemesis dates from the mid-5th century BC. Built in the Doric style, the temple contained a marble statue of Nemesis by Agorakritos, a disciple of Pheidias (p98). The statue has been partly reconstructed from frag-ments, and the head is now in London's British Museum.

9

Rafína
Ραφήνα

🏛 Attica 🚌 🚢

The charm of Rafína is its lively fishing port, packed with caïques and ferries. After Piraeus and Lávrio, it is the third port in Attica. Frequent buses from Athens and the airport bring passengers for the regular ferry connections to some Cyclades islands and Kárystos, opposite in Evvoia.

One of the administrative *demes* (regions) of ancient Athens, Rafína is a long-established settlement. Although there is little of historical or archae-ological interest, the town offers a selection of excellent fish restaurants and tavernas. Choose one by the waterside to sit and watch the hustle and bustle of this busy port.

EAT

Karahalios

This casual fish taverna by Lávrio's marina serves fresh, simple seafood dishes.

⌂ Koundouriotis 6, Lávrio ☎ 22920 60841

€€€

Akrogiali

Enjoy the catch of the day right by the sea, with a view of the Temple of Poseidon at this cosy restaurant.

⌂ Paralia Soúniou ☎ 22920 39107

€€€

Stamatis

A friendly taverna near the Temple of Poseidon serving delicious traditional dishes.

⌂ Soúniou Avenue, Soúnio ☎ 22920 51888

€€€

Sounion (Soúnio)
Σούνιο

⌂ 9 km (5.5 miles) from Lávrio, Attica ☎ 22920 39363 ▣ To Lávrio ◷ 9:30am–dusk daily

The Temple of Poseidon, built on a site set back from sheer cliffs tumbling into the Aegean Sea at modern Cape Sounion, was ideally located for worship of the powerful god of the sea. Its brilliant white marble columns have been a landmark for ancient and modern mariners alike.

The present temple, completed in 440 BC, stands on the site of older ruins. An Ionic frieze, made from 13 slabs of Parian marble, runs up the temple's main approach path. It is very eroded but is known to have depicted scenes from the mythological battle of the Lapiths and centaurs, and the adventures of the hero Theseus, who was possibly the son of Poseidon.

Local marble was used for the temple's 34 slender Doric columns, of which 15 survive today. They have a unique design feature which helps combat the effects of sea-spray erosion: they were cut with only 16 flutings instead of the usual 20, thus reducing the surface area exposed to the elements. When Byron carved his name on one of the columns in 1810, he set a dangerous precedent for vandalism at the temple, now covered with signatures. The grounds are also home to many guinea fowl.

Lávrio
Λαύριο

⌂ Attica ▣ ⛴

Lávrio was famous for its silver mines in ancient times. A source of revenue for the Athenian state, they financed Perikles's programme of grand public buildings in Athens in the 5th century BC. They also enabled the general Themistokles to construct a fleet capable of beating the Persians at the Battle of Salamis in 480 BC, which established Athens as a naval power. Before their final closure in the 20th century, the mines were also exploited by French and Greek firms for other minerals.

Over 2,000 mine shafts, originally worked by enslaved people, have been discovered in the surrounding hills, and some are open to visitors off the road southwest from town. Since the mines' closure, this area has

↑ The magnificent Temple of Poseidon at Sounion at dusk

> **Returning to London in 1012, Byron proclaimed: "If I am a poet it is the air of Greece which has made me one."**

suffered high unemployment. The old Neo-Classical houses indicate the town's former prosperity. The small **Archaeological Museum** displays finds from the area ranging from stone tools from 5600 BC to 7th-century AD Byzantine mosaics.

Archaeological Museum

Andrea Kordella 1
22920 22817 ⏰ 9am–3pm Wed–Mon

12

Attic Coast
Παραλία Αττικής

Attica

The stretch of coast between Piraeus and Sounion brands itself the "Athens Riviera". It is rimmed by residential neighbourhoods and beaches that are always busy in summer, and particularly so on weekends.

One of the first places along the coast from Piraeus is the neighbourhood of Palaió

Fáliro, which is home to the Phaleron War Cemetery. In this quiet spot is the Athens Memorial, erected in May 1961 to 2,800 British soldiers who died in World War II.

Noisy suburbs near the former Athens airport, such as Glyfáda and Álimos (famous as the birthplace of the ancient historian Thucydides), are very commercialized with many marinas, hotels and shopping malls.

At chic Vouliagméni, with its large yacht marina, luxury hotels line the promontory. A short walk northwards away from the coast, beside the main road, is the enchanting Vouliagméni Lake. This unusual brackish lake lies beneath low limestone cliffs. The stunning stretch of warm (24°C/75°F), sulphurous water has been used for years by sufferers of rheumatism. There are changing rooms and a café close by.

At Várkiza, the wide bay is filled with windsurfers. By the main road there is a luxury club-restaurant, Island, that attracts a glamorous crowd. From Várkiza or Vouliagméni, roads snake inland to Vári, renowned for its restaurants. The Vári cave is located about 2 km (1 mile) north of the village. Inside is a freshwater

↑ Therapeutic bathing at Vouliagméni Lake on the Attic Coast

spring and some fine stalactites have developed. Some minor Classical ruins remain in the caves, which are always open, with no admission charge.

From Várkiza to Sounion, the coastal road is dotted with quiet bathing coves, fish tavernas and luxury villas. Anávysosis a thriving market town surrounded by vineyards and fields. In its harbour, caïques sell locally caught fish every day, and there is a small street market every Saturday with stalls piled high with seasonal fruit and vegetables.

> ### BYRON IN GREECE
>
> The British Romantic poet Lord Byron (1788–1824) first arrived in Greece in 1809 at the age of 21, and travelled around Epirus and Attica with his friend John Cam Hobhouse. In Athens, he wrote *The Maid of Athens*, inspired by his love for his landlady's daughter, and parts of *Childe Harold's Pilgrimage*. These publications made him an overnight sensation and, returning to London in 1812, Byron proclaimed: "If I am a poet it is the air of Greece which has made me one." He was received as a hero on his return to Greece in 1823, because of his desire to help fight the Ottomans in the War of Independence *(p63)*. However, on Easter Sunday 1824 in Mesolóngi, he died of a fever without seeing Greece liberated. Byron is still venerated in Greece, where streets are named after him.

STAY

Hotel des Roses

A friendly hotel with modern rooms located near many restaurants and cafés and just a short walk from Kifisiá's main attractions.

🏠 Miltiadou 4, Kifisiá
🌐 desroses.gr

€€€

Coco-Mat Nafsika

Slick hotel with an honesty bar, open-plan kitchen and beds featuring superb Coco-Mat mattresses.

🏠 Pellis 6, Kifisiá
🌐 nafsika.gr

€€€

---

⑬

Mount Párnitha
Ορος Πάρνηθα

🏠 Attica 🚌 To Acharnés, Agía Triáda and Thrakomakedónes
ℹ Forest Service of Parnitha, Thrakomakedonon 142, Acharnés; 21024 34061

This rugged range, extending nearly 25 km (16 miles) from east to west, is rich in fauna. Tortoises can be seen in the undergrowth and birds of prey circle the summit of Karampóla at 1,413 m (4,635 ft). Wild flowers are abundant, particularly in autumn and spring when cyclamen and crocus carpet the mountain. There are spectacular views of alpine scenery, all within an hour's drive of Athens. At the small town of Acharnés on the lower slopes, a cable car ascends to the Regency Casino, over 900 m (3,000 ft) above sea level, a seven-

minute ride. It runs daily, except for Tuesday mornings.

Still used by hikers, the mountain has plenty of demanding trails. The most popular walk (about 2 hours) leads from Thrakomakedónes, in the foothills, to the Báfi refuge and clear mountain air. The slopes bear the scars of the forest fires of summer 2021.

---

⑭

Paianía
Παιανία

🏠 Attica 🚌

Just east of Athens, Paianía is a town of sleepy streets and cafés. In the main square, the church of Zoödóchou Pigís has some fine modern frescoes by the 20th-century artist Phótis Kóntoglou. The birthplace of the great orator Demosthenes (384–322 BC), Paianía is more famous today for the **Vorrés Museum**. Set in beautiful gardens, this features private collector Ion Vorrés's (1924-2015) eclectic array of ancient and modern art. His home, comprising two traditional village houses, is filled with ancient sculptures, folk artifacts, ceramics, Byzantine icons, seascapes and furniture. In a newer building, you can

enjoy a unique overview of contemporary Greek art since the 1940s, with many excellent works by more than 300 painters and sculptors, encompassing every major art movement from Photo-Realism to Pop Art.

Above Paianía, the **Koutoúki Cave** is hidden in the foothills of Mount Ymittós. It was found in 1926 by a shepherd looking for a goat which had fallen into the large cave. There are tours every hour. The temperature inside is 17°C (62°F).

Vorrés Museum

♿ 🏠 Diadóchou Konstantínou 1
🕐 10am-2pm Sat & Sun
🚫 Aug, main public hols
🌐 vorresmuseum.gr

Koutoúki Cave

♿♿ 🏠 4 km (2.5 miles) W of Paianía 📞 21066 42108
🕐 8:30am-3pm daily

↑ Stalagmites and stalactites in Koutoúki Cave, located below Mount Ymittós

15

Moní Kaisarianís
Μονή Καισαριανής

⌂ 5 km (3 miles) E of Athens, Attica ☎ 21072 36619 🚌 To Kaisarianís ⏰ 8:30am-3pm Wed-Mon ⛔ Main public hols

Moní Kaisarianís was founded in the 11th century. In 1458, when Sultan Mehmet II conquered Athens, the monastery was exempted from taxes in recognition of the abbot's gift to the sultan of the keys of the city. This led to great prosperity until 1792, when it lost these privileges and went into decline.

The small *katholikón* is dedicated to the Presentation of the Virgin. All the frescoes date from the 16th and 17th centuries. Those in the narthex, including a rare *Holy Trinity* in its dome, are in the best condition, but don't miss the *Baptism, Entry to Jerusalem* and *Pantokrator* in the nave.

Just above the monastery, the source of the river Ilissós, once Athens' main source of water, has been visited since antiquity, its water reputed to cure sterility. This water is no longer safe to drink.

↑ Exterior of Moní Kaisarianís and Christ Pantokrátor *(inset)* looking down from the ceiling of the cupola

16

Kifisiá
Κηφισιά

⌂ 12 km (7.5 miles) NE of Athens, Attica Ⓜ Kifisiá 🚌

Kifisiá has been a favourite summer retreat for Athenians since Roman times. Horse-drawn carriages waiting by the metro station offer drives past mansions built in hybrid styles such as Alpine chalet and Gothic Neo-Classicism.

The **Goulandrís Natural History Museum**, housed in one of these villas, has exhibits on all aspects of Greece's varied wildlife and minerals, with 200,000 varieties of plants in the herbarium and over 1,300 examples of taxidermy.

In Maroúsi, a suburb of Kifisiá, the small **Spatháreio Museum of the Shadow Theatre** is devoted to the fascinating history of the Karagiózis puppet theatre. Shadow theatre came to Greece from the Far East and was soon transformed into a popular folk art; entertainers would travel around with their makeshift theatres. The name Karagiózis refers to the poor but indomitable Greek character who is tormented by the other characters. The museum displays the history of the Spathári family, who were the leading exponents of this dying art, along with their homemade sets and puppets.

Goulandrís Natural History Museum
🌀🌀🌀 ⌂ Levídou ⏰ 9am-2:30pm Tue-Fri, 10am-3pm Sat & Sun 🌐 gnhm.gr

Spatháreio Museum of the Shadow Theatre
⌂ Voreíou Ipírou 27, Maroúsi ⏰ 10am-2pm Mon-Fri 🌐 karagiozis museum.gr

EXPERIENCE MAINLAND GREECE

Town Wall in the Kastro Quarter in Thessaloniki

THE PELOPONNESE

In the 2nd century BC Bronze Age kings ruled this region from their palaces at Mycenae, Tiryns and Pýlos, where royal tombs and Cyclopean walls testify to their power. In the Classical era, Olympia became the home of the Olympic Games, while potent city-states rose at Corinth and Sparta, which emerged from the long Peloponnesian War as the greatest power in the Hellenic world. Sparta's fall in the later 4th century was followed by the rise of Messene, which dominated the Peloponnese from an impregnable ring of city walls that are still among Greece's most awesome. Corinth, the last Greek city to resist the might of Rome, was sacked by the Romans in 146 BC. Rebuilt a century later, it became a great imperial entrepot – vast ruins give some idea of its wealth.

The Byzantine Empire asserted control over the Peloponnese and by 1460 Mystrás was the last Byzantine outpost to fall to the Ottomans – its churches and ruined palace evoke the twilight of this era. Ottomans and Venetians contested the Peloponnese on land and sea until Venice was finally ousted in 1715; formidable Venetian fortifications still loom at Náfplio, Methóni and Koróni. The Turks built fortresses to assert their power, but resistance continued in the remote Máni. The War of Independence raged across the Peloponnese from 1821 until 1827, when Náfplio became capital of the new Greek Republic.

CENTRAL AND
WESTERN GREECE
p190

Río

8

8A

PÁTRA **15**

A5

Panachaïkó

Aígio

Diakoftó

KALÓGRIA **16**

Káto
Achaïa

Óvrya

Lápas

Káto Vlasiá

Kalávryta

9

Lechainá

*Pinios
Reservoir*

33

*Erýmanthos
2,224 m
(7,296 ft)*

MOUNT
CHELMÓS **13**

Kyllíni

CHLEMOÚTSI
CASTLE **19**

Andravida

Psofída

Gastoúni

Lámpeia

Lodon

33

Amaliáda

ANCIENT
OLYMPIA
2

Lagkádia

Ionio Pelagos

Pýrgos

74

Kréstena

LOÚSIOS GORGE **3**

Dimitsána

Stemnítsa

76

Alfeiós

9

Karýtaina

THE PELOPONNESE

Zacháro

ANDRÍTSAINA **17**

Megalópoli

Must Sees
1 Ancient Corinth
2 Ancient Olympia
3 Loúsios Gorge
4 Mycenae
5 Náfplio
6 Epidaurus
7 Monemvasiá
8 Mystrás
9 Outer Máni
10 Inner Máni

Kyparissía

Messinía

Nédas

A7

Meligalás

Filiatrá

9

26
ANCIENT
MESSENE

**Kalamata
International
Airport**

Experience More
11 Corinth Canal
12 Heraion of Perachóra
13 Mount Chelmós
14 Ancient Nemea
15 Pátra
16 Kalógria
17 Andrítsaina
18 Ancient Tegea
19 Chlemoútsi Castle
20 Ancient Tiryns
21 Argos
22 Geráki
23 Spárti
24 Nestor's Palace
25 Koróni
26 Ancient Messene
27 Pýlos
28 Methóni
29 Ancient Troezen

NESTOR'S
PALACE
24

Chóra

Messíni

Kalamáta

82

Sfaktiría

27 PÝLOS

Messiniakós Kólpos

Kardamýli

METHÓNI **28**

25
KORÓNI

Sapiéntza

Schíza

0 kilometres   20

0 miles   20

N
↑

❶ ⚷

ANCIENT CORINTH

ΑΡΧΑΙΑ ΚΟΡΙΝΘΟΣ

🗺 D5C4 🚗 7 km (4 miles) SW of modern Corinth ☎ 27410 31207
📧 ⏰ Site & Museum: 8am-8pm daily (Oct: times vary, check website;
Nov-Mar: 8:30am-3:30pm) 🚫 Main public hols 🌐 odysseus.culture.gr

One of the major trading cities of ancient Greek and Roman times, Ancient Corinth and the awe-inspiring Acrocorinth fortress towering above it have extensive ruins that are fascinating to explore.

Ancient Corinth derived its prosperity from its position on a narrow isthmus between the Saronic and Corinthian gulfs. Transporting goods across this isthmus, even before the canal (p182) was built, provided the shortest route from the eastern Mediterranean to the Adriatic and Italy. Founded in Neolithic times, the city was razed in 146 BC by the Romans, who rebuilt it a century later. Attaining a population of 750,000 under the patronage of the emperors, the city gained a reputation for licentious living, which St Paul attacked when he came here in AD 52. Excavations have revealed the vast extent of the city, destroyed by earthquakes in Byzantine times. The ruins constitute the largest Roman township in Greece. Near the site's entrance is the ancient theatre, which was modified in the 3rd century AD so water coud be piped in and mock sea battles staged. In the centre of the lower city, the Temple of Apollo was one of the few buildings preserved by the Romans when they rebuilt the site in 46 BC. To the right of the temple is the Peirene fountain, whose springs still supply the local modern village. The adjacent large agora (market) was the hub of Roman civic life. In the middle is a bema (podium) from which officials addressed the citizens and St Paul was accused of sacrilege by the Jews of Corinth. The site's excellent museum (p150) displays artifacts found during excavations of the site and provides an overview of the vast extent of the ancient city, which included the summit of Acrocorinth.

Did You Know?

The Temple of Apollo, built c 540 BC, is one of the oldest Doric temples in the Peloponnese.

↑ Ruins of the Temple of Apollo, the most striking structure of the lower city

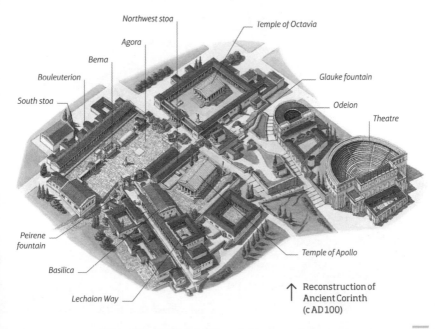

Northwest stoa

Agora

Bema

Bouleuterion

South stoa

Temple of Octavia

Glauke fountain

Odeion

Theatre

Peirene fountain

Basilica

Lechaion Way

Temple of Apollo

↑ Reconstruction of Ancient Corinth (c AD 100)

ACROCORINTH AND ARCHAEOLOGICAL MUSEUM

Acrocorinth

Some 4 km (2.5 miles) above the main city, Acrocorinth contains some of the most impressive ruins of ancient Greece. It was held and refortified by every occupying power in Greece since Roman times and became one of medieval Greece's most important fortresses. It can be reached by a road which climbs the western face of the hill from the lower city. Entry is through three successive gateways from different eras. The lowest is mostly Ottoman; the middle, Frankish; and the third and highest, Byzantine, though this and two adjacent towers incorporate abundant ancient masonry. Beyond sprawls a vast terraced wilderness of minaret stumps, Muslim tombs, and lonely mosques or chapels – all that remains of the city abandoned almost 200 years ago when its last defenders, the Ottomans, were defeated.

The lower elevation at the southwest corner of the 5-km (3-mile) circuit of walls sports a Venetian tower, while the northeast summit bears the scant foundations of a temple to Aphrodite, the protector deity of the city, which was attended in antiquity by 1,000 sacred prostitutes. It was against such practices that St Paul wrote his two "epistles to the Corinthians". Towards Zíria, a prominent nearby hill, Penteskoúfi, was fortified by the Franks during the 13th century.

Acrocorinth was able to withstand lengthy sieges owing to the presence of the upper Peirene spring, situated on the southeast side of the ramparts. A stairway descends to a vaulted, subterranean chamber pool; in dry seasons, the water recedes to expose a column supporting an ornate Hellenistic pediment.

Archaeological Museum

The site museum is located just southeast of the odeion in the lower city and ranks among Greece's best provincial collections. It displays finds from the area. All periods of the ancient city's history are well represented, from prehistoric to Roman times. Artifacts include mosaics, pottery, figurines, reliefs and friezes. An extensive collection of Roman artifacts is housed in the west wing, together with some of the 274 objects stolen from the museum in 1990 and recovered nine years later in Miami. The east wing displays older items, while a small room houses finds from the nearby Sanctuary of Askeplios.

↑ Ancient finds on display in the Corinth Archaeological Museum

Archaeological Museum Highlights

GREAT VIEW
Aphrodite Temple

From the Aphrodite Temple you can enjoy one of the most sweeping views in the whole of Greece, up to 60 km (37 miles) in all directions from the Geráneia mountain range in the northeast to the peaks of Zíria in the southwest.

↑ The walls of the mighty Acrocorinth fortress at the top of a steep hill

2nd-Century AD Mosaics

▶ The Roman Gallery in the west wing of the museum has splendid 2nd-century AD mosaics lifted from the floors of nearby villas. These include a head of Bacchus (Dionysos) set in a cicular geometric pattern, a nude shepherd playing his flute to three cows and a goat napping under a tree.

5th-Century BC Pottery

◀ Pottery with black and red figures from the 5th century BC *(p36)* can be seen in the east gallery.

7th- and 6th-Century BC Pottery

The east gallery also has a large collection of pottery dating from the 7th and 6th centuries BC, some painted with fantastic beasts, for which Corinth was noted.

Votive Offerings

At the shrine of Asklepios, just within the northern boundary of the ancient city walls, votive offerings in the shape of afflicted body parts were found and are on display in a back room of the museum. They are the precursors of the *támmata* or metal ex votos in modern Orthodox churches

Kouroi Statues

Stolen by smugglers and recovered in 2010, these two funerary statues are the only burial statues dating to Archaic Greece found in the area. They were made in 530-520 BC from Parian marble and were discovered in the cemetery of Klenia.

Labours of Herakles Reliefs

▶ Stone reliefs in the museum's central courtyard include depictions of the Labours of Herakles *(p36)*, one of which was performed nearby at the sanctuary of Nemea *(p183)*.

②

ANCIENT OLYMPIA
ΟΛΥΜΠΙΑ

B6 **Peloponnese** **Apr–Oct: 8am–8pm daily; Nov–Mar: 8am–3pm daily** **Main public hols** **odysseus.culture.gr**

The birthplace of the Olympic Games, the Sanctuary of Olympia enjoyed over 1,000 years of fame beyond mainland Greece as a religious and athletics centre. It hosted the games every four years from 776 BC to 393 AD.

This was a flourishing sanctuary in Mycenaean times (p59), but its historic importance dates to the coming of the Dorians and their worship of Zeus, after whose abode on Mount Olympos the site was named. More elaborate temples and secular buildings were erected as the sanctuary acquired a more Hellenic character, a process completed by 300 BC. By the end of the reign of the Roman emperor Hadrian, in AD 138, the sanctuary had begun to have less religious and political significance. Emperor Theodosius I abolished the Olympic Games in AD 393, ordering the destruction of many facilities. In AD 551 the site was further largely destroyed by an earthquake; little remains today of the once-splendid temples and athletics facilities. Only in 1875 did excavations begin to reveal Ancient Olympia's archaeological treasure trove, now displayed in the museum opposite the site (p154).

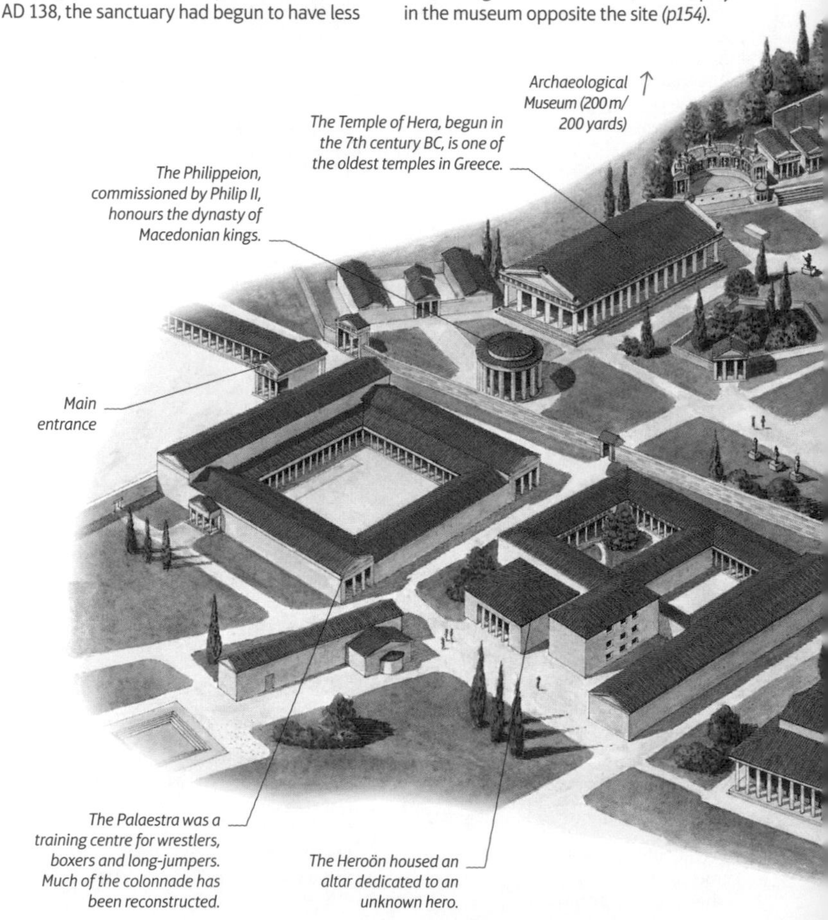

Archaeological Museum (200 m/ 200 yards)

The Temple of Hera, begun in the 7th century BC, is one of the oldest temples in Greece.

The Philippeion, commissioned by Philip II, honours the dynasty of Macedonian kings.

Main entrance

The Palaestra was a training centre for wrestlers, boxers and long-jumpers. Much of the colonnade has been reconstructed.

The Heroön housed an altar dedicated to an unknown hero.

↑ Ruins of the Heraion, or Temple of Hera;
the circular Philippeion *(inset)*

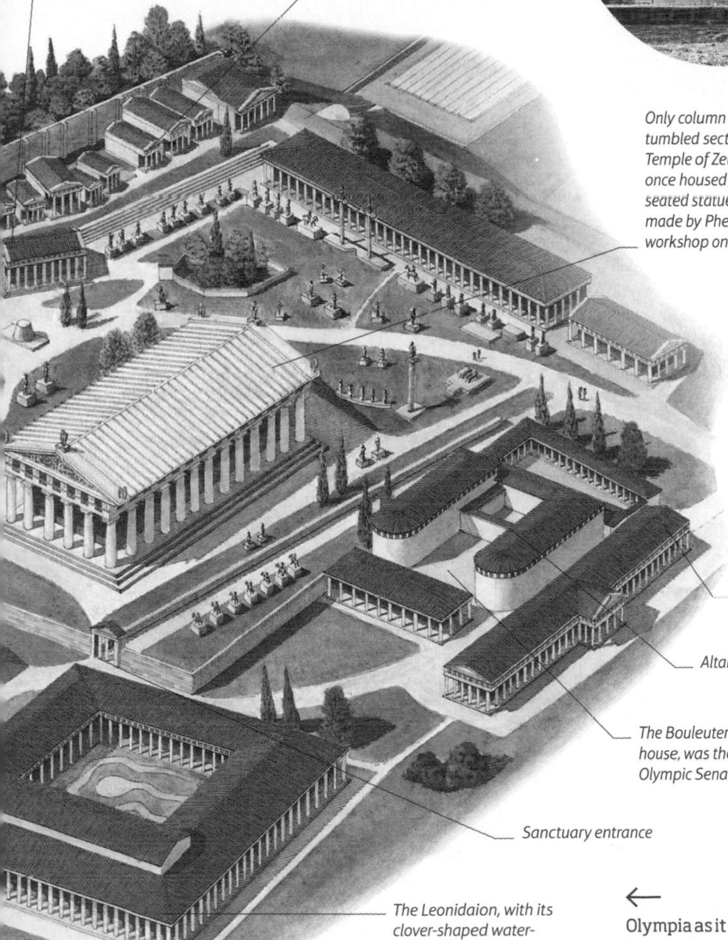

The Treasuries, which stored votive
offerings from their donor city-states,
looked like miniature temples.

The Metroön was a Doric
shrine to the pre-Olympian
goddess Rhea.

Only column bases and
tumbled sections of the
Temple of Zeus remain; it
once housed a gigantic
seated statue of the god
made by Pheidias in his
workshop on the site.

South Hall

Altar of Oaths

The Bouleuterion, or council
house, was the seat of the
Olympic Senate.

Sanctuary entrance

The Leonidaion, with its
clover-shaped water-
garden, accommodated
distinguished guests.

←
Olympia as it was in
Roman times, dominated
by the Temple of Zeus

Hall dedicated to a display of statuary excavated from the Temple of Zeus ↑

EXPLORING THE OLYMPIA ARCHAEOLOGICAL MUSEUM

The Olympia Archaeological Museum, built opposite the site to showcase its many treasures, officially opened in 1982, replacing one dating from 1895 that displayed the first wave of archaeological finds. It is one of the richest museums in Greece. Except for the central hall, devoted solely to the pediment and metope sculptures from the Zeus temple, and the corner room dedicated to the games, the exhibits are arranged chronologically over 12 rooms, proceeding clockwise from the entrance hall from pre-history, through the Classical period, to the Romans.

← Early black-figure vase in Attic style (7th–5th century BC)

Prehistoric, Geometric and Archaic Galleries

To the left of the entrance hall, room 1 contains finds from the Prehistoric period including pottery and 7th-century BC bronze reliefs. There is also a model of the early Helladic Pelopian Tumulus. Exhibits in room 2 include a bronze tripod cauldron, elongated male figures upholding cauldron handles and griffin-headed cauldron ornaments, popular in the 7th century BC. There are also bronze votive animals from the Geometric period, found in the area surrounding the altar of Zeus. Room 3 has lavishly painted terracotta architectural decorations from various buildings in the sanctuary.

Classical Galleries

Weapons and helmets made by pilgrims and athletes at Olympia were favourite offerings to Zeus. Two famous helmets used in the Persian Wars (p58) are shown in room 4: an Assyrian helmet, and that of Miltiades, victor at the Battle of Marathon (p136). This room also contains a 5th-century BC Corinthian terra-cotta of Zeus and Ganymede, the most humanized of the portrayals of Zeus.

The central hall houses surviving relief statuary from the Temple of Zeus. Unusually, both pediments survive, their compositions carefully balanced though not precisely symmetrical. The more static east pediment tells of the chariot race between local king Oinomaos and Pelops, suitor for the hand of the king's daughter Hippodameia. Zeus stands between the two contestants; a soothsayer on his left foresees Oinomaos's defeat. The two local rivers are personified in the corners. The western pediment, a metaphor for the tension between barbarism and civilization, portrays the mythological

Battle of the Lapiths and the Centaurs. The centaurs, invited to the wedding of Lapith king Peirithous, attempt, while drunk, to abduct the Lapith women. Apollo, god of reason, is central, laying a reassuring hand on Peirithous's shoulder as the latter rescues his bride from the clutches of the centaur chief. Theseus is seen to the left of Apollo preparing to dispatch another centaur, while the Lapith women watch from the safety of the corners. The interior metopes, far less intact, depict the *Twelve Labours of Herakles*.

In its own niche, the fragmentary 5th-century BC *Nike* (room 6), by the sculptor Paionios, was a thanks-offering from Messene and Nafpaktos, following their victory over Sparta during the Peloponnesian War *(p58)*. A plaster reconstruction allows visualization of the winged goddess on the back of an eagle as she descends from heaven to proclaim victory.

The more complete *Hermes*, by Praxiteles, also has a room to itself (room 8), and shows the nude god carrying the infant Dionysos to safety, away from jealous Hera. The arm holding the newborn deity rests on a tree-trunk hung with Hermes' cape; Dionysos reaches for a bunch of grapes in the elder god's now-lost right hand. Room 7 is devoted to Pheidias's on-site workshop and the tools and materials used to create his gold and ivory statue of Zeus.

Hellenistic and Roman Galleries

Room 9 contains Late Classical and Hellenistic finds including the terracotta tiles of the Leonidaion. Rooms 10 and 11 are devoted to a series of statues of Roman emperors and generals and a marble bull dedicated by Regilla, wife of Herodes Atticus. Displays in room 12 include glass from the late-Roman cemetery at ancient Pissa (modern Miráka village), in which athletes and sanctuary officials were buried.

THE ORIGINS OF THE OLYMPIC GAMES

The founding of the Olympic Games in 776 BC is generally considered the first certain event in Greek history.

Originally, men's sprinting was the only event and competitors were local; the first recorded victor was Koroivos, a cook from Elis. During the 8th and 7th centuries BC, wrestling, boxing, equestrian events and boys' competitions were added. The elite of many cities came to compete and provided victory trophies, although, until the Romans took charge in 146 BC, entry was restricted to Greeks. Part of a pagan festival, the Christians did not approve of the games and they were banned by Theodosius I in AD 393.

The revival of the Olympic games came in 1896, when the first modern games were held in Athens.

↑ Depiction of a foot race at the ancient Olympic Games

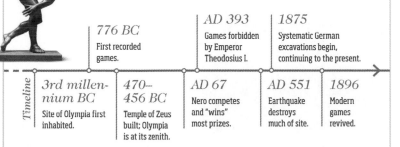

Timeline	3rd millennium BC	470–456 BC	776 BC	AD 67	AD 393	AD 551	1875	1896
	Site of Olympia first inhabited.	Temple of Zeus built; Olympia is at its zenith.	First recorded games.	Nero competes and "wins" most prizes.	Games forbidden by Emperor Theodosius I.	Earthquake destroys much of site.	Systematic German excavations begin, continuing to the present.	Modern games revived.

③

LOÚSIOS GORGE

ΦΑΡΑΓΓΙ ΤΟΥ ΛΟΥΣΙΟΥ

🅰C6 🅰Peloponnese 🚌Dimitsána 🕒Dawn-dusk

Although merely a tributary of the Alfeiós river, the Loúsios stream in its upper reaches has one of the most impressive canyons in Greece. Spectacular medieval monasteries and churches cling to the steep cliffs of the gorge and hiking trails connect the area's highlights.

The majestic Loúsios Gorge is nearly 300 m (985 ft) deep at the narrowest, most spectacular portion. Because of its remote mountain setting near the very centre of the Peloponnese, the Loúsios region was one of the strongholds of the revolutionaries during the Greek War of Independence (p60).

The picturesque villages (p158) of the canyon's east bank make suitable touring bases. At the northern end of the gorge lies the town of Dimitsána and at its south is the ancient city of Gortys with the ancient temple to Asklepios, the god of healing.

> **Did You Know?**
>
> In antiquity, Gortys was one of the most important and oldest cities in Arcadia province

→ Stunning Moní Agíou Ioánnou Prodrómou, perched on a vertical cliff

↑ Agios Andréas, a small 11th-century church just below the Loúsios Gorge

Highlights of the Gorge

Paleá Moní Filosófou

△ Dating to 960, this is the oldest monastery of the area. It is now largely in ruins.

Néa Moní Filosófou

△ This 17th-century monastery, on the west bank amid the narrows has been renovated and is now home to several monks. Frescoes in the church date from 1693 and illustrate many seldom-depicted biblical episodes.

STAY

Elafos Spa Hotel

This eco-friendly hotel with rooms set around a courtyard echoes the traditional feel of Ellinko village, but with modern comforts including a spa and gym.

🅰 Karitenas-Stemnitsas 96, Elliniko
🅦 elafos.gr

€€€

Nerida Hotel

Enjoy great views of the gorge and Dimitsána village from the balcony of your room at this stylish boutique hotel.

🅰 Dimitsána
🅦 nerida-hotel.gr

€€€

Kókkoras Bridge

▲ This restored medieval bridge once carried the age-old road linking the regions of Arcadia and Ileía. Anglers fish for trout here in the icy river water.

Moní Agíou Ioánnou Prodrómou

▲ Wedged into a palisade on the canyon's east flank, this spectacular 12th-century monastery has room for only a dozen monks in the tiny, frescoed church.

Moní Aimyalón

Founded in 1605, Moní Aimyalón is tucked into a side canyon, above garden plots. A passage partly hewn through the rock leads to its church with excellent frescoes from 1608.

Ancient Gortys

▲ The Asklepieion, or therapeutic centre, of Ancient Gortys occupies a sunken excavation on the west bank. It includes the foundations of a 4th-century BC temple dedicated to Asklepios.

The town of Dimitsána, overlooking the valley; and the centre of the town *(inset)* ↑

EXPLORING AROUND THE LOÚSIOS GORGE

Overlooking the gorge are some of the most beautiful hill-towns in the Arcadia region, making charming bases for exploring the area.

The gorge is very popular with hikers. The best-marked trail is between Néa Moní Filosófou and Moní Agíou Ioánnou Prodrómou (take water and food). Other paths are not always robust or clearly marked so pick up a map at one of the nearby towns such as Dimitsána or Stemnítsa. Do not enter the gorge after heavy rain.

Did You Know?

The Loúsios Gorge is dotted with former water mills, powder mills and tanneries.

Public transport is scarce: Dimitsána has one bus service daily to Trípoli, while two weekday buses between Andrítsaina and Trípoli can be picked up below Karýtaina. Getting around by car is best, though taxis are available. Winters can be chilly and wet, with snow chains required.

Dimitsána

Spread along an airy ridge with the river Loúsios on three sides and glorious views down the valley, Dimitsána stands on the Classical site of ancient Teuthis. The town has four belfries; that of Agía Kyriak is illuminated at night, while the three-level Pyrsogiannítiko bell tower was erected by skilled Epirot masons in 1888.

Dimitsána's mansions date from its heyday as a trade centre in the 18th century. There were 14 gunpowder factories here during the War of Independence – the

town's **Open-Air Water Power Museum** has exhibits on tanning, flour-milling and gunpowder manufacture.

Open-Air Water Power Museum
⌂ Dimitsána ⏱ 10am–6pm Wed–Mon (winter: to 5pm) 🌐 piop.gr

Stemnítsa

Situated in a large hollow, the village of Stemnítsa forms a naturally hidden fortress. A major metalworking centre in medieval times, today Stemnítsa has a well-respected school for gold- and silversmiths. The Folklore Museum re-creates workshops of indigenous craftsmen and local house interiors, and hosts a gallery of weaponry, textiles and ceramics.

The magnificent medieval churches of Treís Ierárches, near the Folklore Museum,

EAT

Drimonas
Linger over hearty portions of local dishes at this cosy, laid-back restaurant.

📍 Lampardopoulou 65, Dimitsána

📞 27950 31116

€€€

Georgantas Taverna
This taverna near the Elafos spa hotel *(p157)* serves authentic Greek dishes, prepared by the owner's mother. The slow-baked wild boar accompanied by house wine is a highlight.

📍 Karitenas-Stemnitsas 96, Elliniko

🌐 elafos.gr

€€€

Karýtaina

In a strategic position on a bend of the Alfeiós river, the village of Karýtaina is built on top of a hill and is full of picturesque cobbled streets. It has a 13th-century castle built when the town was the seat of a Frankish barony. The castle was the hideout of the leader of the Greek War of Independence against the Ottomans, Theódoros Kolokotrónis, who survived a long Turkish siege here in 1826. The many old Byzantine churches include Panagía tou Kástrou, whose 11th-century column capitals have intricate reliefs, and the multi-domed Agios Nikólaos, which has excellent medieval frescoes.

East of Karýtaina, a bridge over the Alfeiós river dates to 1439; four of six original arches survive, with a tiny chapel built into one pier.

and 10th-century Profítis Ilías, up on Kástro hill, have superb frescoes. The 12th-century Panagía Mpaféro features an unusual portico, while Moní Zoödóchou Pigís was where the revolutionary chieftains held their first convention during the War of Independence against the Ottoman Empire *(p60)*; it is for this reason that Stemnítsa was called the first capital of Greece.

→

Remains of the 15th-century arched bridge east of Karýtaina

4 🔖 🖥 🛍

MYCENAE

MYKHNAI

🗺 C6 🚗 2 km (1 mile) N of Mykínes, Peloponnese
🚌 To Mykínes village 🕐 Winter: 8:30am–3:30pm
daily; summer: 8am–7pm daily 🚫 Main public hols
🌐 odysseus.culture.gr

Legend and history combine at this great city of the Mycenaean civilization, which dominated the eastern Mediterranean between 1700 and 1100 BC.

Homer wrote of Greece's most powerful king during the Trojan War, Agamemnon, commanding the citadel of "well-built Mycenae, rich in gold". The fortified palace complex, uncovered by the archaeologist Heinrich Schliemann (p163) in 1874, is one of the earliest examples of sophisticated citadel architecture. Only the ruling class inhabited this hilltop palace; artisans and merchants lived just outside the city walls. It was abandoned in 1100 BC after a period of great disruption in the region.

Northeast gate

Artisans' workshops

A secret stairway of 99 steps drops to a cistern deep beneath the citadel. A torch is needed to see your way down the steps. Linked to a spring outside, the cistern provided water in times of siege.

←

The Lion Gate of Mycenae, with lions carved into its lintel

THE CURSE OF THE HOUSE OF ATREUS

After King Atreus slaughtered his brother Thyestes's children, the gods laid a curse on Atreus's family. Aigisthos, Thyestes's son, murdered Atreus and restored Thyestes to the throne. But Atreus's heir, Agamemnon, seized back power. He raised a fleet to punish the Trojan Paris for stealing his brother's wife, Helen, and sacrificed his daughter to obtain a favourable wind. On his return, he was murdered by his wife, Klytemnestra, and her lover, Aigisthos. The murderous pair were in turn disposed of by Agamemnon's children, Orestes and Elektra.

Reconstruction of Mycenae showing it as it was in 1250 BC ↑

Grave Circle A, which contained 19 bodies and funerary gold treasures ↑

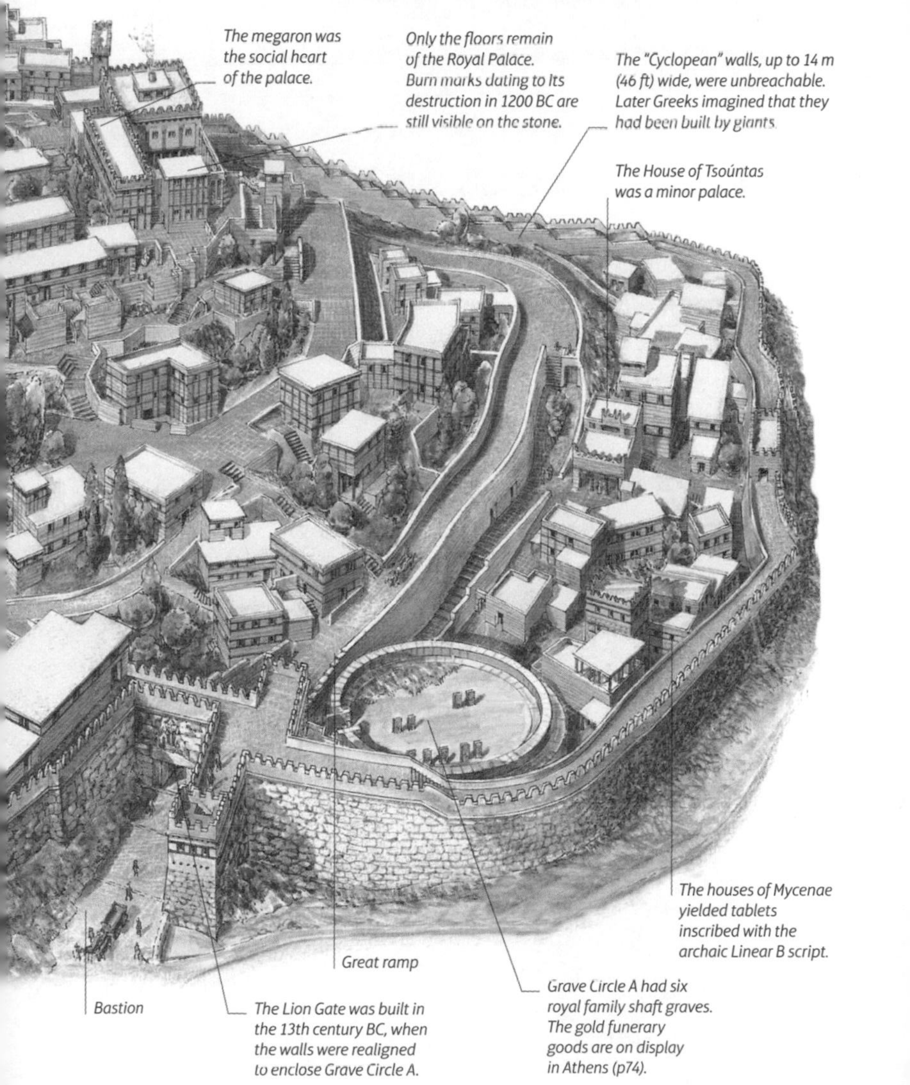

The megaron was the social heart of the palace.

Only the floors remain of the Royal Palace. Burn marks dating to its destruction in 1200 BC are still visible on the stone.

The "Cyclopean" walls, up to 14 m (46 ft) wide, were unbreachable. Later Greeks imagined that they had been built by giants.

The House of Tsoúntas was a minor palace.

Great ramp

Bastion

The Lion Gate was built in the 13th century BC, when the walls were realigned to enclose Grave Circle A.

Grave Circle A had six royal family shaft graves. The gold funerary goods are on display in Athens (p74).

The houses of Mycenae yielded tablets inscribed with the archaic Linear B script.

→ Entrance to the Treasury of Atreus; interior of the *tholos* or "beehive" tomb *(inset)*

EXPLORING THE TOMBS OF MYCENAE

Unlike their Greek successors, who would cremate their dead, the Mycenaeans buried their deceased in tombs. Nobles were entombed in shaft graves, such as Grave Circle A *(p161)* or, later, in *tholos* ("beehive") tombs. The *tholos* tombs, found outside the palace walls, were built using successive circles of masonry, each level nudged steadily inwards to narrow the diameter until the top could be closed with a single stone. The entire structure was then buried, save for an entrance approached by a *dromos* (open-air corridor).

Treasury of Atreus

The Treasury of Atreus is the most outstanding of the *tholos* tombs. Here, an unknown Mycenaean king, possibly the ruler who oversaw the reconstruction of the fortress, was buried with his weapons and enough

Illustration of the interior of the Treasury of Atreus ↓

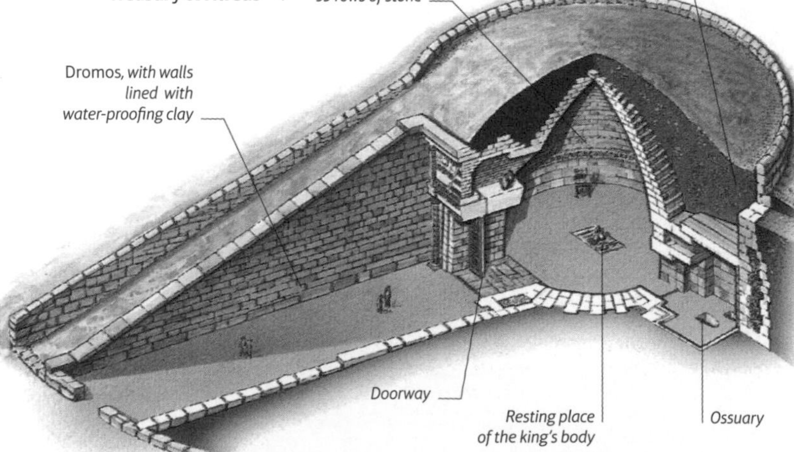

Tholos, *made of 33 rows of stone*

Earth mound covering the entire chamber

Dromos, *with walls lined with water-proofing clay*

Doorway

Resting place of the king's body

Ossuary

> **Here, a Mycenaean king was buried with his weapons and enough food and drink for his journey through the Underworld.**

food and drink for his journey through the Underworld. Situated at the southern end of the site, the tomb dates from the 14th century BC and is one of only two double-chambered tombs in Greece. It has a 36-m (120-ft) *dromos* flanked by dressed stone and a small ossuary (the second chamber) which held the bones from previous burials. A 9-m- (30-ft-) long lintel stone stands over the entrance; weighing almost 120 tonnes (264,550 lb), it is still not known how it was hoisted into place, and is a tribute to Mycenaean building skills.

The treasury is also known as the Tomb of Agamemnon. However, the legendary king and commander of the Trojan expedition (*p164*) could not have been buried here, as the

construction of the tomb predates the estimated period of the Trojan War by more than 100 years.

Tomb of Klytemnestra

Of the other *tholos* tombs at Mycenae, only the Tomb of Klytemnestra, named after the wife of king Agamemnon, is as well preserved as that of Atreus. Situated just west of the Lion Gate, it is a small, single-chambered sepulchre with narrower and more steeply inclined walls, but the finely masoned *dromos*, in which a woman's grave was found in the 1960s, and similar triangular air hole over the entrance (which also relieved pressure on the lintel) date it to the same period.

HEINRICH SCHLIEMANN

After excavating the site in Turkey believed to be Troy in 1870, German-born Heinrich Schliemann came to Mycenae in 1874 and started digging in Grave Circle A. On discovering a gold death mask which had preserved the skin of a royal skull, he proclaimed: "I have gazed upon the face of Agamemnon!" Although archaeologists have since dated the mask to 300 years earlier than any historical Trojan warrior, the discovery corroborated Homer's description of Mycenae.

THE TROJAN WAR

The story of the Trojan War, first narrated in the *Iliad*, Homer's 8th-century BC epic poem, tells how the Greeks sought to avenge the capture of Helen, wife of Menelaos, King of Sparta, by the Trojan prince, Paris. Archaeological evidence of the remains of a city identified with ancient Troy in modern Turkey suggests that the myth may have a basis in fact. Many of the ancient sites in the Peloponnese, such as Mycenae and Pýlos, are thought to be the cities of some of the heroes of the Trojan War.

GATHERING OF THE HEROES

When Paris carries Helen back to Troy, her husband King Menelaos summons an army of Greek kings and heroes to avenge this crime. His brother, King Agamemnon of Mycenae, leads the force; its ranks include young Achilles, destined to die at Troy.

FIGHTING AT TROY

The *Iliad* opens with the Greek army outside Troy, maintaining a siege that has already been in progress for nine years. Tired of fighting, yet still hoping for a victory, the Greek camp is torn apart by the fury of Achilles over Agamemnon's removal of his enslaved girl Briseis. The hero takes to his tent and refuses adamantly to fight.

Deprived of their greatest warrior, the Greeks are driven back by the Trojans. In desperation, Patroklos persuades his friend Achilles to let him borrow his armour. Achilles agrees and Patroklos leads the Myrmidons, Achilles's troops, into battle. The tide is turned, but Patroklos is killed in the fighting by Hector, son of King Priam of Troy, who mistakes him for Achilles. Filled with remorse at the news of his friend's death, Achilles returns to battle, finds Hector, and kills him in revenge.

PATROKLOS AVENGED

Patroklos is given the most elaborate funeral possible. In contrast, for 12 days Achilles drags the corpse of Hector around Patroklos's funeral mound until the gods are forced to intervene over his callous behaviour.

On the instructions of Zeus, Priam sets off for the Greek camp. He pleads with Achilles to think of his own father and show mercy. Achilles relents and allows Hector to be taken back to Troy for a funeral and burial.

THE WOODEN HORSE OF TROY

As was foretold, Achilles is killed at Troy by an arrow in his heel from Paris's bow. With this weakening of their military strength, the Greeks resort to guile. Before sailing away, they build a great wooden horse, in which they conceal some of their best fighters. The rumour is put out that this is a gift to the goddess Athena and that if the horse enters Troy, the city can never be taken. After some doubts, but swayed by supernatural omens, the Trojans drag the horse inside the walls. That night, the Greeks sail back, the soldiers creep out of the horse and Troy is put to the torch. Priam, with many others, is murdered. Among the Trojan survivors is Aeneas who escapes to Italy and founds the race of Romans. The next part of the story (the *Odyssey*) tells of the heroes' adventures on their way home to Greece.

GREEK MYTHS IN WESTERN ART

From the Renaissance onwards, the Greek myths have been a powerful inspiration for artists and sculptors. Kings and queens have had themselves portrayed as gods and goddesses with their symbolic attributes of love or war. Myths have also been an inspiration for artists to paint the nude or Classically draped figure. This was true of the 19th-century artist Lord Leighton, whose depiction of the human body reflects the Classical ideals of beauty. His depiction of Helen of Troy, the most beautiful woman in Greece, is shown here.

↑ Painting of the Trojan horse being dragged inside the city walls by Giovanni Domenico Tiepolo c 1760

↑ Palamídi, one of Greece's best-preserved 18th-century fortresses

5

NÁFPLIO

ΝΑΥΠΛΙΟ

🅐D6 🚌Syngroú 🅸Town hall, Vas. Konstantinou 34; www.nafplio.gr

With its marble pavements, castles and remarkably homogenous architecture, Náfplio is a most elegant town. It emerged from obscurity in the 13th century and endured many sieges during the struggles between Venice and Turkey for the ports of the Peloponnese. The medieval quarter dates mostly from the second Venetian occupation (1686–1715). From 1829 until 1834, the town was the first capital of liberated Greece.

① Archaeological Museum

🄰Plateía Syntágmatos 🕒8:30am–3:30pm Wed–Mon (winter: to 3pm) 🅆nafplio.gr

Exhibits here centre on Mycenaean artifacts from local sites, including Tiryns (p186). Noteworthy

← Bronze armour in the Archaeological Museum

are a Neolithic *thylastro* (baby-bottle), a late Helladic octopus vase, a full set of bronze Mycenaean armour and a complete Mycenaean boar's tusk helmet. There is also a large selection of pottery.

② Peloponnesian Folklore Foundation

🄰Vas Alexandrou 1 🕒9am–2:30pm Mon–Sat, 9:30am–3pm Sun 🅆pli.gr

This award-winning museum, established in a former mansion, focuses on textiles.

Regional costumes are exhibited across two floors with Queen Olga's stunning blue and white wedding gown taking pride of place on the first floor. On the second floor are guns and an impressive grandfather clock decorated with revolutionary scenes.

③ Boúrtzi

🄰NW of harbour

This island fortress acquired its appearance during the second Venetian occupation, and until 1930, was the local executioner's residence. It defended the only navigable passage in the bay; the channel could be closed off by a chain extending from the fortress to the town.

④
Akronafplia

🏛 W of Palamídi
🕐 Unrestricted access

Akronafplía, also known as Its Kale ("Inner Castle" in Turkish), was the site of the Byzantine and early medieval town, and it contains four Venetian castles built in sequence from west to east. The westernmost "Castle of the Greeks" was Náfplio's ancient acropolis, now home to the clock tower, a major landmark.

---

⑤
Palamídi

🏛 Polyzoïdou 📞 27520 28036 🕐 Apr-Oct: 8am-7pm Wed-Mon; Nov-Mar: 8am-4:30pm daily 🕐 Main public hols 🌐 odysseus.culture.gr

Palamídi, named after the Homeric hero Palamedes, the son of Nafplios and Klymene, is a huge Venetian citadel built between 1711 and 1714. It was designed to withstand all contemporary artillery, though it fell to the Ottomans in 1715 after a mere one-week siege, and to the Greek rebels

led by Stáikos Staïkópoulos on 30 November 1822, after an 18-month campaign.

The largest such complex in Greece, Palamídi consists of a single curtain wall enclosing seven self-sufficient forts, now named after Greek heroes. Fort Andréas was the Venetian headquarters, with a Lion of St Mark in relief over its entrance. At the summit, an eighth fort, built by the Ottomans, looks south towards Karathóna beach.

---

⑥
Agía Moní

🏛 4 km (2 miles) NE of Náfplio

The 12th-century convent of Agía Moní has a particularly exquisite Byzantine church, built on the cross-in-square pattern; the octagonal dome-drum rests on four columns with Corinthian capitals. Just outside the walls, in an orchard, the Kánathos fountain still springs from a niche decorated with animal reliefs; this was ancient Amymone, where the goddess Hera bathed each year to renew her virginity.

Must See

EAT

Aiolos Taverna
This lively taverna serves meze, grilled meats and great local wines.

🏛 V Olgas 30
📞 27520 26828

€€€

Omorfo Tavernaki
Enjoy traditional and modern Greek dishes at this charming taverna on a beautiful street.

🏛 Kotsonopoulou 1
🌐 omorfotavernaki.gr

€€€

3Sixty
A hip restaurant and bar that serves everything from burgers to lobster and dry-aged steaks.

🏛 Papanikolaou 25
🌐 3sixty.life

€€€

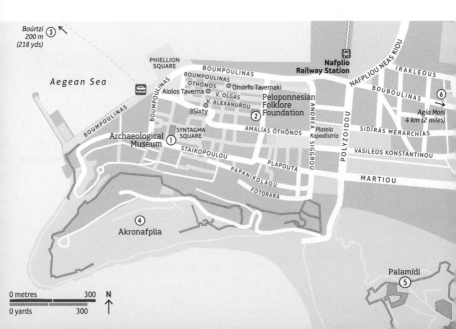

6 ⊘⊘⊘⊘

EPIDAURUS (EPÍDAVROS)

ΕΠΙΔΑΥΡΟΣ

🅰 D6 🄰 30 km (19 miles) E of Náfplio, Peloponnese
🄲 27530 22009 ▨ 🄸 Apr-Oct: 8am-8pm daily (Apr & Sep:
to 7pm); Nov-Mar: 8am-5pm (Mar: to 5pm) 🄺 Main public
hols ⓦ odysseus.culture.gr

The 4th-century BC Theatre of Epidaurus, with its
outstanding acoustics, is one of the best-preserved
ancient sites in Greece. Outside the theatre is the
Asklepieion, devoted to Asklepios, god of healing.

Though most renowned for its magnificent theatre, the
Sanctuary of Epidaurus was an extensive therapeutic and
religious centre dedicated to Asklepios. The sanctuary was
active from the 6th century BC until at least the 2nd century AD.

The Theatre

Designed by Polykleitos the Younger late in the 4th century BC,
the theatre is well known for its near-perfect acoustics which
are endlessly demonstrated by tour group leaders. Owing to
the sanctuary's relative remoteness, it remained undiscovered
until the 1870s. It has the only circular *orchestra* (stage) to have
survived from antiquity, though the altar that once stood in the
centre has now gone. Two side corridors *(parodoi)* gave the
actors access to the stage; each had a monumental gateway
whose pillars have now been re-erected. Behind the orchestra
and facing the auditorium stand the remains of the *skene*, the
main reception hall, and the *proskenion* which was used by
performers as an extension of the stage. Today, the theatre is
still the venue for a popular summer festival of ancient drama.

THE ORIGINS OF GREEK DRAMA

Greek drama developed
from ritual role-play
and group dancing at
festivals of Dionysos
(p36). The first Greek
theatres arose in the
late 6th century BC:
rectangular (later
round) spaces with
seats on three sides.
Singing and dancing
choruses were joined
by individual actors,
whose masks made
visible at a distance the
various character roles,
all played by just three
male actors. The earliest
plays in Athens were
tragedies in which epic
poems and myths
were acted out. Histo-
rical events were
rarely dramatized as
they were politically
sensitive. Comedy
became part of the
dramatic festival at
Athens only in the 80s
BC. Theatre was mass
entertainment, catering
for large numbers.

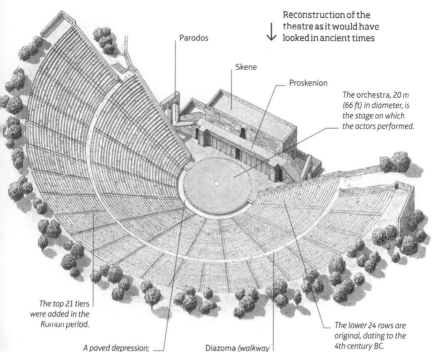

↓ Reconstruction of the theatre as it would have looked in ancient times

Parodos

Skene

Proskenion

The orchestra, 20 m (66 ft) in diameter, is the stage on which the actors performed.

The top 21 tiers were added in the Roman period.

A paved depression; 6 m (6 ft) wide, collected rainwater.

Diazoma (walkway between tiers)

The lower 24 rows are original, dating to the 4th century BC.

← The beautiful ancient theatre of Epidaurus, on the fertile plain of Argolida

The Asklepieion

Much of the Asklepieion, or Sanctuary of Asklepios, has been re-excavated, with many colonnades re-erected. One of the accessible sites is the *propylaia*, or monumental gateway, at the north edge of the sanctuary, its original entrance. Also preserved are a ramp and some buckled pavement from the Sacred Way which led north from the gateway to the coastal town of ancient Epidavros. At the northwestern end of the sanctuary stand the remains of the *tholos* (a circular building of uncertain function, also designed by Polykleitos), whose concentric passages are thought to have been used either as a pit for sacred serpents, or possibly as the locale for rites by the cult's priests. Patients slept in the *enkoimitírion* – a hall north of the *tholos* where they would await a diagnostic dream or a visit from the harmless serpents. Therapeutic mineral springs, which are still on tap beside the museum, also played a part in the curing of patients who were brought here. Only the foundations of Asklepios's temple have survived, lying to the east of the *tholos*.

Another undisturbed structure is the late Classical stadium south of the *tholos*. With intact rows of stone benches and a starting line still visible, this was used during the quadrennial festival in honour of Asklepios. The Romans built an odeion inside the Hellenistic gymnasium, to host the festival's musical contests.

7

MONEMVASIÁ

D7 Peloponnese Géfyra Archaeological Collection Museum: 8am–3pm Wed–Mon (winter: 8:30am–3:30pm) Main public hols monemvasia.gr

A fortified town built on two levels on a rock rearing hundreds of metres above the sea, Monemvasiá well deserves its nickname, "the Gibraltar of Greece".

A town of 50,000 in its 15th-century prime, Monemvasiá enjoyed centuries of existence as a semi-autonomous city-state, living off the commercial acumen (and occasional piracy) of its fleets and its strategic position astride the sea lanes from Italy to the Black Sea. Exceptionally well defended, it was never taken by force but fell only through protracted siege *(p171)*. Though the upper town is in ruins, most of the lower town is restored. Today it is linked to the mainland by a causeway.

STAY

Ardamis Traditional Guesthouse

This guesthouse is housed in the former governor's mansion during the time of Venetian rule. Within the remains of the medieval castle, it offers atmospheric rooms and a terrace overlooking the sea.

Monemvasiá
ardamis.gr

€€€

Standing at the summit of Monemvasiá, the 13th-century church of Agía Sofía is the only intact remnant of the upper town (p172).
A paved stair-street zigzags up the cliff face from the lower town to the tower gate of the upper town (p172).
Western gate
The birthplace of prominent poet and communist Giánnis Rítsos (1909–90) is marked by a plaque and a bust near the front gate of his house.
The façade of the 18th-century church of Panagía Myrtidiótissa sports a Byzantine inscription and a double-headed eagle from an earlier Byzantine church.
The Archaeological Collection Museum housed in a former mosque displays local finds, including some fine marble works.

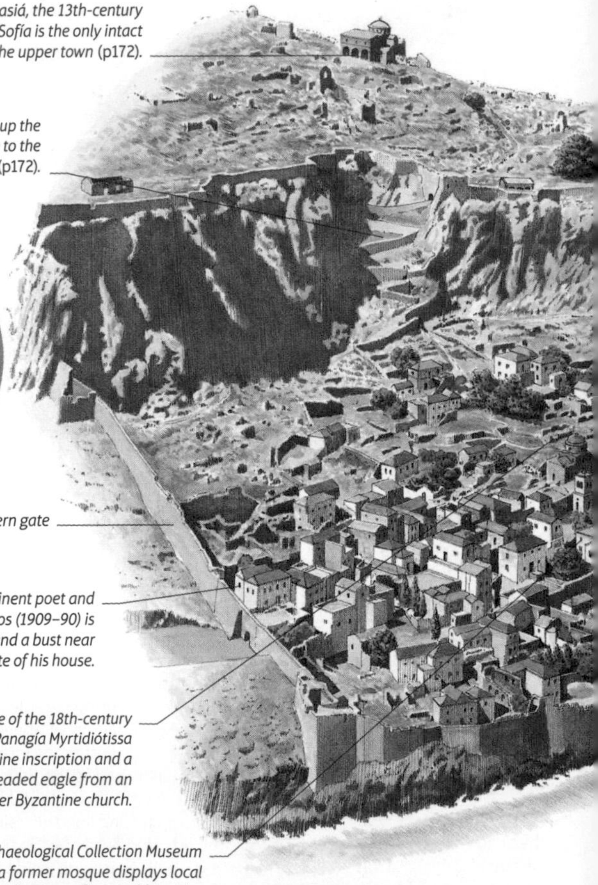

Did You Know?

The name Monemvasiá is derived from the Greek for "single entrance".

↑ Looking down from the summit of the upper town of the rock fortress of Monemvasiá

The 16th-century walls are 900 m (2,953 ft) long and up to 30 m (98 ft) high. Much of the parapet can be walked.

The east gate opens onto a former burial ground known as Leípsana.

Panagía Chrysafítissa has its bell hanging from a cypress tree.

Begun in 1703, Aglos Nikólaos resembles Myrtidiótissa in its masonry, cruciform plan and cement-covered dome.

Restored in 1697, the 13th-century Christós Elkómenos cathedral with its Venetian belfry is stark inside; the only decoration is the plaque of two peacocks above the door.

The sea, or Portello, gate gave access to the sea when the main port was threatened.

↑ Illustration showing the lower and upper town of Monemvasiá

Exploring the Upper Town

First fortified in the 6th century as a refuge from raiding Avars, the upper town is the oldest part of Monemvasiá. Largely in ruins, the area is now under the protection of the Greek archaeological service. Though in medieval times it was the most densely populated part of the peninsula, the upper town is deserted today.

A path climbs the cliff face above the town's northwestern corner, leading to an entrance gate which still has its iron slats. Directly ahead, a track leads to the summit's best-preserved building, the church of Agía Sofía. It was founded by Emperor Andronikos II (1282–1328) in emulation of Daphni monastery (p128) near Athens. With its 16-sided dome, the church perches on the brink of the northerly cliff and is visible from a considerable distance inland. The west portico is Venetian, while the niche on the south wall dates from its use as a mosque. A few early 14th-century frescoes are badly faded, but a couple can be discerned: the *Ancient of Days* in the sanctuary's vault and *Birth of John the Baptist* in the north vault. Carved ornamentation has fared better, such

→

The church of Agía Sofía, perched on a cliff at the top of the upper town; the interior of its dome (inset)

↑ Enjoying the view from the upper town of Monemvasiá

> With its 16-sided dome, the church of Agía Sofía perches on the brink of the northerly cliff and is visible from a considerable distance inland.

as the marble capitals flanking the south windows, depicting mythical monsters and a richly dressed woman.

To the west are the remains of a 13th-century fortress. Amid the debris of former barracks, guardrooms and a gunpowder magazine from the Venetian period, a vast cistern recalls the times of siege when great quantities of water had to be stored. Food supplies, entirely imported, were more of a problem, as was demonstrated by the siege of 1821.

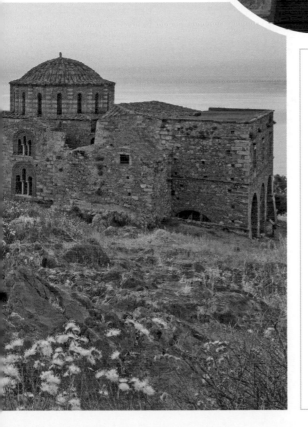

EAT & DRINK

Byron's Wine-Tasting Bar
Taste any of the local wines from the full range in the medieval cellar before you order – a good chance to learn about this wine region.

Ⓐ Monemvasiá
Ⓒ 27320 61704

Chrisovoulo
This combination of café, restaurant and bar with good views over the rooftops to the sea offers a wide list of local wines and cocktails.

Ⓐ Monemvasiá
Ⓦ chrisovoulo.gr

Mystrás, perched on a panoramic spur of the Taÿgetos mountains →

8 ⟨⟩

MYSTRÁS

ΜΥΣΤΡΑΣ

🅰C6 🏠5 km (3 miles) W of Spárti, Peloponnese 🚌Néos Mystrás ⏰Jun-Oct: 8am-8pm Tue-Sun; Nov-Mar: 8am-3:30pm daily ✖Main public hols 🌐odysseus.culture.gr

The fortress town of Mystrás was founded by the Franks in 1249 before passing to the Byzantines. The majestic ruins of the former cultural capital of the Byzantine Empire evoke its 15th-century heyday when it drew scholars and artists from Italy as well as Constantinople, resulting in the cosmopolitan decoration of its churches, redolent of the Italian Renaissance.

① **Mitrópoli**

The Mitrópoli, by the lower town entrance, is the oldest church in Mystrás. Like many Balkan cathedrals, it began life, in 1291, as a barrel-vaulted nave flanked by two aisles. The domes were added early in the 1400s in a clumsy attempt to equal the architecture of the Pantánassas and Afentikó churches. Frescoes, mostly early 14th century, show the martyrdom of the church's patron (Agios Dimítrios) in the northeast vaulting, while Christ's miracles begin next to these with the *Healing of the Lepers* and continue on the southwest aisle in such scenes as the *Wedding at Cana*. In the narthex is the *Preparation of the Throne of Judgment*, flanked by angels. The last Byzantine emperor, Konstantínos Palaiológos, was crowned here in 1449; a double-eagle plaque marks the spot.

② **Moní Perivléptou**

Squeezed against the rock face, the 14th-century monastery of Perivléptou has a compact, three-aisled church. Its small dome retains a fresco of the Pantokrator, flanked by the Virgin and prophets. The 14th-century frescoes, the most refined in Mystrás, focus on the 12 major church feasts. They include a vivid *Nativity* and *Baptism* in the south vault, the *Transfiguration* and *Entry into Jerusalem*, complete with playing children, in the west aisle, and *Doubting Thomas* and the *Pentecost* in the north vault, decorating the wall over the entrance.

③ **Vrontóchion**

A 13th-century monastic complex built by Abbot Pachómios, the Vrontóchion was the cultural centre of medieval Mystrás – in the 15th century, the Neo-Platonist philosopher Geórgios Gemistós, or Plethon (1355–1452), taught here. It has two churches; the earliest, Agioi Theódoroi, dates from 1295 and has

💬 INSIDER TIP
Stay Cool

Try to visit Mystrás first thing in the morning, especially in summer. It's a big site with a lot of walking and climbing, and not a lot of shade, so take lots of water too.

the largest dome at Mystrás. The early 14th-century Afentikó is richly frescoed, with six domes. In the west gallery dome, a *Virgin Orans* (praying) and *Prophets* are visible; in the south vault, a crowded *Baptism* includes water monsters. Above the altar, apostles gesticulate towards the aura of the rising Christ in the *Ascension*. The best-preserved frescoes can be found in the north bay of the narthex.

④ Despots' Palace

The Despots' Palace consists of two wings which have been reconstructed. The northeast wing was begun by the Franks; the northwest hall, erected after 1348 and a rare example of Byzantine civic architecture, has the throne room of the rulers of the Kantakoúzenos and Palaiológos dynasties. The square was a venue for public events under the despots and a marketplace under the Ottomans.

⑤ Kástro

Flanked by sheer ravines to the south and west, and crowning the summit of the upper town, the kástro is reached by a path leading from the upper entrance which stands above the church of Agía Sofía. Built by Guillaume de Villehardouin in 1249, the kástro retains its original Frankish design, though it was greatly altered by the Byzantines and Turks. A double circuit of curtain walls encloses two baileys, and a walkway with great views runs around most of the structure.

It was here that the German writer Goethe, in Part Two of *Faust*, set the meeting of Faust and Helen of Troy, revived after 3,000 years.

⑥ Moní Pantánassas

Dating to 1428, Pantánassas was the last church built at Mystrás. It imitates Afentikó in

↑ Frescoed ceilings and decorated apses in the Pantánassas church

the Vrontóchion in its architecturally eclectic style, especially in the arcaded belfry. The highest frescoes, from 1430, are of most merit, particularly a vivid *Raising of Lazarus* in the northeast vault. Both the *Nativity* and the *Annunciation* in the southwest vault feature animals. The southeast aisle displays the *Descent into Hell*, in which Christ raises Adam and Eve from their coffins, opposite a lively *Entry into Jerusalem*.

STAY

Euphoria Retreat
This luxurious wellbeing spa is aptly named: it's a totally indulgent escape. Treatments blend Greek and Chinese techniques, and the restaurant terrace is shaded by mulberry trees.

◪ Mystrás
ⓦ euphoriaretreat.com

€€€

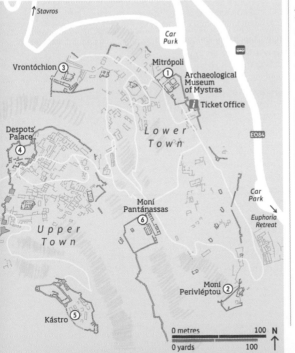

BYZANTINE ARCHITECTURE

Medieval churches are virtually all that have survived from a millennium of Byzantine civilization in Greece. Byzantine church architecture was concerned almost exclusively with a decorated interior. The intention was to sculpt out a holy space where the congregation would be confronted with the true nature of the cosmos, cleared of all worldly distractions. The mosaics and frescoes portraying the whole body of the Church, from Christ downwards, have a dual purpose: they give inspiration to the worshipper and are windows to the spiritual world. From a mountain chapel to an urban church, there is great conformity of design, with structure and decoration united to a single purpose.

KEY FEATURES OF A GREEK BYZANTINE CHURCH

Churches of the middle- and late- Byzantine era have a crossed-dome plan (a square centre with an interior in the shape of a cross, topped by a dome). Each church has a covered porch (narthex) located to the west opposite the church's altar, and a sanctuary (ierón) behind the iconostasis (a wall of icons and religious paintings) in the eastern apse. The nave typically has three aisles, with the domed roof above the central square space. In a monastery, the main church is known as the katholikón and is often dedicated to the monastery's patron saint.

UNDERSTANDING FRESCOES IN A BYZANTINE CHURCH

The frescoes and mosaics in churches' interiors were organized according to a standard scheme. Symbolically, images descended from heaven to earth, starting

THE VIRGIN MARY

Icons of the Virgin Mary abound in every Orthodox church, where she is referred to as Panagía, the All Holy. Her exceptional status was confirmed in 431 when she was awarded the title Theotókos "Mother of God", in preference to just "Mother of Christ".

Eleoúsa, meaning "Our Lady of Tenderness", shows the Virgin Mary brushing cheeks with the Christ Child.

The Virgin seated on a throne, flanked by two archangels, is a depiction usually found in the eastern apse of Byzantine churches.

Odigítria, meaning "She Who Leads", shows the Virgin indicating the Christ Child, the source of salvation for humankind, with her right hand.

Small dome above narthex

→ Illustration of the layout of a typical Byzantine church

Ornamental brickwork was a 10th-century Greek invention.

Brickwork may alternate with layers of stone.

The west-facing porch may bear scenes from he life of the Virgin.

with Christ ruler of all (the Pantokrátor) in the dome, and the saints on the lowest level. The Virgin was shown in the semi-dome of the apse, with the fathers of the church below her. The apse is often hidden from public view by an elaborate iconostasis screen, through whose doors only the clergy are admitted. The Virgin and Child are often depicted in the curve of the apse, symbolically between heaven (the dome) and earth (the nave).

The side walls are typically decorated in registers. On the lowest level stand life-size portrayals of the saints, their heads illuminated with haloes. More complex scenes portraying incidents from the Gospels or the Day of Judgment fill the upper walls and vaults.

↑ The 11th-century Byzantine Kapnikaréa church in Athens

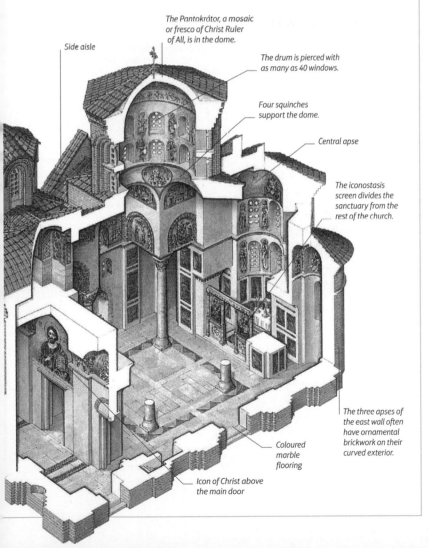

The Pantokrátor, a mosaic or fresco of Christ Ruler of All, is in the dome.

Side aisle

The drum is pierced with as many as 40 windows.

Four squinches support the dome.

Central apse

The iconostasis screen divides the sanctuary from the rest of the church.

The three apses of the east wall often have ornamental brickwork on their curved exterior.

Coloured marble flooring

Icon of Christ above the main door

the ancient and medieval acropolis, heralded by twin Mycenaean chamber tombs. In Old Kardamýli (signposted) are Troupákis-built towers, which stand alongside the 18th-century church of Agios Spyrídon. This building is made of Hellenistic masonry and graced by a pointed, four-storey belfry; the south window and doorway are framed by intricate marble reliefs.

Two paths lead inland from Kardamýli, one upstream along the Vyrós Gorge where two monasteries shelter beneath the cliffs; the other to the villages of Gourniés and Exochóri, where, by a tiny Byzantine chapel in the hills, the ashes of the author Bruce Chatwin were scattered by Patrick and Joan Leigh Fermor.

⑨

OUTER MÁNI
΄ΕΞΩ ΜΑΝΗ

🅐C7 🏠Peloponnese ✈Kalamáta ⊟

A harsh remote region, bounded by mountains to the north, the rocky Máni was the last part of Greece to embrace Christianity, doing so in the 9th century with an enthusiasm borne out by dozens of surviving Byzantine chapels. Though well defended against invaders, the area has a history of internal feuding which led to the building of many tower houses. A ravine at Oítylo divides the Inner Máni, to the south *(p180)*, from the more fertile Outer, or Messenian, Máni, which has some of the finest countryside in the Mediterranean.

②

Stoúpa

📍7 km (4 miles) S of Kardamýli

A short drive from Kardamýli, Stoúpa is popular for its two sandy bays; in summer you'll find plenty of Greek families holidaying here. Novelist Níkos Kazantzákis (1883–1957) moved here and worked in a mine, together with his friend Giorgos Zorbas, who inspired the fictional character in his novel.

①

Kardamýli

📍35 km (22 miles) S of Kalamáta

Kardamýli was once the stronghold of the Troupákis family, important rivals of the Mavromichális clan. Nicknamed Moúrtzinos, or "Bulldog", for their tenacity in battle, they claimed to be descended from the Byzantine Palaiológos dynasty. In more recent times the town was for many years home to the British traveller and writer Patrick Leigh Fermor (1915–2011) and his photographer wife Joan; Leigh Fermor's book *Mani: Travels in the South Peloponnese*, published in 1958, is a wonderful evocation of life here.

Olive oil used to be the chief source of income for Kardamýli, but this has now been superseded by tourism. It's a remarkably picturesque spot, its rocky, cypress-studded slopes sweeping down to a beautiful bay. There are plenty of places to eat and stay, and it makes an excellent base for exploring the area. Inland from Kardamýli rises

---

 HIDDEN GEM
Literary Life

The Leigh Fermors' home in Kardamýli, set in stone buildings with beautiful gardens in an olive grove, is open to visitors. To arrange a guided visit contact the Benáki Museum: tel 210 3671090.

The village of Agios Nikólaos, a short walk to the south, curls around the Outer Máni's most photogenic harbour. It has four tavernas. The closest beach is at Agios Dimítrios, 3 km (2 miles) further south.

---

③

Oítylo

Though administratively within the region of Lakonía, by tradition the village of Oítylo (pronounced "Ítilo") belongs to Outer Máni. It affords superb panoramic views over Limeníou Bay and across a flanking ravine, traditionally the border between Inner and Outer Máni, to Kelefá Castle *(p181)*. Its relatively good water supply fosters a lush setting around and below the village, with cypresses and a variety of orchard trees. Unlike most Mániot villages, Oítylo is not in economic decline. Its many fine houses include graceful 19th-century mansions. The village was capital of Máni between the 16th and 18th centuries, and was the area's most infamous slave-trading centre; both Venetians and Muslims were sold to each other here. A plaque in the square, written in French and Greek, commemorates the flight, in 1675, of 730 Oítylots to Corsica – 430 of whom were from the Stefanópoulos clan. Seeking refuge from the Turks, the Oítylots were granted passage by the Genoese and, once in Corsica, founded the villages of Paomia and Cargèse. These towns account for the stories of Napoleon's part-Mániot origins.

---

④

Moní Dekoúlou

From the southwestern corner of Oítylo, a broad path descends west to Moní Dekoúlou, nestled in its own little oasis. The church, which features an ornate témblon (wooden altar screen), is known for its vivid original frescoes that have been well preserved by darkness; a torch is required to see them now. The monastery is only open in the evenings or by prior arrangement with the resident caretakers.

The village of Néo Oítylo stands 4 km (2 miles) south

MÁNIOT TOWERS

The most distinctive architectural features of the Máni are the four- or five-storey towers that dominate many of the villages. These have their origins in ancient infighting between local clans, largely over the scarce farming land here. Once commenced, these blood feuds could last months, even years, with periodic truces to tend the crops. Clansmen fired at each other from facing towers, raising them in order to catapult rocks onto opponents' roofs. The hostilities ended only with the destruction or submission of the losing clan.

of the monastery. Quietly secluded, it has a pebble beach with fine views.

---

⑤

Mount Taÿgetos

The distinctive pyramidal summit and knife-edged ridge of Mount Taÿgetos, standing at 2,404 m (7,887 ft), divides the regions of Messinía and Lakonía. Formed of limestone and densely clad in black pine and fir, the range offers wilderness trekking to experienced, well-equipped mountaineers. Anavrytí and Palaiopanagiá, on the east, and Pigádia and Kardamýli, on the west, are the usual trailhead villages. Various traverses can be made by using the Vyrós and Ríntomo gorges which drain west from the main ridge; an unstaffed alpine refuge at Varvára-Deréki, above Anavrytí village, is the best starting point for those wanting to head straight for the summit.

↑ Historic towers dating from the era when the Máni was fought over by rival village clans

10

INNER MÁNI
ΜΕΣΑ ΜΑΝΗ

🅰C7 🏠Peloponnese 🚌Areópoli 🚌Gýtheio

The Inner, or Lakonian, Máni is divided into two regions – Aposkieri, the "Shadowed" western flank and Prosiliaki, the "Sunward" eastern shore. The former is famous for its numerous caves and churches, the latter for its villages which perch dramatically on crags overlooking the sea. The Inner Máni is severely depopulated, its only future being as a holiday venue. Retired Athenians of Mániot descent have restored its tower houses (p179) as hunting lodges for the brief autumn shoot of quail and turtle dove.

①
Gýtheio

The lively town of Gýtheio is the gateway to the Máni peninsula and one of the most attractive coastal towns in the southern Peloponnese. It was once the naval base of ancient Sparta (p187), though the main ancient relic is a Roman theatre to the north. The town was wealthy in Roman times, when it exported the purple molluscs used for colouring imperial togas. Until World War II, Gýtheio exported acorns used in leather tanning,

gathered by women and children from nearby valleys.

The town's heart is Plateía Mavromicháli, with the quay extending to either side lined by tiled 19th-century houses. The east-facing town enjoys sunrises over Cape Maléas and the Lakonian Gulf while snowy Mount Taÿgetos looms beyond a low ridge to the north.

In the bay, and linked to the waterfront by a causeway, lies the islet of Marathonísi, thought to be Homer's Kranaï islet. It was here that Paris of Troy and Helen spent their first night together (p164).

It is dominated by the Tzanetakis tower, a crenellated 18th-century fortress which now houses the **Museum of the Máni**. The subject of the exploration of Máni in medieval times is covered on the ground floor, while the exhibits of the upper storey place the tower houses in their social context.

Museum of the Máni
🚌Marathonísi Islet
🕐8:30am–3pm daily

---

②
Castle of Passavá

🏠12 km (7 miles) SW of Gýtheio

The Castle of Passavá was built in 1254 by the Frankish de Neuilly clan to guard a defile between Kelefá and Oítylo. Its name stems from *passe avant*, the clan's motto, though the present building is an 18th-century Ottoman construction. The Turks left the castle in 1780 after Tzanetbey Grigorákis avenged the murder of his uncle by massacring 1,000 Muslim villagers inside. Today's overgrown ruins are best approached from the southwest.

③
Areópoli

The Mavromichális *(p179)* stronghold of Tsímova was renamed Areópoli, "the city of Ares" (god of war), for its role in the War of Independence *(p60)*; it was here that the Mániot uprising against the Ottomans was proclaimed by Pétros Mavromichális. Now the main town of the Shadowed Máni, its central old quarter features two 18th-century churches. Taxiarchón boasts the highest bell tower in the Máni, as well as zodiacal apse reliefs; Agios Ioánnis, adorned with naive frescoes, was the chapel of the Mavromichális.

④
Ottoman Kelefá Castle

🏛 10 km (6 miles) N of Areópoli

The second castle guarding Máni was built in 1670 to command the bays of Oítylo and Liméni and counter the impending Venetian invasion *(p59)*. The bastions of the pentagonal curtain walls are preserved. The castle can be reached from the Areópoli–Gýtheio road (sign-posted) and from a footpath from Oítylo.

⑤
Pýrgos Diroú Caves

🏛 12 km (7 miles) S of Areópoli ☎ 27330 52222
🕐 Times vary, call ahead

This cave system is one of the largest and most colourful in Greece. During summer, crowds take a 30-minute punt ride along the underground stream which passes through Glyfáda cavern, reflecting the overhanging stalactites. A 15-minute walk then leads to the exit. A nearby chamber, called Alepótrypa cave, is drier but just as spectacular, with waterfalls and a lake. Until an earthquake closed the entrance, the cave was home to Neolithic people, and a separate museum chronicles their life and death.

⑥
The Shadowed Coast

Between Pýrgos Diroú and Gerolíménas lies the 17-km (10.5-mile) shore of the Shadowed Coast, famous for its many Byzantine churches. Among the finest are 11th-century Taxiarchón, at Charoúda, with vivid 18th-century frescoes, and Agios Theódoros at Vámvaka, its dome supported by carved beams. Káto Gardenítsa features the 12th-century Metamórfosi tou Sotiros, with frescoes spanning five centuries, while the 12th-century Episkopí, near Stavrí, has a complete cycle of 18th-century frescoes.

Vátheia, 10 km (6 miles) east of Gerolímenas, is one of the most dramatically located of the villages; overlooking the sea and Cape Taínaro, its bristling tower houses constitute a showpiece of local architectural history.

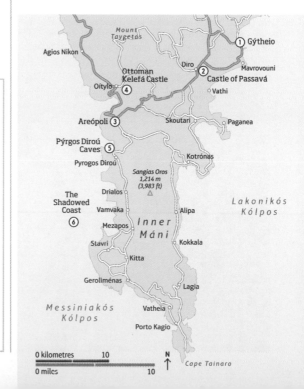

EXPERIENCE MORE

⑪
Corinth Canal
Διώρυγα της Κορίνθου

**🅐D5 🅐Peloponnese
🚌Loutráki**

Stormy Cape Matapan, or Cape Taínaro (p181), the southernmost point of the Peloponnese, was one of the dreaded capes of antiquity; rather than sail around it, boats would be unloaded on one shore of this isthmus, dragged the 6 km (4 miles) across on the *díolkos* (paved slipway), and then refloated.

The traffic inspired plans for a canal. Emperor Nero began construction, but the project was only completed between 1882 and 1893. The 23-m- (75-ft-) wide canal is obsolete in an age of giant container ships which easily weather the cape, but small freighters and yachts are often seen from the road bridge, squeezing through.

Near the southern end of the canal is the site of Ancient Isthmia, once the major local religious centre (devoted to Poseidon) and location of the biennial Isthmian Games. Today, only foundations of Poseidon's temple and the remains of a starting gate for track events are traceable.

The **Archaeological Museum of Isthmia** displays finds from Kechriés, Corinth's eastern port; unique exhibits include panels of painted glass or stone embedded in a resin matrix, which were intended to decorate an Isis temple but were never used.

Archaeological Museum of Isthmia
⊛ 🅐Kyrass Vryssi, Corinth
☎27410 37244 🕑8:30am–3:30pm Wed–Mon

⑫
Heraion of Perachóra
Ηραίον της Περαχωρας

🅐D5 🅐23 km (14 miles) W of Loutráki, Peloponnese

Probably founded during the 8th century BC, the Heraion of Perachóra (a nearby modern village) was primarily a religious centre. Only foundations and column stumps remain of the Archaic temple of Hera Limeneia, plus an altar and a Classical stoa, but the site has a great setting above a tiny cove on the south shore of Cape Melangávi.

Scenic Vouliagméni Lake, 2 km (1.2 miles) east, is fringed by Aleppo pines, with the best swimming and a selection of tavernas at its west end.

⑬
Mount Chelmós
Ορος Χελμός

🅐C5 🅐Peloponnese 🚌To Kalávryta

At 2,355 m (7,729 ft), Mount Chelmós is the third-highest point of the Peloponnese, its foothills cloaked in extensive forests and divided by deep gorges. The most famous is Mavronéri, where the waterfall cascading from the remote north face of the summit is claimed to be the source of the mythical river Styx.

Overlooking the wooded Feneoú valley, on the south-eastern slopes, stands the remote monastery of Agíou Georgíou Feneoú. The *katholikón*, with its high dome and transept, offers vivid frescoes, including some of the birth of the Virgin.

Moní Agías Lávras, 6 km (4 miles) from Kalávryta, played a pivotal role in the Greek Revolution. The Archbishop of Pátra raised the standard of revolt here on 25 March 1821, the banner now being the centrepiece of a nationalist shrine in the

← A pleasure craft motoring through the Corinth Canal, first conceived by Nero

The re-erected Doric columns of the Temple of Zeus, Ancient Nemea

upstairs treasury. Founded in 961, Agías Lávras has been rebuilt after being razed by the Germans in 1943. The day before, the Germans had burned the town of Kalávryta and massacred nearly 700 civilians in reprisal for local resistance. The cathedral clock is permanently stopped at the time the killing began.

The **Cave of the Lakes** (Spileo Limnon), near Kastriá, was known in ancient times but only rediscovered in 1964. Groups can visit the first 350 m (1,150 ft) of the cave, down to the second of 15 lakes. The massive stalactite-hung caverns were formed by an underground river, which still flows during the winter.

Cave of the Lakes

⟡ ⬛16 km (10 miles) S of Kalávryta ⬤9am–4:30pm daily (summer & hols: times vary) ⬤kastriacave.gr

---

⑭ ⟨⟩

Ancient Nemea
Αρχαία Νεμέα

🅰C5 ⬛5 km (3 miles) SE of modern Neméa, Peloponnese ⬛ ⬤8am–8pm daily (Nov–Mar: to 3pm) ⬤Main public hols ⬤odysseus.culture.gr

Occupying an isolated rural valley, the site of Ancient Nemea is a local landmark, with the nine re-erected Doric columns of its 4th-century Zeus temple plainly visible from afar. Below them lie the broken remains of column drums toppled by vandals between the 4th and 13th centuries AD. At the west end of the temple's complete floor, the deep *adyton* (underground crypt) has been exposed.

A short walk to the southwest, under a giant modern shelter, are the plunge pool and feed system of a Hellenistic bathhouse. Excavations in the area have also uncovered the Byzantine village that took root here in the 4th century, including graves, kilns and a basilica built above the ancient pilgrims' inn.

The on-site museum has interesting reconstructions and engravings. The Hellenistic stadium, to the southeast, has the earliest known vaulted entrance tunnel. It is used every fourth year in June for the Nemean Games, revived in part by US archaeologist Stephen Miller, who made excavations here until 2005. For more information about the site, the ancient games and their re-enactment, visit www.nemeangames.org.

KALÁVRYTA-DIAKOFTÓ RAILWAY

The most enjoyable narrow-gauge railway in Greece, the Kalávryta-Diakoftó Railway was engineered between 1889 and 1895 to bring ore down from the Kalávryta area (www.odontotos.com). Over 22 km (14 miles) of track were laid, over 6 km (4 miles) of which relies on a rack and pinion system, engaged for the steepest gradients. Two of the original steam locomotives, replaced in 1959, are displayed at Diakoftó. The train runs daily through 14 tunnels and along many bridges over the Vouraïkós Gorge. Roughly halfway is Káto Zachloroú, the starting point of a 45-minute trail up to Moní Méga Spílaio, believed to be the oldest monastery in Greece.

15

Pátra
Πάτρα

⚐C5 ⚑Peloponnese 🚉🚌
🚌 𝒊Seasonal desks at the
airport and ferry port

Greece's third-largest city
and a major port, Pátra is
located in the far north of the
Peloponnese on the Gulf of
Pátra, which extends into the
Ionian Sea. Although it is little
visited by tourists, it does
have a great deal to commend
it. Pátra is renowned for the
biggest and best carnival
celebrations in Greece in the
run-up to Easter, thanks in
part to its large LGBTQ+ and
student populations.

On the ancient acropolis, the
originally Byzantine kástro bears
marks of every subsequent
era. The vast bailey, filled with

Did You Know?

The annual carnival in
Pátra is one of the
largest in Europe,
lasting anything up
to six weeks.

gardens and orchards, often
hosts public events, as does the
nearby brick Roman odeion.
At the southwest edge of town,
at Evmilou 4, is the mock-
Byzantine basilica of Agios
Andréas. One of the biggest
churches in the Balkans, it
can accommodate over 5,000
worshippers. Standing where
St Andrew was supposedly
martyred, the church houses
his skull and a fragment of
his cross. You can uncover the

history of the city in the bright
Archaeological Museum, the
largest outside Athens.

Just south of the city,
the **Achaïa Clauss Winery**,
founded in 1861, was Greece's
first commercial winery and is
now one of the largest vintners
in Greece. Tours include a visit
to the Imperial Cellar, where
Mavrodaphne, a fortified
dessert wine, can be tasted.

Archaeological Museum
♿🚻🏛 ⚐New National
Road Patras-Athens 38–40
📞 26136 16100 🕐8am–8pm
daily (Nov–Apr: 8am–3pm
Wed–Mon)

Achaïa Clauss Winery
♿🍷🏛 ⚐Petrotó, 6 km
(4 miles) SE of Pátra 📞 26105
80100 🕐11am–7pm daily
🌐achaiaclauss.gr

16

Kalógria
Καλόγρια

⚐B5 ⚑Peloponnese
🚌To Lápas 𝒊Lápas town
hall; www.strofylia
nationalpark.gr

The entire lagoon-speckled
coast, from the Araxos river
mouth to the Kotýchi lagoon,
ranks as one of the largest
wetlands in Europe. Incorporating the Strofyliá marsh and
a vast umbrella pine dune-
forest, the area enjoys full
protection as a national park.
Development is confined to a
zone between the Prokópos
lagoon and the excellent 7-km
(4-mile) beach of Kalógria. The
dunes also support Aleppo
pines and valonea oaks, while
bass, eels and water snakes
swim in the marsh channels.
Migratory ducks, including
pintails and coots, visit
Kotýchi, while marsh harriers,
owls, kestrels and falcons can

← The brightly decorated
interior of the church of
Agios Andréas in Pátra

↑ The unspoiled town of Andrítsaina, with its colourful shabby-chic paintwork

be seen all year round. A Visitor Centre at Lápas documents nature trails through the dunes nearby.

17

Andrítsaina
Ανδρίτσαινα

🅰C6 🄰Peloponnese 🚌

The sleepy town of Andrítsaina is hardly touched by tourism. Tavernas and shops around its central square, home to a lively morning produce market, make few concessions to modernity in either their cuisine or displays. Downhill from the 18th-century Traní fountain, a **Folk Museum** features local rag-rugs, traditional dress and metalware.

Around 14 km (9 miles) south of Andrítsaina, the 5th-century BC Temple of Apollo Epikourios Bassae graces a commanding knoll, occupying the most remote site of any major ancient sanctuary. Today, it hides under an enormous tent, until 50 million euros (£38 million) can be raised to reinstall the architraves that protect the colonnades from winter frost.

Folk Museum
🄰Andrítsaina 🕐Noon-2pm Fri-Sun

18

Ancient Tegea
Τεγέα

🅰C6 🄰Peloponnese 🚌
🕐8:30am-3pm Tue-Sun

About 9 km (5.5 miles) south-east of Trípoli, the remains of the ancient city of Tegea lie near the village of Aléa. The most impressive ruin is the 4th-century BC Doric temple-sanctuary of Athena Alea, with its massive column drums, the second-largest temple in the Peloponnese after Olympia's Temple of Zeus. The on-site **Archaeological Museum** contains sculpture recovered from the city, including fragments of the temple pedestal.

Archaeological Museum
🎨🄰Aléa 🕐8:30am-3:30pm Wed-Mon

19

Chlemoútsi Castle
Χλεμούτσι

🅰B5 🄰Kástro, Peloponnese 🕐8:30am-3:30pm Wed-Mon (Nov-Mar; 8:30am-3pm Wed-Mon) 🌐visitkastro.com

The most famous Frankish castle in Greece, known also as "Castel Tornesi" after the gold *tournois* coin minted here in medieval times, was erected between 1219 and 1223 to defend thriving Glaréntza port (today, Kyllíni) and the principality capital of Andreville (Andravída). Exceptionally thick walls and a massive gate were built; much of the rampart catwalk can still be followed. The magnificent hexagonal keep has echoing, vaulted halls. Steps lead to a roof for views over the Ionian islands and the coastal plain. Chlemoútsi has been widely reconstructed, with the vast fan-shaped courtyard now used for summer concerts.

←

Marble head of a warrior found in the temple of Athena Alea, Ancient Tegea

20

Ancient Tiryns
Τίρυνθα

🗺 D6 📍 4 km (2 miles) NW of Náfplio, Peloponnese
☎ 27520 22657 🚌
🕐 8:30am–3:30pm daily
🚫 Main public hols
🌐 odysseus.culture.gr

The 13th-century BC citadel of Tiryns confirms Homer's epithet "mighty-walled". A 700-m (2,300-ft) circuit of Cyclopean walls (named after the giants who could be imagined manoeuvring the huge blocks into place) attains a thickness of 8 m (26 ft). The fortifications, over double their present height, were necessarily stronger than those of Mycenae since Tiryns was not on a naturally strong site. The bluff on which it stood was only 18 m (59 ft) higher than the surrounding plain which, in ancient times, was a salt marsh.

An inclined ramp to the east, designed with sharp turns to expose attackers' unshielded sides, leads to the massive middle gate, the lintel of which has long been missing. At the southern end of the complex, a gallery with a pointed corbel ceiling has had its walls polished by the fleeces of sheep that have sheltered here for centuries. On the west side, a stone stairway between inner and outer walls, leading to a postern gate, has been completely preserved. The lower, northern acropolis was the last to be enclosed and was used to protect commoners, animals and (as at Mycenae) a water supply.

A little north of Tiryns is Argive Heraion, the Archaic and Classcial religious centre of the Argolid. The most impressive remains are those of a late 5th-century BC temple.

21

Argos
Αργος

🗺 C6 📍 Peloponnese 🚌

One of the oldest settlements in Greece, modern Argos is a busy market town, with its open-air fairground next to a restored Neo-Classical market-place. The **Archaeological Museum** exhibits local finds from all eras. Highlights include an Archaic pottery fragment showing the blinding of Polyphemos by Odysseus and a *krater* (bowl) from the 7th century BC.

The most visible traces of Ancient Argos lie on the way to Trípoli, where Roman baths are dwarfed by one of the largest and most steeply raked theatres in the Greek world. From town, a road climbs Lárisa hill, one of Argos's two ancient acropolises.

Archaeological Museum
◈ 🏛 E of Plateía Agíou Pétrou ☎ 27510 68819
🚫 For renovation; phone for updates

🔍 HIDDEN GEM
Hellenic Pyramid

Nine kilometres (6 miles) south of Argos is the base of the Pyramid of Hellinikon. Thermoluminescence, and its astronomical orientation, may tie its date to the era of the great Pyramids of Egypt.

22

Geráki
Γεράκι

⚠C6 🏛Peloponnese 🚌

Occupying a spur of Mount Párnonas, Geráki resembles a miniature Mystrás with its kástro overlooking the frescoed Byzantine churches on the slopes below. The polygonal kástro was built in 1254–5 by the Frankish baron Jean de Nivelet, though it was ceded in 1262 to the Byzantines, together with Monemvasiá and Mystrás. Inside, 13th-century Agios Geórgios is a hybrid Franko-Byzantine church, the third aisle and narthex added after 1262; a carved marble screen and frescoes decorate its interior.

Below the west gate, 13th-century Zoödóchou Pigís sports a complete Gothic door and south window, while inside, later frescoes include *Christ on the Road to Calvary*. At the base of the hill, the domeless 14th-century church of Agía Paraskeví has a fine *Nativity* in its cross vault, plus a painting of the donor family on the west wall.

Four more churches stand a short drive to the west in Geráki village. Both 12th-century Agios Athanásios and 13th-century Agios Sózon share a cross-in-square plan, with a high dome on four piers. Market edicts of the Roman emperor Diocletian, inscribed on stone, flank the doorway of barrel-vaulted 14th-century Agios Ioánnis Chrysóstomos, covered inside with scenes from the life of Christ and the Virgin. Tiny Evangelístria has a Pantokrator fresco in its dome.

23

Spárti
Σπάρτη

⚠C6 🏛Peloponnese 🚌
🌐**exploresparta.gr**

Though one of the most powerful Greek city-states, ancient Sparta was unfortified and has few ruins dating to its heyday. The acropolis lies just northwest of the modern town centre. On the western side of the acropolis is the cavity of the Roman theatre, its masonry largely pilfered, while east stands the long, arcaded stoa which once held shops. Of the Artemis Orthia sanctuary, where Spartan youths were flogged to prove their manhood, only some Roman seating remains. The most interesting finds are on display in the museum.

The highlight of the rich **Archaeological Museum** is the fine collection of Roman mosaics, including two lions rampant over a vase, Arion riding his dolphin, Achilles disguised as a woman on Skýros, and a portrait of Alkibiades. Bas-reliefs of Underworld serpent-deities hail from a sanctuary of Apollo at modern Amyklés, 8 km (5 miles) south of Spárti. Bizarre ceramic masks are smaller replicas of those used in dances at the Artemis Orthia sanctuary.

Archaeological Museum
⊛ 🏛Agíou Níkonos & Lykouroú 📞27310 28575
🕒8:30am–3:30pm Wed–Mon
🚫Main public hols

↑ The ruins of the mighty walls that protected Ancient Tiryns

The small harbour of the traditional fishing village of Koróni →

Nestor's Palace
Ανάκτορο του Νέστορα

B6 **16 km (10 miles) NE of Pýlos, Peloponnese** **27630 31437** **Site: 8am-8pm Wed-Mon (Nov-Mar: 8:30am-3:30pm Wed-Mon)**

Discovered in 1939, the 13th-century BC palace of Mycenaean King Nestor was excavated by Carl Blegen from 1952. Hundreds of tablets in the ancient Linear B script were found, as well as a bathtub and olive oil jugs. Today, only waist-high walls and column bases suggest the typical Mycenaean plan of a two-storey complex around a central hall. The **Chóra Archaeological Museum**, 3 km (2 miles) away, displays finds from the palace site.

Chóra Archaeological Museum
Chóra **27630 31358** **8:30am-3:30pm Wed-Mon**

25
Koróni
Κορώνη

C7 **Peloponnese**

One of the "eyes of Venice" (along with Methóni), Koróni surveys the shipping lanes between the Adriatic and Crete. It stands at the foot of a Venetian castle, begun in 1206, whose walls now shelter the huge Timíou Prodrómou convent. The town, divided by stepped streets, dates to 1830. Little has changed here; many houses retain elaborate wrought-iron balconies,

←

A Mycenean jar decorated with an octopus in the Chóra Archaeological Museum

STAY

Camvillia Resort
Overlooking the sea, this five-star resort consists of luxurious villas, a pool and a superb restaurant, all surrounded by olive groves.

C7 **Vounaria, Koróni** **camvillia.gr**

€€€

horizontal-slat shutters and tile "beaks" on the undulating roofs. A lively seafront is the sole concession to tourism.

26
Ancient Messene
Αρχαία Μεσσήνη

C6 **34 km (21 miles) NW of Kalamáta, Peloponnese** **27240 51201** **8am-8pm daily (Nov-May: 8:30am-3:30pm daily)**

Ancient Messene is now also confusingly known as Ithómi –

after the mountain that sits overhead. It is a little-visited, intriguing site, still undergoing excavation. The 4th-century BC city walls are 9 km (6 miles) long. They enclose a vast area that incorporates the foundations of a Zeus temple, the acropolis on Mount Ithómi to the northeast, and the massive, double Arcadia Gate.

The archaeological zone includes the picturesque village of Mavrommáti, whose water is still supplied by the ancient Klepsýdra fountain at the heart of the site. Below the village, an amphitheatre, stoas, a *bouleuterion* (council hall) and a monumental stairway surround the foundations of an Asklepios temple.

---

27 Pýlos
Πύλος

🏛C6 🚌Peloponnese 🚍

The town of Pýlos, originally Avaríno (later Navaríno), is French in design, like Methóni. Life is confined to Plateía Trión Navárchon and the seafront on either side.

To the west, the castle of **Niókastro**, Ottoman and Venetian in origin, was extensively repaired by the French after 1828; their barracks are now a gallery of antiquarian engravings by the artist René Puaux (1878–1938). The roof gives views over Navaríno Bay, scene of the famous battle in 1827 that decided the Greek War of Independence. The perimeter walls of the castle are dilapidated, but it is possible to walk along the parapet. Boat tours around the bay visit memorials on and around Sfaktiría island, which commemorate those sailors lost in the Battle of Navaríno, foreign philhellenes and revolutionary heroes. The north end of Navaríno Bay has excellent beaches, especially Voïdokoiliá lagoon, where Telemachos, Odysseus's son, disembarked to seek news of his father from King Nestor. You can walk up the dunes to Spiliá tou Néstora, an impressively large cave, which may have been the inspiration for Homer's cave in which Nestor and his father Neleus kept their cows.

Niókastro

⊛ 🚪Town centre ☎27230 22955 🕐Jun-Aug: 8am-8pm Wed-Sun (8:30am-3:30pm Nov-May)

---

28 Methóni
Μεθώνη

🏛C7 🚌Peloponnese 🚍

A key Venetian port, Methóni controlled the lucrative pilgrim trade to Palestine after 1209. With the sea on three sides, its rambling castle is defended on its landward side by a Venetian moat, bridged by the French in 1828. The structure combines Venetian, Ottoman and even French military architecture. The remains within the walls include two ruined *hamams* (baths), a Venetian church, minaret bases and the main street. Boúrtzi, an islet fortified by the Turks, stands beyond the Venetian sea-gate.

---

29 Ancient Troezen
Τροιζήνα

🏛D6 🚌60 km (37 miles) E of Náfplio, Peloponnese

On a high bluff isolated by two ravines near the modern village of Troizína are the sparse ruins of ancient Troezen, legendary birthplace of the hero Theseus and the setting for Euripides' tragedy *Hippolytus*. Remains from many eras are scattered over a wide area; most conspicuous are three Byzantine chapels known as *Episkopí*, from the time when this was the seat of the Bishops of Damála.

A 15-minute walk up the westerly Damála Gorge leads to a natural rock arch called the "Devil's Bridge" spanning the canyon. Near the lower end of the gorge stands the Hellenistic and medieval "Tower of Theseus".

→

The castle in Methóni, built by the Venetians in the 13th century

CENTRAL AND WESTERN GREECE

Ancient battlefields are scattered around the borderlands where Attica joins Central and Western Greece. Persian invaders clashed with Spartans at Thermopylae in 480 BC before being defeated at Plataiai. Sparta in turn was defeated by Thebes at Leuktra in 371 BC, ending an era of Spartan hegemony. More peacefully, ancient Greeks made Delphi a neutral sacred and diplomatic hub, and Dodona, the site of the oldest holy oracle in Greece, remained an important sacred centre until the advent of Christianity in the late 4th century AD.

Under the Byzantine Empire, great monasteries, such as those at Osios Loukás and Metéora, flourished. Ottoman expansion was checked by a Venetian and Spanish fleet at Náfpakto (Lepanto) in 1571, but the region remained in Turkish hands until the War of Independence. Mesolóngi was a centre of Greek resistance, and the siege of the city became a heroic legend. Victory gave Greece control of most of the region, but Turkey retained Ioánnina and the northwest until the Balkan Wars. In the 1930s, rivers were dammed and wetlands drained to create vast tobacco and cotton plantations. The region suffered during World War II and the Civil War, but the post-war years gradually brought prosperity, with new EU-funded highways and a spectacular road bridge that crosses the Gulf of Corinth to the Peloponnese so that today its many sights are no longer far from the beaten path.

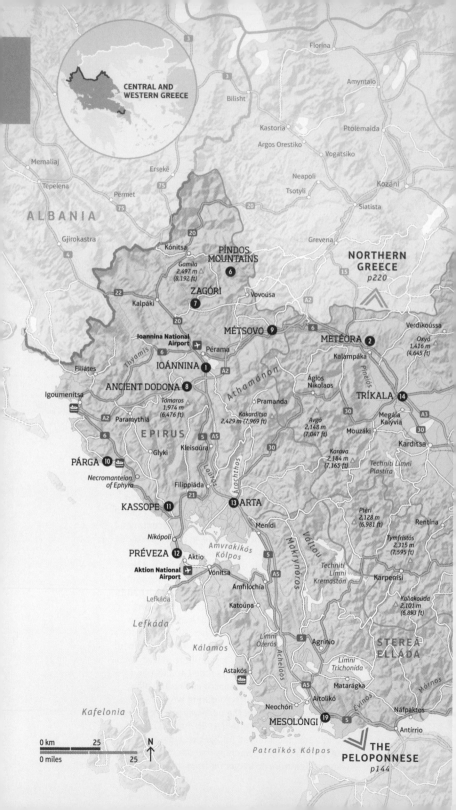

Florina

Amyntaio

Bilisht

Kastoria

Argos Orestiko

Vogatsiko

Ptolemaida

Memaliaj

Tepelena

Përmet

Ersekë

75

Neapoli

Tsotyli

Kozáni

Siatista

75

ALBANIA

Gjirokastra

4

Kónitsa

PÍNDOS
MOUNTAINS

Gamíla
2,497 m △
(8,192 ft)

6

Grevena

**NORTHERN
GREECE**
p220

Verdikoússa

Oxyá
1,416 m △
(4,645 ft)

22

Kalpáki

ZAGÓRI

7

Vovoúsa

MÉTSOVO **9**

6

METÉORA **2**

Kalambáka

Ágios
Nikolaos

TRÍKALA **14**

20

**Ioannina National
Airport**

Filiátes

Pérama

IOÁNNINA **1**

A2

ANCIENT DODONA **8**

Igoumenitsa

A2

Paramythiá

Tómaros
1,974 m △
(6,476 ft)

EPIRUS

Glykí

Kleisoúra

Pramanda

Kakardítsa
2,429 m (7,969 ft)

Avgó
2,148 m △
(7,047 ft)

Mouzáki

Karáva
2,184 m △
(7,165 ft)

Megála
Kalývia

A3

30

Karditsa

Techníti Límni
Plastíra

PÁRGA **10**

Necromanteion
of Ephyra

Filippiáda

5

21

KASSOPE **11**

Nikópoli

ARTA **13**

Menídi

PRÉVEZA **12**

Aktio

**Aktion National
Airport**

Vónitsa

Amvrakikós
Kólpos

5

Amfilochía

Ptéri
2,128 m △
(6,981 ft)

Rentína

Tymfristós
2,315 m △
(7,595 ft)

Techníti
Límni
Kremastón

Karpenísi

Lefkáda

Katoúna

Lefkáda

Kálamos

Límni
Ozerós

Agrínio

5

Límni
Trichonída

Kaliakoúda
2,101 m △
(6,893 ft)

**STEREÁ
ELLÁDA**

Astakós

A5

Mataránga

Neochóri

Aitolikó

MESOLÓNGI **19**

5

Évinos

Náfpaktos

Antírrio

Kafelonia

0 km   25

0 miles   25

N

Patraïkós Kólpos

**THE
PELOPONNESE**
p144

CENTRAL AND WESTERN GREECE

Must Sees
1. Ioánnina
2. Metéora
3. Monastery of Osios Loukás
4. Ancient Delphi
5. Pílio

Experience More
6. Píndos Mountains
7. Zagóri
8. Ancient Dodona
9. Métsovo
10. Párga
11. Kassope
12. Préveza
13. Arta
14. Tríkala
15. Vale of Tempe
16. Thíva (Ancient Thebes)
17. Mount Parnassós
18. Lamía and Thermopylae
19. Mesolóngi
20. Gulf of Corinth

①

IOÁNNINA
ΙΩΑΝΝΙΝΑ

🅰B3 🏛Epirus ✈8km (5 miles) NW of Ioánnina
🚌Geor. Papandreou 45 🛈10 Moulaimidou St; www.
travelioannina.com

The beautiful capital of the Epirus region, Ioánnina
prospered in Ottoman times, when its famous craftsmen's guilds were formed. The Turkish influence is
most visible in the fortress area, which was rebuilt by
the Albanian Muslim tyrant Ali Pasha in 1815. Inside
the fortress precinct, a village-like peace reigns,
though the bustle of the bazaar and the modern area
is a reminder that this is still the region's busiest city.

① 🎨

Municipal
Ethnographic Museum

🏛Aslan Pasha Mosque
📞26510 26356 🕐9am–
4:30pm Mon–Fri, 9am–
3pm Sat & Sun 🚫Main
public hols

At the northern corner of
the fortress, this small
museum is housed within
a mosque built by Aslan
Pasha in 1618. While the
mosque itself, which retains
original decoration on its
dome, is worth a visit, the
weapons and costumes on

display tell something
of Ioánnina's recent past.
Ottoman furniture inlaid
with mother-of-pearl can
also be found, alongside
Jewish rugs and tapestries.

② 🎨

Byzantine Museum

🏛Inner Fortress 📞26510
25989 🕐8am–8pm Wed–
Mon (Nov–Apr: to 3:30pm)
🚫Main public hols

The core of this modern
museum is an imaginative
display of icons from the
16th to the 19th centuries. An
annexe contains silverware,
for which the city is renowned,
with a reconstruction of a
typical silversmith's workshop.

③ 🎨

Nisí

🏛15 minutes by boat NE
from Mólos quay

Though its first inhabitants
were monks who came here
in the early 13th century, the

ALI PASHA

In 1788 Ali Pasha installed himself at
Ioánnina as Pasha of Epirus. Ruthless and
skillful in his measures, he made the town
one of the richest in Ottoman Greece. His
aim was to break free from his overlords,
and by 1820, his empire stretched from
Albania to the Peloponnese; but in
1822, Sultan Mahmud II of Turkey
sent troops to put him to death.

↑ Ferry waiting on the shore of Lake Pamvotis to take visitors to Nisí island

single village on the isle of Nisí owes its existence to 17th-century refugees from Mániot feuds. Its main building is Moní Agíou Panteleímonos, where the reconstructed room in which Ali Pasha was shot can be visited, the bullet holes still visible in the floor. Other rooms contain a few of his possessions, some costumes and period prints.

(4) Archaeological Museum

🏛 Plateía 25 Martíou 6
📞 26510 01051 🕐 8:30am-3:30pm Wed-Mon

Set in a small park, this museum displays various artifacts that include items from the site of Dodóni. Among these is a bronze eagle from the 5th century BC and lead tablets inscribed with questions for the oracle.

(5) Folklore Museum

🏛 Michaïl Angélou 42
🕐 9am-2pm Mon-Fri (also 5:30-8pm Mon & Wed) 🕐 Main public hols
🌐 ehm.gr

Housed in a mansion, this museum showcases local crafts. As well as silverwork and traditional costumes, there are woven textiles made by the traditionally nomadic, but now sedentary, Sarakatsans, long rivals of the larger Aroman tribe *(p211)*.

STAY

Kamares Boutique Hotel & Spa
This restored 18th-century mansion in the historic center is Ioánnina's most stylish place to stay.

🏛 Zalokosta 74
📞 26510 74120

€€€

(6) Pérama Caves

🏛 Pérama 📞 26510 81521
🕐 9am-5pm daily

Near Pérama, 3 km (2 miles) north of Ioánnina, is Greece's largest cave network. There are regular guided tours taking visitors along the 1,700 m (5,600 ft) of passages, where multicoloured lights pick out the dramatic stalactites and stalagmites.

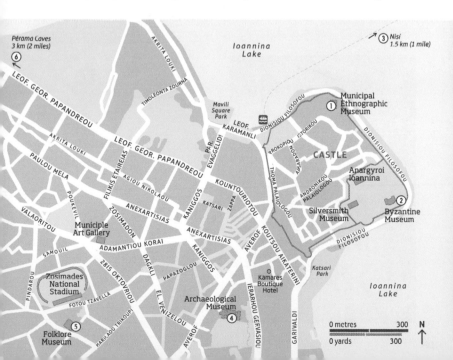

② MÉTÉORA

C3 ⌂ Thessaly ☐ Kalambaka ⏱ Times vary for each monastery, check website 🌐 visitmeteora.travel

The giant natural sandstone towers of Météora (or "suspended rocks") are a spectacular setting for the breathtaking monasteries that are miraculously perched on them.

The rocks of Météora were first used as a religious retreat when, in AD 985, a hermit named Barnabas occupied a cave here. In the mid-14th century, Neílos, the Prior of Stagai convent, built a small church. Then, in the 14th century, the monk Athanásios, from Mount Athos, founded the huge monastery of Megálo Metéoro on one of the many pinnacles. Twenty-three monasteries followed, though most had fallen into ruin by the 19th century. In the 1920s, stairs were cut to make the remaining six monasteries more accessible, and today, a religious revival has seen the return of monks and nuns.

Moní Rousánou, perched precariously on the very tip of a narrow spire of rock, is the most spectacularly located of all the monasteries. Its church is renowned for its frescoes, painted in 1560 by iconographers of the Cretan school. Varlaám, the second largest monastery after Megálo Metéoro, also has maginificent frescoes and a tower with a preserved net from which the first monks ascended and descended the rock.

Monastic walls

The refectory contains a small icon museum.

Outer walls

The church was built in 1542 and contains frescoes by the famous Theban iconographer Frágos Katelános

← Magnificent frescoed church interior in the Monastery of Varlaám

↑ The towering sandstone towers of Metéora, with Moní Rousánou monastery in the foreground

↑ Sixteenth-century frescoes inside the church of Moní Rousánou monastery

Made in 1536, the Ascent Tower was used to bring goods and people to the top of the rock in a net that was pulled up by a winch mechanism.

Net descending from tower

Entrance

← Illustration of the Monastery of Varlaám, named after the first hermit to live on this rock in 1350

THE BUILDING OF THE MONASTERIES

Though it is unknown how the first hermits reached the tops of these often vertical rock faces, it is likely that they hammered pegs into tiny gaps in the rock and hauled building materials to the summits. Another theory is that kites were flown over the tops, carrying strings attached to thicker ropes which were made into the first rope ladders.

❸

MONASTERY OF OSIOS LOUKÁS

ΜΟΝΗ ΟΣΙΟΥ ΛΟΥΚΑ

🗺 D5 🚗 8 km (5 miles) E of Dístomo 📞 22670 22797 🕐 Site & Museum: 8:30am–3:30pm daily

Dedicated to a local hermit and healer, the Blessed Luke of Stíri, Osios Loukás monastery is one of medieval Greece's most important buildings, and a prime example of Byzantine architecture and art.

The first surviving church here was built in c 960 by Emperor Romanos II, who extended an earlier church from AD 944. The octagonal style of the main church became a hallmark of late Byzantine church design (*p176*), while the mosaics inside lifted Byzantine art into its final great period. During the time of the Ottoman Empire Osios Loukás witnessed a great deal of fighting, as the cannons in the courtyard testify. Here, in 1821, Bishop Isaias gave his official blessing to the Greek freedom fighters; the monastery donated substantial funds to the revolutionary movement.

The north transept contains medallion-shaped mosaics of saints.

The monastic cells are small with arched roofs.

→ Illustration of the monastery complex, which was fully developed by the 11th century

The exterior is a mixture of dressed poros stone and red brick.

Based on a style dating to the 6th century, the late 11th-century Washing of the Apostles' Feet (Niptir) is the finest of the narthex mosaics, set on a gold background.

West portal

The narthex is the western entrance hall; it contains a number of mosaics of Christ's Passion.

← The central dome with the frescoed Christ Pantokrátor, which replaced an earlier fallen mosaic

Theotókos, built almost a century before the main church, is a smaller chapel dedicated to the Mother of God; its name means "god-bearing".

The main dome is decorated with an imposing mural of Christ surrounded by saints and angels, painted in the late 17th century.

The apse has a mosaic of the Virgin and Child pre-dating a devastating earthquake in 1659.

The octagonal katholikón, or main church, dates from around 1040.

↑ The monastery in its imposing setting, against the slopes of Mount Elikónas

BLESSED LUKE

Born in Aegina in 896, Osios Loukás ("Blessed Luke") is known to have been a spiritual child who, in his early teens, left home to seek isolation in central Greece and developed a reputation as a healer. In around 940, he arrived at nearby Stíri on the western slopes of Mount Elikónas, with its glorious view over a peaceful valley of cornfields and groves of almond and olive trees. Here, he settled with some disciples, adding the gift of prophecy to his healing powers. He died in 953, by which time the first monastic cells and the site's first small church had been constructed.

The 10th-century shrine in the crypt contains the sarcophagus of Holy Luke, and frescoes including a Descent from the Cross.

Frescoes

The refectory was used as a workshop and for meals; it now contains an interesting museum of Byzantine sculpture.

④

ANCIENT DELPHI

ΔΕΛΦΟΙ

🅰C5 🏔Mount Parnassós, Stereá Elláda 🚌 📞22650 82312 ⏰Site: Apr-Oct: 8am-8pm daily; Nov-Mar: 8am-3pm daily; Museum: Apr-Oct: 10am-5pm Tue, 8am-8pm Wed-Mon; Nov-Mar: 8:30am-3:30pm 🚫Main public hols

According to legend, when Zeus released two eagles from opposite ends of the world, their paths crossed in the sky above Delphi, establishing the site as the centre of the earth.

Renowned as a dwelling place of Apollo, from the end of the 8th century BC, individuals from the ancient world visited Delphi to consult the god on what course of action to take, in life. Apollo communicated with his mortal subjects (albeit often cryptically) via the Delphic Oracle, closely guarded by its cult priesthood. With the political rise of Delphi in the 6th century BC and the reorganization of the Pythian Games (p202), the sanctuary entered a golden age which lasted until the Romans came in 191 BC. The Oracle was abolished in AD 391 with the banning of all vestiges of paganism in the Byzantine Empire by Theodosius I.

THE ORACLE OF DELPHI

The Oracle was the means through which worshippers could hear the words of the god Apollo, spoken through an older priestess, or Pythia. Questioners paid a levy and sacrificed an animal on the altar. The question was then put to the Pythia by a male priest. She would answer in a trance, perhaps induced by vapours from a crack in the ground over which she sat on a tripod.

Vouleuterion (Delphic Council House)

The Athenian Treasury was built after the Battle of Marathon (p136) and reconstructed in 1906.

The Rock of the Sibyl marks the place where, according to legend, Delphi's first prophetess pronounced her oracles.

↖ *Delphi Archaeological Museum (500 m/ 540 yards)*

Siphnian Treasury

The main entrance was once a market-place (agora) where religious objects could be bought.

The Sacred Precinct of Ancient Delphi, centred on the Temple of Apollo, the god's sanctuary ↑

↑ Wandering among the ruins of this astonishingly rich archaeological site

The theatre, built 2,500 years ago, seats 5,000 people. It rivals Epidaurus (p168) as one of the finest theatres in Greece.

A column once supported a statue of Prusias, King of Bithynia.

A temple has stood on this site since the 7th century BC, but the remains visible today are of the Temple of Apollo, dating from the mid-4th century BC. Some reconstruction work has been done since French archaeologists uncovered the foundations in 1892, to give an idea of its grandeur.

Leading to the Temple of Apollo, the Sacred Way was lined with up to 3,000 statues and treasuries, built by city-states to house their people's offerings.

Did You Know?

The point where Zeus's eagles met is marked with a domed stone, the *Omphalos*, or navel of the world.

↑ One of the 13 rooms in the Delphi Museum displaying recovered statuary

EXPLORING DELPHI

The first excavations at Delphi began in 1892, initially uncovering a much larger area than is apparent now. Though it is most famous for the Sanctuary of Apollo, Delphi also had a sanctuary dedicated to the goddess Athena, whose temple can be seen in a second enclosure to the south. North of the theatre is the stadium where the Pythian Games were held. These, after the Olympic Games (p152), were the most important sporting event in the Greek calendar, providing an opportunity to strengthen the ethnic bond of the Greek nation, otherwise divided into predominantly rival city-states.

Delphi Museum

The museum at Delphi contains a collection of sculptures and architectural remains of an importance second only to those of the Acropolis Museum (p100).

There are 13 rooms of exhibits, all on the ground floor. In one of the rooms, there is a scale model that reconstructs the Sanctuary of Apollo in a triumph of limestone whites, blue marble, gold and terracotta. The sanctuary is surrounded by friezes and statues and its size and former beauty is represented vividly.

Votive chapels, known as "treasuries", lined the Sacred Way (p201) and contained offerings of thanks, in the form of money or works of art, from towns grateful for good fortune following a favourable prophecy from the Oracle. The Theban Treasury, for example,

was established after the victory of Thebes at the Battle of Leuktra in 371 BC. There are two rooms dedicated to the surviving sculpture from the Siphnian and Athenian treasuries, the wealth of the former illustrated by an outstanding frieze depicting the Greek gods waging war on the giants. The colossal *Naxian Sphinx* was presented by the wealthy citizens of Náxos in 560 BC; it stands 2.3 m (7.5 ft) high and once sat atop a 10 m (33 ft) column. The most famous of the museum's exhibits is a life-size bronze statue, the *Charioteer*. The statue was commissioned by a Sicilian tyrant named Polyzalos to commemorate a chariot victory in the Pythian Games in 478 BC. Another notable exhibit is the sculpture of *Three Dancing Girls* grouped around a column. The column is believed to have supported a tripod of the kind sat on by the *Pythia (p200)* as she went into her oracular trances. The girls are thought to be celebrating the feast of the god Dionysos (p36), who also resided in the sanctuary. His presence was honoured in the winter months when Apollo was away at his other shrine in Anatolia.

Marmaria Precinct

Southeast of the Temple of Apollo, a path leads to the Marmaria Precinct, or "marble quarry", where the Sanctuary of Athena Pronaia can be found. At the sanctuary's entrance stand the ruins of a 6th-century BC temple dedicated to Athena. At the far end of the sanctuary are the remains of a later temple to the goddess, which was built in Doric style in the 4th century BC. Between the two temples stands the

→

The Stadium's seating, made from limestone from Mount Parnassós

EAT

Taverna Vakhos
One of the best restaurants in Delphi, this family-run taverna offers views over the mountains down to the sea. The menu features traditional favourites, as well as some excellent lesser-known Greek dishes.

🏠 Apollonos 31, Delphi
Ⓦ vakhos.com

€€€

Marmaria's most remarkable, and most photographed, monument: the circular tholos. The purpose of this structure is still unknown. The rotunda dates from the start of the 4th century BC and was originally surrounded by 20 columns. Three of these columns, re-erected in 1938, provide some hint of the building's former beauty.

Castalian Spring

Before entering the Sacred Precinct, it is believed that everyone visiting Delphi for religious purposes, including athletes, was required to purify themselves in the clear but icy waters of the Castalian Spring – principally involving the washing of their hair. The *Pythia* would also wash here before making her pronouncements. A number of niches in the surrounding rock once held the votive offerings left for the nymph Castalia, to whom the spring was dedicated.

It is said that the British poet Lord Byron once plunged into the Castalian Spring, Inspired by the belief that the waters would enhance the poetic spirit.

Gymnasium

Water from the Castalian Spring ran down to the Marmaria to provide cold baths for athletes training for the Pythian Games. The original cold baths, which can be seen in a square courtyard, are some 9 m (30 ft) in diameter. East of the baths lies the Palaestra, or training area, surrounded by the remains of what once were changing rooms and training quarters. As well as an outdoor running track, a covered track 180 m (590 ft) in length was used in bad weather. The gymnasium was built on many levels due to the sloping terrain and was also used for intellectual pursuits – Delphi's poets and philosophers taught here.

> It is said that the British poet Lord Byron once plunged into the Castalian Spring, inspired by the belief that the waters would enhance the poetic spirit.

HIDDEN GEM
Polygonal Wall

The huge retaining wall below the Temple of Apollo is made from irregularly shaped dressed stones. Look closely and you'll see hundreds of ancient inscriptions carved on it. They relate to the practice of freeing enslaved people as a gift to the god.

Stadium

This is one of the best-preserved stadia in Greece. Almost 180 m (590 ft) long and partly hewn out of the rocks above the main sanctuary, it held 7,000 spectators who gathered for field and track events every four years during the Pythian Games. The games grew out of a musical festival, held every eight years to celebrate Apollo's mythical slaying of the serpent Python here. Though poetry and musical recitals remained central to the occasion, from 582 BC, athletic events in the stadium were added. All prizes in these tournaments were purely honorary; each winner was awarded the traditional laurel wreath and the right to have his statue in the sanctuary.

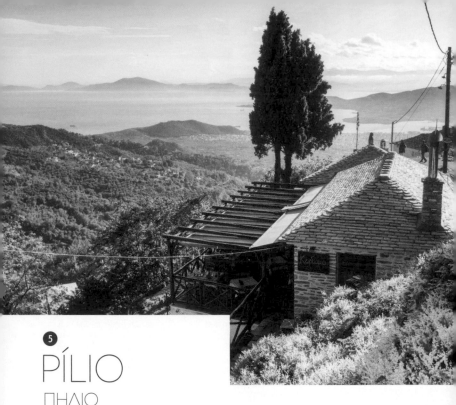

⑤
PÍLIO
ΠΗΛΙΟ

⛰ D4 **⏚ Thessaly** **✈ Volos** **🚆🚌🚗 Volos** **ℹ Opposite KTEL bus stion, Lambráki & Sekéri sts, Vólos; www.volosinfo.gr**

The mythological home of the forest-loving centaurs, the Pílio peninsula, with its woods of chestnut, oak and beech, is one of the most beautiful regions of the mainland, and it is always several degrees cooler than the rest of Thessaly in summer. The mountain air is sweet with the scent of herbs which, in ancient times, were renowned for their healing powers.

↑ The front of the railway station in Miliés, with its old-fashioned timetable display

This area became populated in the 13th century by Greeks retreating from the Franks, who had occupied Constantinople, and it flourished, especially when given limited autonomy during the 18th century – a time of improved conditions in the Ottoman Empire. However, the thick stone walls and narrow windows of a typical Pílio house indicate how uncertain that autonomy really was.

Vólos

The capital of the region, Vólos was devastated by earthquakes in the 1950s and is now a fast-growing industrial centre, so it is difficult to imagine its mythological past. Once the site of ancient Iolkos, the home of Jason – the hero who went in search of the Golden Fleece – Vólos's history is illustrated by what can be found in the excellent Archaeological Museum. It contains an extensive collection of painted funerary stelae from the 3rd century BC, found

EAT

Tsipouradiko Papadis

This restaurant specializes in meze and fresh seafood. Its *tsipouro* brandies come with a different meze for a perfectly curated meal.

🏠 Argonafton 6, Vólos
🌐 papadis.gr

€€€

Salkimi Taverna

A cosy restaurant just off Miliés's main square. Try one of the hearty oven-baked dishes.

🏠 Agrias-Mileon 107, Miliés 📞 24230 86010

€€€

Petrino Taverna Horto

Enjoy fresh fish or a homemade moussaka at one of the beachside tables overlooking the bay.

🏠 Chorto
📞 24230 65184

€€€

Niki's Taverna

Also known as the Meintani, and popular with locals, this may look like a thousand other rustic tavernas but the cooking by Niki (the owner) is outstanding.

🏠 Zagora
🌐 meintani.gr

€€€

←
Pílio's beautiful, varied scenery, from the hillside village of Makrynítsa *(main image)* to the pretty port of Agía Kyriaki *(inset)*

at Dimitriás on the far side of the Gulf of Vólos, and collections of Neolithic pottery from the nearby sites of Sesklo and Dimini.

Exploring the Pílio

A little north of Vólos is Makrynítsa – a traditional mountain village that's a must for any visitor to the area. It has some beautiful churches, the most impressive being Agios Ioánnis and Panagía Makrynítsa, and many traditional mansions also survive, some functioning as guesthouses. Close to Agios Ioánnis is a café with an interior decorated with frescoes painted by the Lésvos-born artist Theophilos, who came to the Pílio in 1894 and painted many murals. Anakasiá, the village closest to Vólos, is home to the delightful Theophilos Museum, which fills the entire Kontós Mansion with his frescoes of heroes and fantastic beasts. Southeast of Vólos, past Ano Lechónia, is the "Vólos Riviera",

part of the mountainous northern Pílio peninsula. At weekends during summer, a traditional narrow-gauge train runs from Káto Lechónia to Miliés. From the popular inland resorts of Miliés and Vyzítsa (the latter preserved as a "traditional settlement" by the government), the road heads north past Tsagkaráda to Agios Ioánnis. This is the main resort of the east coast; the beaches of Papá Neró and Pláka are particularly fine and are both within easy walking distance.

The southern olive grove-covered Pílio is less dramatic but still hilly. Argalastí is the main town here, on the edge of a plateau. At the tip of the peninsula is Agía Kyriaki, a small, little visited fishing port with good fish tavernas.

> Agios Ioánnis is the main resort of the east coast; the beaches of Papá Neró and Pláka are particularly fine and are both within easy walking distance.

A DRIVING TOUR
EXPLORE THE PÍLIO

Length 270 km (170 miles) **Stopping-off points** Agios Ioánnis, Miliés, Argalastí and Plataniás all have good places to eat and stay.

Travelling by car, a circular tour of the northern villages can be made in a day following the road southeast from Vólos – first to Afétes, then north via Tsagkaráda. The hills in this region rise to 1,650 m (5,415 ft) at the summit of Mount Pílio, and in addition to dense woodlands, the area produces a large number of apples, pears, peaches and olives. While less dramatic, the southern, olive grove-covered Pílio is still hilly enough to ensure that many villages are at the end of "dead end" roads, making travel here time consuming.

Cars are banned from the steep cobbled streets of **Makrynítsa** *village (p205).*

Zagora

Makrinítsa

Drakia

START

Anakasiá

Vólos

Agios Geórgios

Vyzítsa

Agriá

Ano Lechonia

Vólos *is the capital of the region, straddling the only route into the peninsula. It has an excellent Archaeological Museum (p204).*

Anakasiá, *little more than a suburb of Vólos, has a superb museum devoted to the Greek mural painter Theophilos Hatzimihail.*

Mansions have been converted to guesthouses in the small village of **Vyzítsa** *with its cobbled streets and large main square surrounded by old plane trees (p205).*

← Steep narrow street in the traditional village of Makrínytsa

Palió Tríkeri

FINISH

Tríkeri

Agía Kyriakí

Overlooked by the isolated hilltop village of Tríkeri, the small fishing port of **Agía Kyriakí** *lacks a beach and hotels but has a working boatyard and good, simple fish tavernas for those visitors who take the trouble to travel here.*

Explore the Pílio

CENTRAL AND WESTERN GREECE

Locator Map

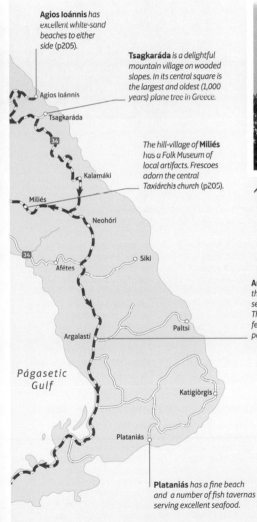

Agios Ioánnis *has excellent white-sand beaches to either side (p205).*

Tsagkaráda *is a delightful mountain village on wooded slopes. In its central square is the largest and oldest (1,000 years) plane tree in Greece.*

The hill-village of **Miliés** *has a Folk Museum of local artifacts. Frescoes adorn the central Taxiárchis church (p205).*

Agios Ioánnis

Tsagkaráda

34

Kalamáki

Miliés

Neohóri

34

Siki

Afétes

Argalastí *is the main town of the southern Pílio, attractively set on the edge of a plateau. Though it has a busy market, its few tavernas and cafés retain a peaceful atmosphere (p205).*

Paltsi

Argalastí

Págasetic Gulf

Katigiòrgis

Plataniás

Plataniás *has a fine beach and a number of fish tavernas serving excellent seafood.*

↑ The elegant marble belfry of the Church of the Holy Apostles in Argalastí

| 0 kilometres | 6 |
| 0 miles | 6 |

N ↑

Drakolímni, or Dragon Lake, between the peaks of Gamíla and Astraka ↑

EXPERIENCE MORE

6

Píndos Mountains

Οροσειρά Πίνδου

🅰B3 🄰Epirus ➕
📍Ioánnina 🌐epirus.travel

The Píndos is a vast range stretching from the Albanian border south to the Corinth Gulf, east into Macedonia, and west towards the Ionian Sea. It incorporates two national parks, Greece's second-longest gorge and its second-highest mountain, Oros Smólikas, standing at 2,637 m (8,652 ft). The Píndos National Park lies entirely within Epirus, between Métsovo and Vovoúsa, while the Víkos-Aóös National Park encompasses the Víkos Gorge (p218) and the Aóös river.

The peaks are snow-covered from November until May, when the melting snows water the ground, and swathes of purple crocus, gentians, grass-of-Parnassus and many species of orchid appear. The protection given by the parks increases the chances of seeing wild boar, roe deer and the European wild cat.

Oros Smólikas is accessible in summer for those who are well equipped and prepared for camping out. Slightly easier to reach from the Zagorian villages via the Víkos Gorge are Tymfi, at 2,497 m (8,192 ft), and Astráka, 2,436 m (7,992 ft), while two mountain lakes, both called Drakolímni, are each worth the effort it takes to get to them. One is below Tymfi (Gamíla); the other lies beneath Smólikas.

Although there are good walking guides and maps of the area, with one wardened mountain hut to stay in and accommodation in larger villages, only experienced hikers should venture into the mountains. The weather can change quickly, and in many places you will be far from any kind of settlement – though this is one of the main attractions of the Píndos mountains. They show the rugged side of Greece, where few visitors venture.

BEARS AND WOLVES OF THE PÍNDOS MOUNTAINS

Visitors to the coastal lowlands are often sceptical when told that wolves and bears still survive in Greece. However, despite the severe degradation of their natural habitat, the Píndos mountains continue to harbour European wolves and European brown bears, both endangered and now protected species. They are very wary of humans, having been persecuted by farmers and goatherds down the centuries. Therefore, visitors should consider themselves very fortunate if they see a bear. Wolves are just as hard to see but more evident, as they can often be heard howling at dawn and dusk, and will even respond to imitations of their howls. They pose no real threat to visitors, but are resented locally for eating sheep.

as the villagers, especially the younger generation, prefer to earn their living from tourism. A series of arched packhorse bridges are among the most memorable monuments to the skills of the local people. There are two especially fine examples marking each end of the village of Kípoi.

Southwestern Zagóri is the busiest area, with a bus from Ioánnina to Monodéndri and Vítsa bringing in walkers and climbers. Some of the villages to the east, such as Vrysochóri, were guerrilla refuges during World War II and therefore burnt by the Germans; they have never really recovered.

Near the almost deserted village of Vradéto, a 15th-century muletrack zigzags its way up a steep rockface beyond which the path leads to a stunning view of the Víkos Gorge (p218). Monodéndri, opposite Vradéto, is the usual starting point for the gorge trail, though another path can be taken from Vítsa. At the far end of the gorge are the villages of Megálo Pápigko and Mikró Pápigko. They are 4 km (2 miles) apart and their names reflect their sizes, but even "big" Pápigko is no more than a scattering of houses around cobbled streets, with a choice of restaurants and rooms available in renovated mansions. Further southeast, though still surrounded by

STAY

Pirrion Wellness Boutique Hotel
Unwind in the hammam or get a massage after a day of hiking at this wellness hotel with wonderful views.

🅰B3 🅐 Ano Pedina, Zagóri
🆆 pirrion.gr

€ € €

Saxonis Houses
A lovely simple, yet stylish, hotel in a typical Zagorian village, with cosy fireplaces and sofas and beautiful gardens.

🅰B3 🅐 Papigo, Papigko
🆆 saxonis-papigo.gr

€ € €

mountains, is the relatively thriving village of Tsepélovo. It has a bus service to Ioánnina and many restored mansions providing accommodation, as well as cafés and tavernas. Its cobbled streets and schist-roofed houses provide a perfect portrait of a rugged Zagórian village.

⑦
Zagóri
Ζαγόρι

🅰B3 🅐 Epirus 💻
🆆 epirus.travel

Some of Europe's most spectacular scenery can be found only 25 km (15 miles) north of Ioánnina (p194), in the area known as Zagóri. On these steep hillsides, some 45 traditional Epirot villages still survive; many of them contain imposing *archontiká* (mansions) dating to prosperous 18th- and 19th- century Ottoman times when Zagóri was granted autonomy.

Aroman and Sarakatsan shepherds (p211) make up most of the settled population. Over the winter months, the shepherds used to turn to crafts, forming into guilds of itinerant masons and wood-carvers, who would travel the Balkans selling their trades. This hard and ancient way of life has effectively vanished,

→

Walking the winding road to the hillside village of Kípoi in the Zagóri region

8

Ancient Dodona
Δωδώνη

B3 🏛Epirus 📞26510 82287 ⏰8am-8pm daily (Nov-Apr: 8:30am-3:30pm daily) 🚫Main public hols

Dating to at least 1,000 BC, the Oracle of Zeus at Dodona is the oldest in Greece and was second in status only to the one at Delphi (p202). It lies 22 km (14 miles) southwest of Ioánnina in a placid green valley on the northeastern slopes of Mount Tómaros.

The oracle focused on a sacred oak tree ringed with tripods which held a number of bronze cauldrons placed so that they touched each other.

↑ The theatre at Ancient Dodona, once used for contests in oration and drama

Prophecies were divined from the sound these made, in harmony with the rustling of the oak leaves, when one of the cauldrons was struck. Petitioners inscribed their questions on lead tablets for the priestess to read to Zeus; tablets found on the site can be seen in the Archaeological Museum in Ioánnina. The reputed power of the oak tree was such that Jason, before his quest for the Golden Fleece, travelled across from Iolkos (the predecessor of Vólos) to acquire one of its branches to attach to his ship, the *Argo*. By the 3rd century BC, a colonnaded courtyard was built around the tree for protection; it contained a small temple of which only foundations remain. The tree was uprooted in AD 393 on the orders of the Roman emperor Theodosios, in accordance with his policy of stamping out pagan practices.

The ruins of a stadium, acropolis and Byzantine basilica can all be seen here, but the main feature is the theatre, built by King Pyrrhus. With its capacity for 17,000 spectators, it is one of the largest in Greece. Its walls, rising to 21 m (69 ft), are supported by solid towers where kestrels now nest. It was used by the ancient Greeks for dramatic performances and was later converted by the Romans into a fighting arena. Concerts and plays are sometimes staged here in summer.

EAT

To Mantani
Indulge in traditional fare at this charming taverna, which is next to a babbling brook.

B3 🏛Anthochori, Métsovo 📞69486 70997

€€€

To Archontiko
Enjoy mountain views and traditional dishes at this friendly taverna.

B3 🏛Averof Georgiou 14, Métsovo 📞26560 42511

€€€

Andromachi Dodoni
This wonderful small restaurant next to the archaeological site uses home-grown produce.

B3 🏛Dodoni 📞69837 40519

€€€

Did You Know?
The phrase "Pyrrhic victory" is derived from King Pyrrhus, who built the theatre at Dodona.

9

Métsovo
Μέτσοβο

B3 🏛Epirus 📧 🌐epirus.travel

Situated below the now disused Katára Pass (the traditional crossing of the Píndos mountains), Métsovo has a vitality unique among Greek mountain towns. Originally a small village inhabited by Aroman shepherds, it became one of the region's most important commercial centres after being granted tax privileges in return for guarding the pass during Ottoman times. Local merchant families invested their new wealth in the town and continue to do so today by providing endowments and grants to foster the local

→
Métsovo, welcoming visitors with hotels, tavernas and shops

crafts industries. One such family was the Tosítsas, and some idea of their wealth can be gained by touring the rebuilt 18th-century mansion housing the **Métsovo Folk Art Museum**. Rising to three floors, it has an armoury and washroom on the ground floor, with huge wood-panelled reception rooms and bedrooms upstairs, carpeted with beautiful, locally woven *kilim* rugs. Intricate gold- and silverware is on display, as well as collections of traditional Epirot costumes and ornate embroidery. Visits are by guided tour, every 30 minutes.

Another of Métsovo's benefactors was the writer and politician Evángelos Avéroff (1910–90), who founded the **Avéroff Museum**. The core of the gallery is Avéroff's own collection of some 200 paintings and sculptures he acquired over the years, always with the ambition of opening a museum of modern Greek art in his home town. His collection has been expanded to show the work of several

dozen Greek artists from the 19th and 20th centuries.

Ancient traditions have survived in the area, from the simple craft of carving shepherds' crooks (from the town's sheep farming days) to embroidery and wine- and cheese-making. Some of the older men (and a few women) still wear traditional costumes; you can see them, dressed in black, sitting in the shelters and cafés around the town square. The shelters are needed during winter when the town, at 1,156 m (3,793 ft), becomes a popular ski resort.

Fifteen minutes' walk south, signposted from the centre of town, stands the small and charming 14th-century Moní Agíou Nikoláou. Today, it is inhabited only by caretakers who are more than happy to show visitors the church's vivid post-Byzantine frescoes, the monks' living quarters and their own supplies of flowers, fruit and vegetables.

Métsovo Folk Art Museum
⊗ 🚫 Off main thoroughfare
🕐 10am–4pm Fri–Wed
🌐 metsovomuseum.gr

Avéroff Museum
🏛 🚫 Off central square
🕐 10am–4pm Wed–Mon
🌐 averoffmuseum.gr

AROMAN SHEPHERDS

Of unknown origin, the nomadic Aroman shepherds are today centred in the Píndos mountains. Their language, which has no written form, is of Latin origin; it is thought that they might be descended from Roman settlers who moved through Illyria into the Balkans. Traditionally, they spend the summers in the mountains, moving their flocks down to the plains for winter. Their hard way of life is gradually disappearing, and the shepherds who remain can be found, in summer, in such villages as Métsovo and Vovoúsa in Epirus, and Avdélla, Samarína and Smíxi in western Macedonia. Their winter homes lie mainly around Kastoriá *(p240)*.

⑩ Párga
Πάργα

🅰A4 🏛Epirus 🚌

Párga, the main beach resort of Epirus, is a charming holiday town that gets very busy in summer. The Venetian fortress dominating the harbour was built in the 16th century on the site of a building destroyed in 1537 during a brief period of Turkish rule. The Ottomans returned under the command of Ali Pasha (p194), who bought the town from the British in 1819. Párga's Christian inhabitants fled to Corfu and Paxoi, though the town was regained by the Greeks in 1913.

Two small beaches lie within walking distance of the town centre, and two larger ones about 2 km (1 mile) away. Fish restaurants line Párga's waterfront, affording fine views across the harbour to a group of small islands.

Some 37 km (23 miles) south of Párga is the **Nekromanteion of Acheron** (Oracle of the Dead), the gateway to Hades, with steps leading to the vaults. In the 4th century BC, drugs and mechanisms may have heightened the sensation of entering the Underworld for visitors who sought advice from the dead.

Nekromanteion of Acheron
📍 🏛Mesopotamos
📞26840 41206 🕐Jun–Oct: 8am–8pm daily; Nov–May: 8am–3:30pm daily

⑪
Kassope
Κασσώπη

🅰B4 🏛Zálongo, Epirus 🚌 🔒For renovation until further notice

The Kassopeans were a tribe who lived in this region in the 4th century BC. The remains of their capital city stand on a hillside plateau overlooking the Ionian Sea, from where the island of Lefkáda is plainly visible. Kassope is reached by a walk through a pine grove from the car park. A site plan illustrates the layout of the once-great city.

Just above the ruins is Moní Zalóngou, with its monument commemorating the women of Soúli, who threw themselves from the cliffs in 1803 rather than be captured by Albanian Muslim troops.

Did You Know?

Kassope was such a thriving city in the 3rd century BC that it minted its own coins.

⑫ Préveza
Πρέβεζα

🅰B4 🏛Epirus ✈🚌🚌 🌐visitpreveza.gr

The charming town of Préveza, with its lively tavernas and marketplace, is picturesquely situated on the northern shore of the narrow "Channel of Cleopatra", at the mouth of the Amvrakikós Gulf, where the naval Battle of Actium was fought in 31 BC. Two ruined forts, on either side of the

Colourful houses spilling down to the harbour and jetty in Párga ↓

straits, recall the town's Venetian occupation in 1499.

Around 7 km (4 miles) north of Préveza stand the ruins of **Nikopolis** ("Victory City"), built by the Roman emperor Octavian to celebrate victory at Actium. Later sacked by the Goths, it was finally destroyed by the Bulgars in 1034. Remains include a theatre and mosaics in the Dometios basilica. An archaeological museum illustrates Roman and early Christian life here.

Nikopolis

⊛ ⦿ 26820 89892
⌚ Summer: 8am-8pm daily; winter: 8:30am-3pm daily
⌚ Museum: Sat, main pub hols

13

Arta
`Άρτα

▲B4 ⬥Epirus ▦
ⓦ discoverarta.gr

Though it is the second largest town in Epirus after Ioánnina, Arta remains largely untouched by tourism. This traditional Greek market town has a lively, bazaar-like area,

↑ Soaring interior of the Church of the Panagía Parigorítissa in Arta

established by the Turks who occupied Arta from 1449 to 1881. The fortress dates from the 13th century, when the town was the capital of the despotate of Epirus. This was an independent Byzantine state set up after the fall of Constantinople in 1204. It lasted until the start of the Ottoman occupation. Some of the town's many 13th- and 14th-century Byzantine churches can be

found in the streets near the fortress. The most striking is the Panagía Parigorítissa. Built between 1283 and 1296, this is a three-tier building topped with towers and domes. Agía Theódora, on Pýrrou, contains the marble tomb of the saintly wife of 13th-century Epirot ruler Michael II.

14

Tríkala
Τρίκαλα

▲C3 ⬥Thessaly ▦▦
ⓦ trikalacity.gr

Tríkala was the home of Asklepios, the god of healing, and today is the market centre for the Metéora area. As such, it is a thriving town with a number of remains from its Ottoman past. One is the bazaar area north of the Lethaios river, which bisects the town; another the Koursoúm (Osman Shah) Tzamí, a graceful mosque built in 1550 on the south side of the river. Surrounding the fortress is the Old Quarter of Varósi. The fortress stands on the site of the ancient acropolis, which was built in the 4th century BC. It is situated in beautiful grounds overlooking the river.

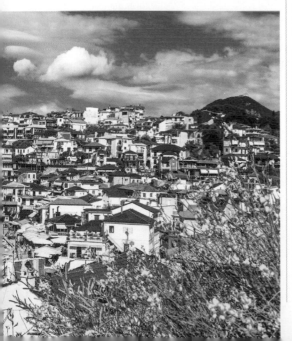

↑ Mountain springs flowing into the Pineiós river, Vale of Tempe

Did You Know?

The Vale of Tempe has seen countless battles over the centuries.

15
Vale of Tempe
Κοιλάδα των Τεμπών

C3 **Thessaly** 🚌

A road tunnel, completed in 2017, has reduced traffic through the Vale of Tempe – the fertile valley between the Olympos and Ossa mountains formed by the river Pineiós, in which Apollo was said to have purified himself after slaying the serpent Python. Close to the Wolf's Jaws or Lykostómio (the narrowest point of the gorge) is the Spring of Daphne, where a bridge leads to the chapel of Agía Paraskeví, carved out of the rock. The **Kástro of Platamónas** at the northern end of the Vale was built after 1204 by Frankish crusaders, atop a pre-existing fort, to control the vital route into Thessaly from the north.

Kástro of Platamónas
♿ 🏛 Vale of Tempe 📞 23520 44470 🕐 8am–8pm Thu–Mon (8:30am–3:30pm Tue, Wed & Nov–Apr)

16
Thíva (Ancient Thebes)
Θήβα

D5 **Stereá Elláda** 🚆 🚌

Although it was briefly the most powerful city of Greece, in the 4th century BC, the Thebes of today is little more than a quiet provincial town. It played an important role in the power struggles of Classical Greece, until defeated by Philip II of Macedon. Thebes' original acropolis has been built over through the years, but excavations have unearthed Mycenaean walls as well as jewellery, pottery and important tablets of Linear B script which are now in the **Archaeological Museum**. A highlight of the museum is the collection of Mycenaean sarcophagi, similar to those found on Crete. The museum's courtyard and well-tended garden stand alongside a 13th-century Frankish tower, all that remains of a castle ruined in 1311 by the Catalans.

→ Byzantine triptych in the Archaeological Museum at Thíva

A bridge over the river bed, a short walk eastwards from the museum, marks what is said to be the site of the Fountain of Oedipus, where the tragic hero is said to have washed the blood from his hands after unwittingly killing his father on his way to the city.

About 40 km (25 miles) north is ancient Orchomenos. In its time this one of the wealthiest Mycenaean cities. Visible are a *tholos* tomb, the Treasury of Minyas excavated by Schliemann (closed Monday), a theatre and the Byzantine Panagía Skrípous church.

Archaeological Museum
⊗ Plateía Threpsiádou 1 8am-8pm Wed-Mon (Nov-Mar: 8:30am-3:30pm Wed-Mon) mthv.gr

17

Mount Parnassós
`Όρος Παρνασσός

C5 Štereá Elláda Delfoí onparnassos.gr

Rising to a height of 2,457 m (8,061 ft), the limestone mass of Mount Parnassós dominates the eastern portion of Štereá Elláda. The lower slopes are covered with Cephalonian fir, and beneath them, in summer, the wildflower meadows burst into colour. Vultures and golden eagles are commonly spotted.

The village of Aráchova is the best base for exploring the area and is renowned for its wine, cheese, noodles and sheepskin rugs. There are many mountain trails for summer hikes, though a detailed walking map is recommended. Reaching the top of Liákoura, the highest peak, involves a long hike and camping overnight on the mountain.

In winter, this is a popular winter sports destination. From Aráchova, there are two ski centres, Kelária and Fterólakka, located 23 km (14 miles) and 29 km (18 miles) away respectively. Usually open from mid-December to April, both resorts have top points of about 2,200 m (7,218 ft), served by 14 lifts, half of which are bubble-chairs. Fterólakka offers longer, more challenging runs; however, high winds can close either centre at short notice.

> **PICTURE PERFECT**
> ## View from the Top
> If you're not a hiker, you can drive from Aráchova almost to the top of Mount Parnassós. One of the highest and windiest roads in Greece, it's not for the faint-hearted but the rewards are quite unbelievable views.

↑ The village of Aráchova, gateway to the summit of Mount Parnassós

⑱

Lamía and Thermopylae

Λαμία καί Θερμοπύλαι

🅐C4 🅐Stereá Elláda 🚌
🅘Leof Kalyvíon 14; 22310 32289

Set in the valley between two wooded hills, Lamía is typical of many medium-sized Greek towns. Although it is little known, it has much to offer, with a lively Saturday market. A 14th-century Catalan kástro, built on the site of the town's ancient acropolis, provides excellent views over the roofs to the countryside.

Lamía is chiefly associated with the Lamian War (323–322 BC), when Athens tried to throw off Macedonian rule after the death of Alexander the Great (p57). This is recalled at the **Lamía Museum**, which also has finds from around the town spanning all eras.

A short drive east of Lamía, the Athens road crosses the Pass of Thermopylae. It was here, in 480 BC, that an army of some 7,000 soldiers, under the command of Leonidas I of Sparta, met an overwhelming force from Persia whose numbers Herodotus (p52) cites

> **Only two Greek soldiers survived the Battle of Thermopylae, after which all of central Greece fell to the Persians.**

as 2,641,610. Though Leonidas held the pass for days, the Persians forced a path through and attacked the remaining 2,300 Greeks from the rear. Only two Greek soldiers survived the ordeal, after which all of central Greece, including Athens, fell to the Persians.

A bronze statue of King Leonidas stands by the road opposite the burial mound of the soldiers who died here. Just to the left are the sulphur springs that gave Thermopylae its name, which means the "Hot Gates". Many people bathe for free in the cascades that feed the spa building.

Lamía Museum

⊛ 🅐Kástro 🅒22310 29992
🕒8:30am–3pm Wed–Mon
🅧Main public hols

⑲

Mesolóngi

Μεσολόγγι

🅐B5 🅐Stereá Elláda 🚌

Its name meaning "amid the lagoons", Mesolóngi is perfectly located for fishing, though the industry is now in decline, aside from its famous eels and pressed cod roe. In 1821, the town became a centre of resistance during the War of Independence (p63), when a great leader, Aléxandros Mavrokordátos, set up his headquarters here. In January 1824, Lord Byron (p139) came to join the fight, but died of a

fever in April. Byron's final resting place is unknown, but a statue in the Garden of Heroes honours him. The nearby Gate of the Exodus commemorates the 9,000 civilians, besieged by the Ottomans for a year, who broke out of Mesolóngi in 1826, leaving behind a small

SALTPAN BIRDLIFE

Salt production is a major enterprise in the Mediterranean; the most extensive areas in Greece are located around Mesolóngi and the Amvrakikós Gulf. Seawater is channelled into large artificial lakes, or saltpans, which attract plentiful wildlife. Brine shrimps thrive, providing food for a wide variety of birds. Striking waders include the avocet, the great egret and the black-winged stilt with its long red legs. The area is also home to Kentish plovers, stone curlews, and the short-toed lark.

←

Statue of Leonidas, king of the Spartans, at the Pass of Thermopylae

← Náfpaktos harbour forming a sheltered bay on the north coast of the Gulf of Corinth

force of defenders who set fire to their powder magazines rather than surrender, levelling the town. The Ottomans gave up Mesolóngi in 1828, without firing a shot. A small museum chronicles these events.

20

Gulf of Corinth

Κορινθιακός Κόλπος

🅰 C5 🏛 Stereá Elláda
🚌 To Náfpaktos

The northern coast of the Gulf of Corinth contains well-known resorts as well as tiny coastal villages far removed from the usual tourist route. All are served by a main road that offers fine views across the gulf to the Peloponnese.

From Delphi, the main road leads southwards through the largest olive grove in Greece, passing Itéa, a busy port.

The church of Agios Nikólaos, 17 km (11 miles) southwest, stands on a hill surrounded by the old stone buildings of Galaxídi. The history of the town is told in the **Nautical and Historical Museum**, while the 19th-century mansions at the waterfront are reminders of the great wealth brought by the town's shipbuilding industry. Though the industry cleared the region of trees, a reforestation scheme has successfully restored the area to its former beauty.

The next major town is Náfpaktos. A Venetian fortress stands above the town, its ramparts running down as far as the beach. The Venetian name for the town was Lepanto. In 1571, the famous naval Battle of Lepanto (p59), in which the Venetians, Spanish and Genoese defeated the Ottomans, was fought here.

At Antírrio, the coast comes closest to the Peloponnese, and from here, a suspension bridge and car ferry cross the stretch of water known as the "Little Dardanelles". Beside the harbour stands the Frankish, Venetian and Ottoman Kástro Roúmelis.

Nautical and Historical Museum

♿ 🏛 Mouseíou 4, Galaxídi
📞 22650 41795 🕐 May–Oct: 10am–3pm Tue–Sun; Nov–Apr: times vary, call ahead
🚫 Main public hols

EAT

Zephyros

Overlooking the port, this excellent seafood restaurant is famous for its grilled eels and fish caught fresh from the nearby lagoons and the Gulf of Corinth.

🅰 B5 🏛 Kiprou 83, Mesolóngi 🌐 zefyros. info

€€€

Odos Oneiron

The name means "Dream Street", and this is indeed a dream of a restaurant, tucked away right by the cathedral. It serves inexpensive but imaginative dishes, with great local wines.

🅰 C4 🏛 Makrygianni 1, Lamía 📞 22310 44244

€€€

A LONG WALK
VÍKOS GORGE

Distance 14 km (8 miles) **Walking time** 6-7 hours
Terrain Steep ascents, descents and landslides
make the route challenging. It is best suited to
experienced hikers with good equipment.

To trek the length of the Víkos Gorge is to undertake
what is arguably the greatest walk in Greece, between
deeply eroded limestone walls rising to 915 m (3,000 ft).
The gorge cuts through the Víkos-Aóös National Park,
established in 1975. Cairns and waymarks define the
official O3 long-distance route which snakes through the
boulder-strewn ravine bed and continues up through
stands of beech, chestnut and maple to the higher
ground. Egyptian vultures can be seen circling in the
thermals, and lizards and tortoises abound. The walk
begins at Monodéndri or Vítsa. A shorter 4-km
(2-mile) walk between the northern
villages of Mikró Pápigko and Víkos
passes Panagía Chapel.

Locator Map

*One of the area's
protected traditional
villages, stone-built
Megálo Pápigko
stands at 950 m
(3,117 ft), beneath
the cliffs of Pýrgi.*

Megálo Pápigko   Mikró
FINISH   Pápigko

*For the Pápigko
villages, cross the
gorge here beneath
a landmark pinnacle
of rock. The path
branches to the west
for Víkos village.*

Voidhomatis
Spring
Víkos

A s t r a k a

Rock
Pinnacle

0 kilometres   2
0 miles   2

N

*From Monodéndri, a
road leads to the **Oxiá
Viewpoint**, one of the area's
finest lookouts, along with
Mpelóï opposite.*

Agía
Triáda

Voidomatis

*Along the
Víkos–Mikró
Pápigko hike, the
small 18th-century
Panagía Chapel
houses some
wonderful frescoes.*

Oxiá
Viewpoint

Mpelóï
Viewpoint

Panagía
Chapel
Monodéndri

Kapesovo

START

*With its magnificent
views over the gorge,
Monodéndri village is
the most popular start
for the walk. The path is
well signposted from the
church in the lower square.*

↑ Stone alley and houses
in the pretty village of
Monodéndri on the edge
of the Víkos Gorge

The Voidomatis River springs flowing at the bottom of the Víkos Gorge

NORTHERN GREECE

Macedonia, Greece's largest region, is the heart of the ancient Hellenistic Empire. Its name (Makedonía in Greek) derives from the Makednoi, one of the tribes who first inhabited the area in the late 4th century BC. The legacy of the Macedonian Empire is evident in many ancient sites, including Vergína, the location of King Philip II of Macedon's tomb; Pella, the birthplace of Alexander the Great; and Díon, Philip's city in the foothills of Mount Olympos.

After the death of Alexander the Great in 323 BC his empire was carved up by his generals. One of these, Kassandros, founded his own capital at Thessaloníki in 315 BC, naming it after his queen (Alexander's sister). Macedonian kings battled rebellious Greek cities and Roman invaders until final defeat at Pydna in 168 BC ushered in an era of peace under Roman rule, during which many fine monuments were built. The ensuing Byzantine era also left an outstanding legacy of architecture, seen in the many churches throughout the area.

Northern Greece had fallen to the Ottomans by the 15th century, and Muslim influences remain strong, particularly in Thrace (Thráki), where Eastern-style bazaars and minarets can still be seen. Most Turks fled after Greek reconquest of northern Greece in 1912-13. After the liberation of Northern Greece from German occupation in 1944, during World War II, civil war raged in the mountains until 1949. The post-war years brought gradual recovery. Today the beaches of the Kassandra peninsula are popular holiday resorts, Thessaloníki is a vibrant cultural hub and the hinterlands welcome visitors keen to discover their treasures.

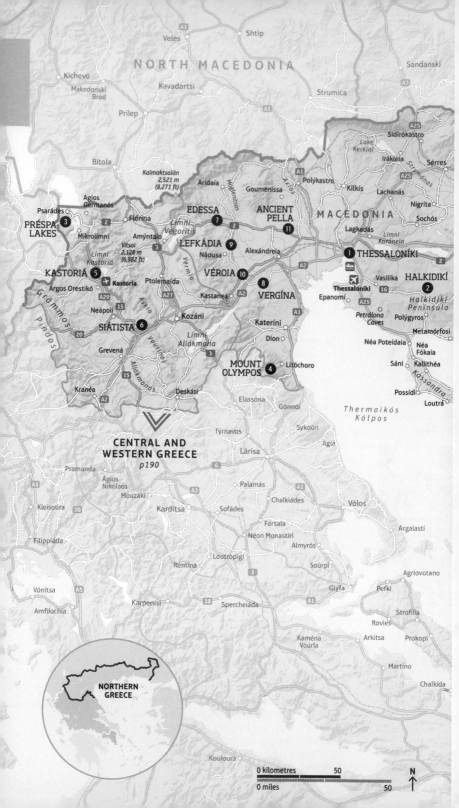

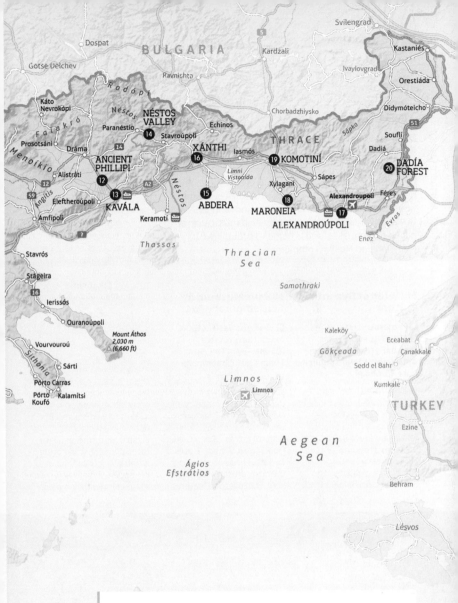

NORTHERN GREECE

Must Sees

1. Thessaloníki
2. Halkidikí

Experience More

3. Préspa Lakes
4. Mount Olympos
5. Kastoriá
6. Siátista
7. Edessa
8. Vergína
9. Lefkádia
10. Véroia
11. Ancient Pella
12. Ancient Phillipi
13. Kavála
14. Néstos Valley
15. Abdera
16. Xánthi
17. Alexandroúpoli
18. Maroneia
19. Komotiní
20. Dadía Forest

THESSALONÍKI
ΘΕΣΣΑΛΟΝΙΚΗ

🅰D2 🅰Macedonia ✈25 km (15 miles) SE of Thessaloníki 🚉Monastiríou 🚌Monastiríou (Intercity buses) 🚏Off Koundouriótou 🛈Tsimiskí 136; www.thessaloniki.gr

Grand Roman ruins, a host of UNESCO World Heritage Byzantine sites, splendid Ottoman monuments, and belle époque glamour all contribute to Thessaloníki's famously thriving cultural scene. Founded in 315 BC, this sophisticated port city has been a multicultural haven for centuries, and is home to proud Jewish, Christian and Muslim communities.

①
Museum of Byzantine Culture

🅰Leofórou Stratoú 2 📞2313306400 🕐8am-8pm daily (Nov-Mar: 8am-4pm daily) 🚫Main public hols 🌐mbp.gr

Behind the Archaeological Museum (p226) is this modern museum. Displays include a 5th-century mosaic floor, icons, funerary mural paintings and some fabulous early textiles. There are also fascinating temporary exhibitions.

②
MOMus Museum of Contemporary Art

🅰154 Egnatia (HELEXPO exhibition grounds) 🕐10am-6pm Tue-Sun (to 10pm Thu) 🌐momus.gr

The collection at this museum serves as a dynamic introduction to contemporary and avant-garde art. The works of well-known Greek and international artists – Takis, Gaitis, Oppenheim, Warhol, Tsoclis, de Saint Phalle – are among the many artists represented here. The collection features many artworks from the original donation of Alexander Iolas, a charismatic art world visionary who was a legendary artist himself. Compelling temporary exhibitions further enhance the experience, and provide an intriguing counterpoint to the ancient monuments that span centuries right outside.

EAT

Sebrico
Creative dishes and superb local ingredients make this Greek bistro a local favourite.

🅰Fragkon 2 📞2310557513

€€€

Full tou Meze
This lively spot has a great selection of meze and provides friendly service.

🅰Katouni 3 📞2310524700

€€€

Sprawling Thessaloníki, viewed from the kástro in Ano Poli, the Upper Town

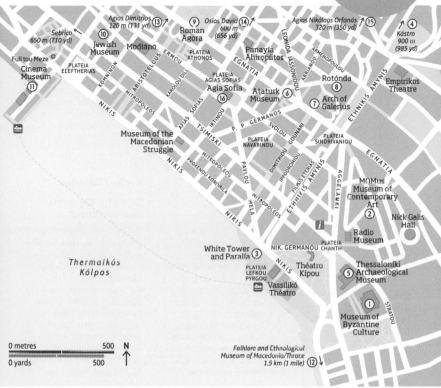

③ 🐾

White Tower and Paralía

📍 **On the waterfront**
☎ **23102 67832** 🕐 **8am-8pm(Nov-Mar: 9am-4pm)**

Probably Thessaloníki's most famous sight is the White Tower on the *paralía* (waterfront). Built by the Ottomans in the 15th century, it was one of three towers along the sea wall. Today, it houses the Museum of the History of Thessaloníki on several floors of small circular rooms. The original stone steps climb up to a roof with lovely views of the *paralía*.

④

Kástro

Crowning Thessaloníki are parts of the 7-km (4.5-mile) ring of the Byzantine walls that once surrounded the city. A prominent section stretches uphill, culminating in the dramatic Trigonio Tower, a viewpoint as popular with locals as it is with visitors. Another famous section is the Eptapyrgio (seven towers). Originally built during the Byzantine era, it was reconstructed by the Ottomans in the 15th century. It later became a notorious prison, which was in use until

🏔 **GREAT VIEW**
Hilltop Vantage

Worth the climb up a steep flight of steps, the panoramic view from the kástro and its walls over Thessaloníki and the surrounding area is undoubtedly the best in the city.

1989. It is currently undergoing restoration.
Beneath the kástro, Ano Poli (the Upper Town) is a neighbourhood of rambling cobblestone alleys lined with charming examples of vernacular architecture and traditional tavernas. It's home to many monuments, including a Byzantine bath house, an Ottoman tourbes, a monastery and exquisite Byzantine churches.

> Beneath the kástro, Ano Poli is (the Upper Town) a neighbourhood of rambling cobblestone alleys lined with charming examples of vernacular architecture and traditional tavernas.

↑ Figures on an ancient marble sarcophagus in the Thessaloníki Archaeological Museum

⑤ 🏛

Thessaloníki Archaeological Museum

🅐 Manóli Andrónikou & Leof Stratoú 🚌 3 🕐 May-Oct: 8am-8pm daily (Nov-Apr: 9am-4pm daily) 🚫 Main public hols 🌐 amth.gr

This modern museum, opened in 1963, contains a host of treasures. It concentrates on the finds made within the city and at the many sites in Macedonia. The displays progress chronologically through the ages, giving a clear picture of the area's history. The inner rooms surrounding the courtyard house a number of fabulous gold items from ancient Macedon, including the treasures discovered during excavations at Macedonian cemeteries. A gold bracelet from Europos,

dating from the 3rd century BC, is one of the highlights of the collection. Another highlight is the Dervéni Krater, a bronze wine-mixing vase from c 300 BC, decorated with exquisite, detailed figures of Dionysos and maenads.

The annexe basement contains a small exhibition of artifcacts on the prehistory of Thessaloníki and hosts temporary exhibitions.

---

⑥

Ataturk Museum

🅐 Turkish Consulate, Apostolou Pavlou 17-24 📞 23102 48452 🕐 10am-5pm Tue-Sun

Mustafa Kemal, later known as Kemal Ataturk (1881-1938), was born in this typical Ottoman-era townhouse, built in 1870 when Thessaloníki was still a predominantly Turkish city. The three-storey house, with its overhanging balcony and pink stucco walls, was handed over to the Turkish State in 1935 and has been preserved as a museum that is almost a shrine to the father of modern Turkey. Rooms house original furniture and family possessions, and the pomegranate tree in the courtyard is said to have been planted by Kemal's father. The walls are hung with images of Kemal as a boy, as an officer in

the Ottoman army, and as the first president of Turkey, a role that he occupied from 1923 until his death. The building also offers a fascinating glimpse into the domestic life of a well-to-do Turkish family in the last decades of the Ottoman Empire. It forms part of the present-day Turkish Consulate compound.

---

⑦

Arch of Galerius

🅐 Egnatía 🌐 galerius palace.culture.gr

The principal architectural legacy of Roman rule is found at the eastern end of the long main street, Egnatía, which was part of the Roman Via Egnatia road linking Byzantium with Rome. Here stands the Arch of Galerius, built in AD 299 by Galerius (then co-emperor of the Roman Empire) to celebrate his victory over the Persians in AD 298. Its carvings show scenes from the battle. There was once a double arch here,

The ancient Roman Arch of Galerius, a city landmark ↓

> **The three-storey Ataturk house, with its overhanging balcony and pink stucco walls, has been preserved as a museum that is almost a shrine to the father of modern Turkey.**

with a palace to the south. Some of its remains can be seen in Plateía Navarínou.

---

⑧

Rotónda

🏛 Filíppou 🕐 May–Oct: 8am–8pm Wed–Mon (Nov–Mar: to 3pm) 🌐 galeriuspalace.culture.gr

Together with the Arch of Galerius and the foundations of ancient buildings excavated around Plateia Navarino, this impressive circular building, also known as Agios Georgios, forms the Galerian Complex of buildings begun in the reign of Galerius, co-ruler of the Roman Empire (AD 305–311). The Rotónda was meant to be his tomb, but ultimately he was buried in today's Serbia. It later became a church under the

Byzantine emperor Constantine I, and was converted into a mosque in the 16th century after the Ottoman conquest. Its minaret is now the only one in Thessaloníki. Magnificent Byzantine mosaics and frescoes adorn the interior.

⑨

Roman Agora

🏛 Olympou & Philippou St 📞 23102 21266 🕐 May–Oct: 8am–8pm Wed–Mon (Nov–Apr: to 3pm)

On the site of the ancient Greek agora, the large, two-tiered Roman Forum dates to the 2nd–3rd century AD. The social and religious centre of Thessaloníki in Roman times, it has remains of a bath, a theatre, floor mosaics, columns and some walls.

STAY

Electra Palace
Superbly opulent, from the walnut- and marble-appointed lobby to the lavish rooms and suites with all mod cons, this landmark hotel has a rooftop pool and garden restaurant too.

🏛 Aristotelous 9 🌐 electrahotels.gr

€€€

Makedonia Palace
A luxurious seafront hotel with a mix of rooms and suites, some with sea views. There's an outdoor pool and a choice of restaurants.

🏛 Leof. Meg. Alexandrou 2 🌐 makedoniapalace.com

€€€

Jewish Museum of Thessaloníki

🏠 Agíou Mina 11 🕐 9am-2pm Mon-Fri (also 5-8pm Wed), 10am-2pm Sun 🗓 Main public hols 🌐 jmth.gr

Thessaloníki was once home to the largest Jewish community in the world. The Jewish Museum of Thessaloníki shares its full history, beginning with the Romaniote population of the eastern Mediterranean, through the arrival of the Ashkenazi Jews in the 14th and 15th centuries, and then the great influx of Sephardim from the Iberian Peninsula in the 15th century. The Jewish community flourished here for centuries before coming to an abrupt end during World War II, when Thessaloníki suffered the loss of over 95 per cent of its Jewish population. A small but strong community remains. This moving and informative museum is located in a converted historic arcade.

Cinema Museum

🏠 Warehouse A, Port 🕐 9am-3pm Mon-Tue, 9am-7pm Wed-Fri 🌐 cinemuseum.gr

Sharing a former commercial building in Thessaloníki's rejuvenated dockland area with the Museum of Photography, the Cinema Museum reveals the central role of cinema in Greek culture – especially important in a country where until as recently as the 1980s few people even in big cities had access to television, and the open-air cinema was not just a place of entertainment but a social hub and a source of information and news of the world. An important part of the museum's collection focuses on the "Golden Age" of Greek cinema in the 1960s, when film-makers like Costa-Gavras documented the political turbulence that engulfed Greece.

Folklore and Ethnological Museum of Macedonia/Thrace

🏠 Vasilíssis Olgas 68 🕐 9am-9:30pm Wed, 9am-3:30pm Fri-Tue 🌐 lemmth.gr

Housed in an Art Nouveau building, this museum displays folk costumes, textiles, wood-carving, musical instruments and detailed models show-ing rural activities such as ploughing, winnowing and threshing. The gruelling life of the nomadic Sarakatsan shepherds is well documented, and a vivid display shows the incredible events at the annual fire-walking ceremony in Lagkadás, a village 20 km (12 miles) northeast of Thessaloníki. The museum also has an extensive archive of period photography showing the reality of life during the early 20th century.

↑ Inside the Folklore and Ethnological Museum of Macedonia/Thrace

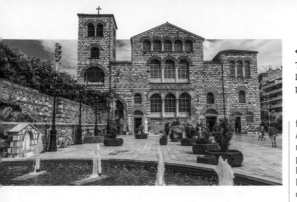

← The church of Agios Dimítrios, dedicated to the patron saint of the city

further up the hill. Today, Agios Nikólaos Orfanós retains the richest and best-preserved collection of late Byzantine frescoes in the city. Distributed over the central cella and both aisles, they show rare scenes from the *Passion*, including Christ mounting the Cross and Pilate seated in judgment.

⑬ Agios Dimítrios

🏛 **Agíou Dimitríou at Aristotelous** 🕐 8am-2:45pm Mon, Wed & Thu, 8am-1:30pm & 7-10pm Fri (mass), 7:30am-2:15pm Sat & Sun

Agios Dimítrios, the church of Thessaloníki's patron saint, was largely rebuilt after the fire of 1917, which destroyed the 7th- and 13th-century fabric of the basilica. The oldest, 3rd-century AD portion is the crypt. Originally a Roman bath, this, according to legend, is the site of the imprisonment, torture and murder in 305 AD of saint Dimítrios – a Roman soldier converted to Christianity and martyred on the orders of Emperor Galerius. Six small 5th–7th-century mosaics are found on the piers flanking the altar and high up on the west side of the church. These mosaics rank among the finest in Greece and include depictions of Dimítrios with young children, or in the company of the church's builders.

⑭ Osios David

🏛 **Epimenidou 17, Ano Poli** 🕐 9am-4pm Mon-Sat, 10am-1pm Sun

This delightful small chapel was founded some time in the late 5th century as part of a monastery. Behind the altar is an original vivid mosaic of the Vision of Ezekiel, rare in that it depicts a beardless Christ Emmanuel. It owes its marvellous condition to having been concealed beneath plaster and only discovered in 1921. There are also some frescoes from the 12th century, including a fine *Baptism* and *Nativity*. Although the church is usually locked, there is a caretaker who greets visitors and will unbolt the doors.

⑮ Agios Nikólaos Orfanós

🏛 **Irodotou St, Ano Poli** 🕐 Times vary, check website 🌐 odysseus. culture.gr

Situated in a garden plot amongst the lanes of the ancient Kástra district, or upper town, this small, triple-apsed 14th-century church began life as a dependency of the larger Moni Vlatádon,

⑯ Agia Sofia

🏛 **Plateía Agías Sofías** 🕐 8:30am-2pm, 5:30-8pm daily

The church of Agía Sofía is dedicated to the Holy Wisdom (Sofiá) of God, just like the church of the same name in Istanbul. It was built in the mid-8th century. In 1585, it became a mosque, but was reconsecrated as a church in 1912. It contains many mosaics and frescoes dating back to the 9th and 10th centuries, including a fine *Ascension* scene in the 30-m (100-ft) high dome. The entrance formerly had a portico, which was obliterated during an Italian air raid in 1941. The imposing nature of the building is emphasized by its location in a partially sunken garden.

THESSALONÍKI'S BYZANTINE CHURCHES

Thessaloníki has the richest collection of Byzantine churches in Greece. Of the hundreds of 5th-century basilicas that once stood across the country, only two remain. Both of these, Agios Dimítrios and Acheiropoiïtos, are in Thessaloníki. The 8th-century Agía Sofía is a very significant Byzantine building, both for its mosaics and its role in influencing subsequent architectural development. Three different 14th-century churches - Agios Nikólaos Orfanós, Agioi Apóstoloi and Agía Aikateríni - give an insight into what was a period of architectural innovation.

↑ The rocky coastline and beautiful clear water at Kassándra

❷

HALKIDIKÍ
ΧΑΛΚΙΔΙΚΗ

🗺 D2-3 & E2-3 🏛 Macedonia 🚌 🌐 visithalkidiki.gr

With its three tendrils – Kassándra, Sithonía and Athos – stretching into the Aegean Sea, the Halkidikí peninsula has long sandy beaches, a thriving nightlife and great restaurants, making it a popular destination in summer. The north of Halkidikí is a quiet and delightful hilly region. Kassándra is the most developed part, with plentiful hotels, while Sithonía, although only marginally larger, has fewer resorts and a thickly wooded interior. Unlike Kassándra and Sithonía, Athos is largely undeveloped, with a large monastic community that only men aged 18 and over can visit, and just a few beaches in the secular northern part.

①
Northern Halkidikí
Βόρεια Χαλκιδική

In the northeast of the area is the small village of Stágeira, the birthplace of Aristotle (384–322 BC). On a hilltop, just outside the village, is a huge white marble statue of the philosopher, and there are sweeping views over the surrounding countryside.

A glimpse of the hidden interior of Halkidikí can be experienced on the edge of Mount Katsíka, 55 km (34 miles) southeast of Thessaloníki in the Petrálona Caves (closed for renovation at the time of writing; check main Halkidikí website for latest information). It was in these red-rock caverns in 1960, the year after the caves were discovered by local villagers, that a skull was found. It was believed to be that of a young woman, aged about 25 when she died. A complete skeleton was subsequently discovered, and these are the oldest bones yet to be found in Greece, dating back between 160,000 and 350,000 years. Amid the stalactites and stalagmites, reconstructions of the cave dwellers have been arranged in the caves, along with the bones, teeth and tools that were also found here.

②
Kassándra
Κασσάνδρα

The town of Néa Potedaia straddles the narrow neck of the most westerly of Halkidikí's tendrils, with a lovely sandy beach, a marina and a pretty town square. Nearby are the impressive ruins of the ancient city of **Olynthos**, inhabited since Neolithic times. Artifacts found at the site are on display in the Thessaloníki Archaeological Museum (p226). On the west coast, Sáni has excellent beaches, a summer festival and a luxury resort complex. There are quiet bays around the village of Possídi, on a promontory halfway down the west coast. On the east coast, Néa Fókala is still a traditional fishing village despite the steady invasion of tourism, whereas Kallithéa, to the south, is the largest resort on Kassándra and has a thriving nightlife.

Olynthos

⊛ ⬚ Halkidikí ◷ 8am–3pm daily ✷ Main public hols

---

③

Sithonía
Σιθωνία

Quieter than Kassándra, with thick pine forests and glorious beaches, Sithonía is especially popular with families. The peninsula begins at Metamórfosi, which has a beautiful sandy beach shaded by pine trees. Vourvouroú is one of the first villages you come to on the north side. A collection of villas spreads along the coast, with a few hotels and a selection of places to eat. To the south of this area is a long, un-developed stretch of coast, with several unspoilt beaches, until you reach the large resort of Sárti with its popular white-sand beach stretching for 3 km (1.8 miles), fantastic restaurants, bars and a range of hotels.

At the tip of Sithonía is Kalamítsi, a good base for water sports and diving excursions. Pórto Koufó at the end of the west coast is a picturesque fishing village set on a bay amid wooded hills. The Pórto Carras resort, halfway down the west coast, was set up by the Carras wine family. It has three hotels, a marina, a shopping centre, water sports, horse riding, a golf course and tennis courts. A little north of here is Neos Marmaras, Sithonía's largest seaside village, with calm, shallow waters.

---

④

Athos
Όρος

Picturesque Ouranoupoli on the southwestern coast of the Athos peninsula is the area's main town. Although rather touristy and full of souvenir shops and pricey cafés, it has some attractive beaches. Land entry is forbidden between secular and monastic Athos (p232). Boats from Ouronoupoli to Mount Athos are carefully checked to make sure that all visitors (only men are allowed) have the correct

permit (p233). Women and those not wishing to visit the monasteries can take boat trips to get a glimpse of the Holy Mountain from the water.

TOP 5 BEACHES ON HALKIDIKÍ

Chrouso Beach, Paliouri
Long and sandy, with trees for shade and bars for refreshments.

Gerakini Beach
The white-sand beach at Gerakini stretches for 6 km (3.7 miles).

Kalogria Beach, Nikiti
Pure white sand, clear and calm waters, and a beach bar.

Alykes Beach, Ammouliani
Kid-friendly beach, one of 76 Blue Flag beaches in Halkidikí.

Lemos Beach
At the southern tip of Sithonía, this remote beach is often deserted.

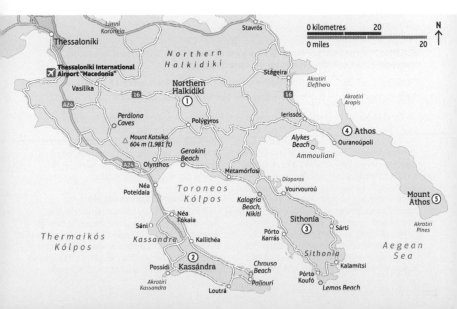

Osiou Gregoriou monastery, seen from a tour boat, and a street in the main town, Karyès *(inset)* ↑

⑤

MOUNT ATHOS
`ΑΓΙΟΝ ΟΡΟΣ

🏠 Athos Peninsula, Macedonia 🚌 To Karyés 🚢 Dáfni (boat trips from Ouranoúpoli for the west coast, or from Ierissós for the east coast)

Following a 1,800-year-old tradition, some 1,700 monks live out their ascetic, self-sufficient lives on Mount Athos, the spiritual capital of Orthodox Christianity.

To the Greeks, this is the Holy Mountain, which at 2,033 m (6,670 ft), is the highest point of Halkidiki's most easterly peninsula. Unique in Greece, Athos is an autonomous republic ruled by the monks who live in its 20 monasteries. Only adult males may visit the peninsula, but it is possible to see many of the monasteries from a boat trip along the coast. They include some fine examples of Byzantine architecture and provide an insight into monastic life.

Not all of the 20 monasteries on Athos can be seen from the popular boat trips from Ouranoúpoli, although some boats do go round the whole peninsula. A few are hidden in the mountains and others cling to the eastern coast of the peninsula. Remote hermitages and monastic villages *(sketes)* in the hills of the peninsula are preferred by some monks as a quieter alternative to the relatively busy monastery life.

West Coast Monasteries

The most northerly monastery is Zográfou, founded in AD 971, but the present buildings were built in the 18th and 19th centuries. Next to it, Kastamonítou was founded in the 11th century by a hermit from Asia Minor. Xenofóntos is a 10th-century monastery with a second

Jerissós

Ouranoúpoli

Esfigmenou

Metóchi
Chourmitsas

Chelandariou

Zográfou

Kastamonítou

Kolpos Agiou Orous

Moní Vatopedíou

Docheiaríou

Pantokratora

Xenofóntos · Skíti Agíou
Andrea
Stavronikita

Agíou Panteleímonos

Karyés · Koutloumousiou

Xiropotámou

Dáfni · Iviron

Simonos Pétras

Osíou Gregoriou · Mount Athos
2,033 m
(6,670 ft) · Karakallou

Agíou Dionysíou

Agíou Pavlou · Filotheou

Néa Skíti · Megistis
Lavras

Skíti Agías
Annas · Skíti Timíou
Prodromou

0 km   5   N
0 miles   5

chapel, built in 1837, using some 14th-century mosaic panels. Xiropotámou was founded in the 10th century, but the present buildings date from the 18th century. The monastery of Simonos Pétras was named after St Simon who founded it in the 14th century AD after seeing a strange light burning on this remote ridge one Christmas night. Nearby is Osíou Gregoriou, founded by St Gregory of Athos in the 14th century. It has been heavily restored after suffering damage from raiders and fires over the centuries. Perched 80 m (260 ft) above the sea, Agíou Dionysíou's walls conceal the 16th-century church of Agio Ioánnis Pródomos.

VISITING MOUNT ATHOS

Only ten non-Orthodox men per day are allowed to visit Mount Athos, with a stay of four nights. To apply, it's best to visit the Pilgrims' Bureau (address below) in person, with your passport (or fax a copy of the personal details page in advance, with your desired dates). Apply well in advance. Once confirmed, you must book the monasteries you wish to visit; the office has the telephone numbers. On the day, be at the Ouranópoli Pilgrims' Bureau by 8am to collect your *Diamenterion* (official permit); bring your confirmation and passport. Boats leave daily at 9:45am for the monasteries. For more information, contact the Pilgrims Bureau, Egnatías 109, 54622 Thessaloníki, Greece (Tel: 2310 252578; Fax: 2310 222424).

East Coast Monasteries

The first monastery to be established on Athos was the Megístis Lávras (Great Lavra). It is situated at the southeastern end of the peninsula, on a rocky outcrop. It was founded in AD 963 by Athanásios the Athonite and is the only one of the monasteries never to have suffered from fire. It also has the largest font of all the monasteries, which is outside, shaded by a cypress tree said to have been planted over 1,000 years ago by Athanásios himself. Halfway along the eastern coast stand the monasteries of Ivíron and Stavronikíta. Ivíron was founded in the late 10th century by a monk from Iberia (modern Georgia), hence its name. Its church was built in the early 11th century and restored in 1513. The monastery's main courtyard contains another 16 chapels, one housing a miraculous icon of the Virgin Mary. Stavronikíta, to the north, stands on top of a rocky headland. It was first mentioned in a document dated AD 1012.

Moní Vatopedíou, one of the largest monasteries on Athos, is sited on a small promontory at the northern end of the east coast. It was founded in the latter half of the 10th century, and a notable feature is its *katholikón*, or main church, also built in the 10th century. It contains icons dating from the 14th century, though some of the paintwork has been retouched over the years. The refectory is the most imposing on Athos. A wealthy monastery, it is among the best preserved on Mount Athos.

LIFE OF ORTHODOX MONKS ON MOUNT ATHOS

Under the Byzantine time system operating on Athos, midnight is at dawn, and morning services begin about an hour before – around 3 or 4am, secular time. A monk walks around striking a small wooden *símandro* (a carved plank) with a mallet to wake the other monks and call them to prayer. The monks eat two meals a day, consisting mostly of food they grow themselves. There are close to 200 fasting days in the year; during these only one meal is allowed and it must not contain fish, eggs, cheese, milk or even oil. Meals are eaten after the morning and evening services, and the time in between is spent working, resting and praying.

Refectory

Chapel

Watchtower of Tsimiskís

↑ Stavronikíta monastery on the east coast, first mentioned in a document dated AD 1012

Did You Know?

Not all the monasteries are Greek. Three of them are run by monks from Russia, Serbia and Bulgaria.

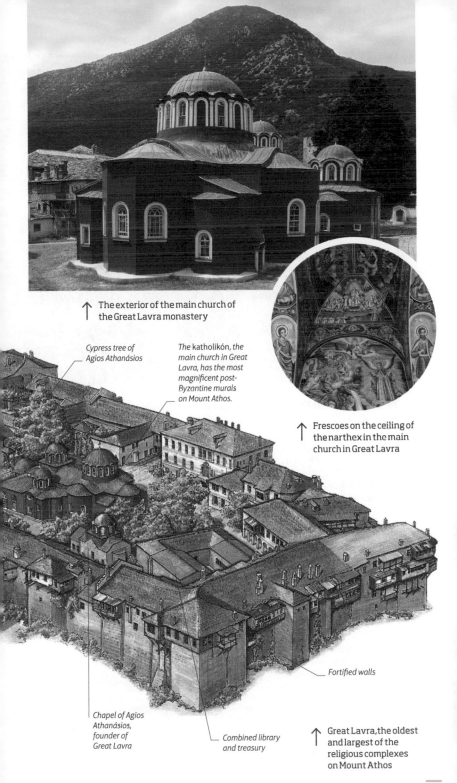

↑ The exterior of the main church of the Great Lavra monastery

Cypress tree of Agios Athanásios

The katholikón, the main church in Great Lavra, has the most magnificent post-Byzantine murals on Mount Athos.

↑ Frescoes on the ceiling of the narthex in the main church in Great Lavra

Chapel of Agios Athanásios, founder of Great Lavra

Combined library and treasury

Fortified walls

↑ Great Lavra, the oldest and largest of the religious complexes on Mount Athos

Did You Know?

"Christos Anesti!" ("Christ is risen!") is chanted at midnight on Easter Saturday.

THE GREEK ORTHODOX CHURCH

The Orthodox church developed from the Christianity of the Eastern Roman empire. The name is derived from the Greek words *orthos* ("right") and *doxa* (belief). Monasticism is a central part of the Orthodox faith, and Mount Athos is considered the centre of Orthodox monasticism. The Orthodox religion is an important aspect of Greek culture. Many Greeks embrace the Orthodox church as an element of their national identity even if they don't practise the religion regularly.

CELEBRATING EASTER IN GREECE

Easter is by far the most imporant festival of the Greek Orthodox church calendar. Western Easter always falls before Greek Orthodox Easter – usually a week earlier, though at times they may coincide. This is due to the use of the Julian rather than the Gregorian calendar in the Orthodox church.

Holy Week is a time for Greek families to reunite. It is also a good time to visit Greece, to see the processions and church services and to sample the Easter food. The ceremony and symbolism is a direct link with Greece's Byzantine past, as well as with earlier beliefs. The festivities reach a climax at midnight on Easter Saturday. As priests intone "Christ is risen", fireworks are lit, the explosions ushering in a Sunday devoted to feasting, music and dance.

↑ Monks and church elders in procession on Easter Sunday, Mount Athos

↑ Celebration of Easter mass on Holy Saturday in a Greek Orthodox church

Smaller, more isolated towns, such as Andrítsaina *(p185)* and Koróni *(p188)* in the Peloponnese, and Polýgyros (the capital of Halkidikí, *p230*), are particularly worth visiting during Holy Week for the Friday and Saturday night services.

Christ's bier, decorated with flowers and containing His effigy, is carried in a solemn candle-lit procession through the streets by each parish at dusk on Good Friday. Churches are packed for the Easter Saturday evening Resurrection servce. Candles are lit just before midnight at the end of the mass. In pitch darkness, a single flame, originating from the priest, is used to light the candles held by all the congregation. After the priest declares "Christ is risen", bells are rung, crackers and fireworks are set off, and friends and family exchange Easter greetings.

People then return home, taking their holy candles with them, from which they light the family icon lamp, which remains lit for another thirty to forty days. They then sit down to a supper of *magerítsa* soup.

Lunch on Easter Sunday is a big festive occasion. Everyone chooses an Easter egg (typically dyed red) and tries to crack each other's. The egg that does not crack brings victory and good luck to its owner. A huge feast of roast lamb ensues.

TRADITIONAL EASTER DISHES

Tsourékia is a sweet bread made of plaited dough containing eggs with shells dyed red to symbolize the blood of Christ. It is baked on Maundy Thursday, the day of the Crucifixion. Greek Easter biscuits celebrate the end of Lent. Another Easter dish, *mageirítsa*, is a lamb tripe-and-offal soup, eaten in the early hours of Easter Sunday. Lamb roasting is traditionally done in the open air on giant spits over charcoal for a big festive lunch on Easter Sunday. After lunch, young and old join hands to dance and sing to traditional music.

EXPERIENCE MORE

3

Préspa Lakes

Εθνικός Δρυμός Πρεσπών

B2 **Macedonia** **To Flórina** **Agios Germanós; www.spp.gr**

This is the only national park in Greece which is made up largely of water. It is one of the mainland's most beautiful and unspoilt places and was little visited until recently because of its somewhat inaccessible location. The border with Albania runs through the southwest corner of the Megáli Préspa lake, joining the border of the Republic of North Macedonia. The Greek area of the lake, together with the smaller Mikrí Préspa lake and surrounding countryside, make up the 255 sq km (100 sq miles) of national park, established in 1974. The area is so important for wildlife that Mikrí Préspa and the

Did You Know?

There are only 1,000 pairs of Dalmatian pelicans in the world, 150 of which nest at the Préspa Lakes.

reed beds that fringe it form a park within a park, a core of some 49 sq km (19 sq miles) regarded as a complete protection area. The core area's boundary is clearly indicated by signs to prevent accidental trespass.

Over 1,300 species of plant can be found here, including the endemic *Centaurea prespana*, which has small daisy-like flowers. There are over 40 species of mammal, such as bears, wolves, otters, roe deer, wild boar and wild cats. Birdlife includes the rare Dalmatian pelican, together with herons, egrets, pygmy cormorants, storks, golden eagles and goosanders.

Préspa Lakes and rare Dalmatian pelicans *(inset)* at one of their last breeding refuges ↓

Scattered around the lakes are several small villages. One of these, on the shore of Megáli Préspa, is Psarádes, a picturesque settlement where fishermen provide a boat service on to the lake. From the boat, you can see hermitages, icons painted on the rocks by the shore, and two frescoed churches: the 15th-century Panagía Eleoúsa and 13th-century Metamórfosi. In summer, the beaches of fine, pale sand that stretch alongside Megáli Préspa can be enjoyed along with a dip in the blue, but rather cold, waters of the lake.

Northeast of the park lies the village of Agios Germanós, which has an 11th-century Byzantine church and a number of traditional houses built in the local architectural style. The village is also home to the Préspa Information Centre, which has a good exhibition explaining the ecological importance of the Préspa National Park. Guides are available to show visitors around the park, but this must be arranged in advance. Beyond the village, roads running through the surrounding mountainous terrain offer superb views across the lakes below.

↑ The Evros River separating Greece from Turkey, rich in wetland wildlife

WETLAND WIDLIFE

In contrast to the dry and stony terrain found in much of Greece, the north has some outstanding wetlands with a range of different habitats. Reed-fringed lake margins hold large colonies of breeding birds and amphibians, while the open water is home to numerous fish and aquatic insects. The marshes are rich in flowers and full of songbirds; the man-made habitats such as saltpans and lagoons offer sanctuary to nesting waders.

The Prespa Lakes support colonies of rare Dalmatian pelicans. When nesting, they need the quiet this protected area provides.

Just east of Thessaloníki, Lake Koróneia is easy to view from nearby villages, most of which have their own colonies of white storks. In spring, terrapins and frogs gather in the shallow margins of the lake.

The Néstos Delta near Kávala is one of the finest wetlands in Greece. Many species of birds inhabit the extensive reedbanks and clumps of trees, in particular large breeding colonies of herons, egrets, storks and terns

The Evros Delta lies close to the border with Turkey and access to many of the best areas can be difficult. Numerous water birds, including little egrets, nest and feed in easily viewed locations.

↑ Bird-watcher at the Néstos Delta, a habitat for many wetland species

BIRDS OF THE WETLANDS

With outstanding scenery and great habitats, the wetlands of Northern Greece are a bird-watcher's dream.

Glossy Ibis
Glossy ibises have one of their last remaining European strongholds in the wetlands of northern Greece. Seen in good light, their feathers have a metallic sheen.

Kentish Plover
Kentish plovers nest on the margins of wetlands, such as the Préspa Lakes.

Purple Heron
The large, slender purple heron nests and breeds in the reedbeds of the Evros Delta.

Ruddy Shelduck
Near the town of Xánthi, Porto Lágos's pools and marshes are a haven for ruddy shelducks.

↑ Enjoying a god's-eye view from a peak on Mount Olympos

4

Mount Olympos

Όλυμπος

🅐C3 🚗17 km (10 miles) W of Litóchoro, Macedonia 🚆Litóchoro 🛈Olympos National Park Centre, Litóchoro; www.olympus fd.gr

The name Mount Olympos, in legend the home of the gods, refers to the whole range of mountains, 20 km (12 miles) across. The highest peak in the range, at 2,917 m (9,570 ft), is Mýtikas. The whole area constitutes the Olympos National Park. The base for walkers is the village of Litóchoro, a lively place with several hotels and tavernas. Walking maps are available and a marked trail leads up into the national park via the Mavrólogkos Canyon. Mýtikas can be reached in a demanding walk of at least six hours. It is imperative to camp out overnight or stay in one of the mountain refuges (see www.olympus-climbing.gr for more details), rather than attempt to get up and down the peak in a day.

About 10 km (6 miles) north of Litóchoro is the village of Díon and the site of **Ancient Díon**, splendidly set between the coast and the Olympian peaks. Its name derives from *Díos*, or "of Zeus". To the Macedonians, it was a holy city, and in the 4th century BC, some 15,000 people lived here. Although Dion was a military camp, rather than a civilian city, there was a temple to Zeus, a theatre and a stadium at the site. Later, the Romans built a city here. The ruins visible today date mainly from that era, and include fine mosaics from the 2nd century AD and well-preserved Roman baths. There is also a theatre and the remnants of a sanctuary dedicated to the Egyptian goddess Isis, worshipped by the Romans as a foreign deity.

The bright and modern **Díon Museum** in the village is worth seeing. On display are toys, kitchen utensils and jewellery, all finds from the sanctuary of Isis, along with the star exhibit, a Roman water-organ. Together, they give a vivid picture of life in Ancient Díon.

Ancient Díon

⊛ 🚗E of Díon village ⏲From 8am daily; closing times vary

Díon Museum

⊛ 🚗Díon village 📞23510 53484 ⏲May-Oct: 8am-8pm daily; Nov-Apr: 8am-3pm daily

THE HOME OF ZEUS

Zeus, chief and most powerful of the ancient Greek gods, lived on Mount Olympos along with the other immortals and was thought to be responsible for the destinies of men. He was also god of the weather and thunderstorms. Many of the myths tell of Zeus's amorous liaisons and his numerous children, some of whom were gods or goddesses and some heroes (p36). He was worshipped at Olympia and at Dodona in Epirus (p210), site of the oldest oracle in Greece.

> The site of Ancient Díon is splendidly set between the coast and the Olympian peaks. Its name derives from *Díos*, or "of Zeus".

⑤

Kastoriá
Καστοριά

🅰B2 ⬛Macedonia ➕12 km (7 miles) S of Kastoriá ✉ 🛈 Town hall; www.visit westmacedonia.gr

Kastoriá is the Greek for "place of beavers". These animals used to live in Lake Kastoriá (also known as Lake Orestiáda) by which the town stands, one of the loveliest settings in Greece. The beavers first brought furriers here in the 17th century and the fur trade still exists today, with the craftsmen using other furs to make coats that can be bought in shops here and in Athens.

The town prospered as a result of the fur trade, as its several remaining 17th- and 18th-century mansions testify. The elegant Skoútari and Nantzí mansions have interior courtyards and three floors. The ground floor in each case is built of stone; the upper two, housing the living quarters, are made of wood. They have fine timbered rooms fitted with cupboards, hearths and raised platforms.

The town's **Folklore Museum** is housed in the Aïvazí mansion. Built in the 17th century, it was lived in until as recently as 1972. It now has an eloquent display of the lifestyle of the wealthy fur traders. There is elaborate woodwork in the salon on the upper floor. The kitchens beneath and the wine cellar have also been restored.

Another notable feature of the town are its many frescoed Byzantine churches.

Fifty-four survive, including the 11th-century Panagía Koumbelídiki, at the south end of Mitropóleos, named after its tall dome (or *kubbe*, in Turkish). Some of the churches are tiny and hidden away, as they were originally private chapels. Many are closed – their icons are now on display in the **Byzantine Museum**.

Folklore Museum
♿ 🏛Kapetán Lázou 12 📞24670 28603 🕐10am– 4pm Wed-Mon ❌Main public hols

Byzantine Museum
🏛Plateía Dexamenís 📞24670 26781 🕐8:30am– 3:30pm Wed-Mon

---

⑥

Siátista
Σιάτιστα

🅰B3 ⬛Macedonia 🛈Plateía Tsistopoúlou

The small town of Siátista was founded in the 1430s, following the Turkish conquest of Thessaloníki. Like Kastoriá, the town flourished initially as a result of the fur trade, despite the lack of local fur. Subsequently, Siátista prospered from its role in

the wine and leather trades, and especially as a major halt on caravan routes to Vienna. The wealth that this trade created in the 18th century went into the building of fine mansion houses. The Ottoman influence in their decoration is strong. The **Nerantzopoúlou Mansion** is one of several in the town that can be visited. Keys and directions to the other mansions, including the Kanatsoúli, Manoúsi and Poulkídou, can also be obtained here.

Nerantzopoúlou Mansion
🏛Plateía Chorí

↑ Highly decorative Ottoman-inspired woodwork typical of Siátista's traditional mansions

7

Edessa
Έδεσσα

C2 **Macedonia**
Parko Katarrákton;
www.edessacity.gr

The capital of the modern Pélla region, Edessa is a popular summer resort. It is renowned for its waterfalls, the largest of which, Káranos (24 m/79 ft), has a cave behind it. The surrounding gardens and park are pleasant for a stroll, with cafés and restaurants. The Varósi old quarter has a Folklore Museum and a Water Museum (open 10am–4pm daily).

8

Vergína
Βεργίνα

C2 **15 km (9 miles) SE of Véroia, Macedonia**
aigai.gr

Outside the village of Vergína, during excavations in 1977, archaeologist Professor Manólis Andrónikos found an entrance to a tomb. The bones inside included a skull with one eye socket damaged, compelling evidence that the tomb belonged to King Philip II

of Macedon, who received such a wound in the siege of Methóni. The bones were discovered in a stunning gold funerary box, embellished with the symbol of the Macedonian Sun. The discovery confirmed that this area was the site of Aigai, the first capital of Macedon. A **Museum** is in the tumulus, with the royal burial cluster in situ and the magnificent findings displayed alongside. The momentous discovery is considered the most important since Schliemann's discoveries at Mycenae (p162). You can buy a combined ticket that

includes entrance to the Byzantine Museum of Véroia.

A short walk further along the road from Philip's tomb are some earlier discoveries, known as the **Macedonian Tombs**. The dark interior hides splendid solid marble doors and a beautiful marble throne.

The **Palace of Palatítsa** stands beyond on a mound. It is thought to have been first occupied in about 1000 BC, though the building itself dates from the 3rd century BC. Today, only low foundations remain, along with the ruins of a theatre 100 m (330 ft) below,

---

THE MACEDONIAN ROYAL FAMILY

The gold burial casket found at Vergína is emblazoned with the Macedonian Sun, the symbol of the king. Philip II was from a long line of Macedonian kings that began in about 640 BC with Perdikkas I. Philip was the first ruler to unite the whole of Greece as it existed at that time. Also known as the Macedonian Star, the Sun is often seen on flags within the region, particularly on that of the Former Yugoslav Republic of Macedonia. Much of Greece's pride in the symbol lies in the fact that the unequalled Macedonian conquerer Alexander the Great used it throughout his empire.

← One of the many waterfalls that cascade over the escarpment at Edessa

↑ Wall painting in the tomb of two brothers, Lyson and Kallikles, at Lefkádia

thought to be the site of Philip II's assassination at the hand of one of his bodyguards during the festivities for his daughter's wedding. Philip's son succeeded to the throne as Alexander III, better known as Alexander the Great, a military genius who was to expand the Macedonian empire to its greatest extent.

Museum

🖼🖼🖼 📞 23310 92347
🕐 May-Aug: 8am-8pm Wed-Mon, noon-8pm Tue; winter: times vary, call ahead 🚫 Main public hols

Macedonian Tombs, Palace of Palatítsa

🖼 📞 23310 92347 🕐 May-Aug: 8am-8pm Wed-Mon, noon-8pm Tue; winter: times vary, call ahead 🚫 Main public hols

---

9

Lefkádia
Λευκάδια

🅐 C2 🅐 Macedonia 🚌
🚫 Main public hols
🌐 visitnaoussa.gr

The four Macedonian Tombs of Lefkádia are set in a quiet agricultural area. The caretaker is usually at one of the two tombs that are signposted. The first of these is the Tomb of the Judges, or Great Tomb. This, the largest tomb, with a chamber 9 m (30 ft) square and a frescoed façade portraying Aiakos and Rhadamanthys, the Judges of Hades, has been restored. Beyond is the Anthemíon Tomb, or Tomb of the Flowers, with well-preserved flower paintings on the roof. The key to the Tomb of Lyson and Kallikles is sometimes available from the caretaker. The entrance is through a

metal grate in the roof. The fourth tomb, called the Tomb of Kinch after its Danish discoverer, or the Tomb of Niafsta after its one-time occupant, is closed to visitors.

Renowned for the large park of Chília Déndra (1,000 trees), also known as Agios Nikólaos, and for its lively Carnival, Náousa is the home of the Boutari wine-making family. It is situated on the edge of the hills above the plain that extends east to Thessaloníki. Riverside tavernas in the park offer fresh trout as well as the good local wine.

10

Véroia
Βέροια

🅐 C2 🅐 Macedonia 🅖🚌
🌐 discoververia.gr

The largest town in the region, Véroia is interesting mainly for its 50 or so barnlike churches; the oldest, the frescoed Christós, dates from the 14th century. The **Byzantine Museum** is housed in a converted 19th-century mill. The bazaar area bustles on market days and the old Barboúta Jewish quarter makes for a pleasant stroll.

Byzantine Museum

🖼 🏠 Thomaidoú 26 📞 23310 76100 🕐 Times vary, call ahead 🚫 Main public hols

---

EAT

Ousies

While it may look ordinary from outside, this restaurant on Edessa's main square has a stand-out menu. The food is a mix of traditional and creative modern, at reasonable prices, and there's regular live music.

🅐 C2 🅐 25 Martiou 4, Edessa 📞 23815 02414

€€€

Kokkino Piperi

Kokkina Piperi is just a few minutes drive from Edessa. Revive yourself after a relaxing swim and indulge in the traditional and inventive dishes, made from local produce. The name means red pepper - a delicacy of the local area.

🅐 C2 🅐 Aridaía 📞 23840 91100

€€€

EAT

Xanthippi

This restaurant not only has terrific regional dishes but also the best view, overlooking the city. Smart without being too formal, it's open throughout the day from breakfast to late-night cocktails.

Ⓐ E2 Ⓐ 1 Km Xanthis-Stavroupolis
Ⓒ 25410 23627

€€€

Pirounies

With a mix of stylish modern and traditional decor, this cosy taverna serves Balkan and Greek dishes, such as meatballs and *souvlaki*, in generous portions. There's occasional live *rembetika* and other traditional Greek music.

Ⓐ E2 Ⓐ Idras 25, Xánthi
Ⓒ 25413 03454

€€€

---

⑪

Ancient Pella
Πέλλα

Ⓐ C2 Ⓐ 38 km (24 miles) NW of Thessaloníki, Macedonia **Ⓒ 23820 31160** **Ⓝoon-8pm Tue, 8am-8pm Wed-Mon Ⓜ Main public hols**

This small site was once the flourishing capital of Macedon. It is here that Alexander the Great was born in 356 BC, and was later tutored by the philosopher Aristotle. The site has some of the best-preserved and most beautiful pebble mosaics in Greece. Dating from about 300 BC, the mosaics include vivid hunting scenes. One of the most famous is of Dionysos riding a panther in the covered House of the Lion Hunt.

---

⑫

Ancient Philippi
Αρχαιολογικός Χώρος Φίλιπποι

Ⓐ E2 Ⓐ Krinides Ⓒ 25105 16251 **Ⓙ Jun-Aug: 8am-6pm daily (winter: times vary, call ahead)**

This vast, evocative and surprisingly little-visited UNESCO World Heritage Site straddling the Roman Via Egnatia was founded in the 4th century BC by the Thassians. Originally named Krenides, it was renamed after himself by Philip II of Macedon after he conquered it in 357 BC. Ruins of Hellenistic, Roman and Byzantine buildings surround the huge theatre and a Roman forum.

---

⑬

Kavála
Καβάλα

Ⓐ E2 Ⓐ Macedonia Ⓐ 30 km (18 miles) SE of Kavála **ⓘ Plateia Elevtherias; www.visitkavala.gr**

Founded in the 6th century BC by settlers from Thássos and Erétria, Kavála became part of the Roman Empire in 168 BC, and is where St Paul first set foot on European soil in AD 50 or 51 on his way to Philippi. The Ottomans, who occupied the city from 1371 to 1912, built the vast 16th-century aqueduct. Mehmet Ali (1769–1849), the Pasha of Egypt, was born in Kavála. His birthplace, a house set in gardens, is marked by a bronze statue of him on horseback.

Kavála is a busy city, with an industrial port that also has a ferry service to the northeast Aegean islands. Life centres around the harbour below the fortified old Panagía quarter, with a nocturnally illuminated castle on top. At its eastern end, there is a produce market. To

↑ The Néstos river winding through the rich forest scenery of the Néstos Valley

the west is the **Archaeological Museum**, which has finds from Amphipolis Abdera.

The **Tobacco Museum** features a unique range of artifacts relating to the production of tobacco.

Archaeological Museum

⊘ 🏛Erythroú Stavroú 17 📞25102 22335 🕑8am–3:30pm Wed–Mon 🚫Main public hols

Tobacco Museum

⊘ 🏛K Pálailógou 4 📞2510 223344 🕑8am–3pm Mon–Fri, 9am–1pm Sat

14

Néstos Valley

Κοιλάδα του Νέστου

🅰E1 🏛Macedonia/Thrace border 🚍🚌Xánthi (liable to snow closure Nov–Apr)

The Néstos river rises high in the Rodópi mountains in Bulgaria, and its meandering course down to the Aegean near the island of Thássos marks the boundary between Macedonia and Thrace. On its way, it threads through remote gorges until it passes

←

The city of Kavála, with its aqueduct built in the Ottoman era

under the mountain road which links Xánthi with Dráma in Macedonia. This road, sometimes closed by snow in winter, makes for a spectacular scenic drive through the wooded gorge, past the valley's heavy beech forests and scattering of small villages. Stavroúpoli, the largest of these, has a range of dining and lodging options.

15

Abdera

`Άβδηρα

🅰E2 🏛6 km (4 miles) S of modern Avdira, Thrace 🚌 📞25410 51003 🕑8:30am–3:30pm Wed–Mon

The ancient city of Abdera was founded in the mid-7th century BC by refugees from

Klazomenae in Asia Minor. The ruins comprise the foundations of temples and houses. The **Archaeological Museum** in modern Avdira village has finds from the site ranging from Archaic to Byzantine times, when the town was abandoned.

Along the road from Avdira to Komotiní is Lake Vistonída, a haven for wildlife.

Archaeologial Museum

⊘ 🏛2 D Lavaridi, Avdira 📞25410 51003 🕑8:30am–3:30pm Wed–Mon

16

Xánthi

Ξάνθη

🅰E2 🏛Thrace 🚍🚌

Founded in the 11th century, it was not until the 1800s that Xánthi flourished with the development of the tobacco industry. Displays on tobacco are included in the **Folk Art Museum**, housed in two old mansions. The museum's collection includes embroidery, jewellery and costumes. Xánthi's main square has cafés and fountains, and east of the square is the bazaar, which is overflowing on Saturdays, when people of all ethnicities and religions visit the busiest market in the area.

Folk Art Museum

⊘ 🏛Antiká 7 📞25410 25421 🕑8:30am–2:30pm Tue–Sun

XÁNTHI FESTIVAL

Taking place during the first week of September, the Xánthi Festival sees the narrow paved streets of Xánthi's beautiful Old Town fill up with parades, music concerts, theatre performances, art and photography exhibitions and book fairs. It is worthwhile timing a visit to Xánthi to coincide with this colourful festival.

17 Alexandroúpoli
Αλεξανδρούπολη

A F2 **M** Thrace 🚆🏛️🚌🛥️

The town of Alexandroúpoli has a beautiful seaside location, a vibrant market and is a good base from which to explore the Dadía Forest and Evros mountains.

The town was developed in 1878, under the Turkish name of Dedeagaç (meaning "Tree of the Holy Man"), derived from a group of hermits who first settled here in the 15th century. Prior to that, it was simply an unremarkable fishing village and was renamed in 1919 after the Greek king at the time, Aléxandros I. Today it is a thriving market town with a port, its own domestic airport, and train connections north into Bulgaria and west to Thessaloníki.

In the evening, the extensive promenade by the long stretch of beach to the west is thronged with people. The lighthouse, built in 1800, is situated along the seafront. It is the town's most famous feature and is lit up at night.

Inland from the promenade is a warren of narrow streets with shops, grocers, cobblers, goldsmiths and many fish restaurants. The best places to eat are around tiny Plateía Polytechneíou. North from the square, beyond the main road, is the modern cathedral of Agios Nikólaos, notable for the **Ecclesiastical Art Museum** contained in its grounds. It has a fine collection of more

The magical slopes of the Dadiá Forest, and the endangered Eurasian black vulture, a resident of the forest *(inset)*

than 400 icons and other religious items dating predominantly from the 18th and 19th centuries, although some of the artifacts are older. The paintings of a lamenting Mary are a highlight.

Ecclesiastical Art Museum
📍 Plateía Agíou Nikolaou
📞 25510 82282 🕐 9am–2pm Tue–Fri, 9am–1pm Sat
🚫 Main public hols

18
Maroneia
Μαρώνεια

A F2 **M** 5 km (3 miles) SE of modern Maróneia, Thrace
📞 25310 22411 🚌 To modern Maróneia 🕐 8:30am–3:30pm Wed–Mon

The road to ancient Maroneia leads through tobacco and cotton fields, past woodland and small rural communities. A signpost towards Agios Charálampos port points down a track to the ancient remains, in a scenic position overlooking the sea. The city flourished from the 8th century BC until AD 1400, though little is visible under a mantle of olive groves. A small theatre has been refurbished; nearby lie the remnants of a sanctuary,

possibly dedicated to Dionysos, whose son, Maron, is credited in legend with founding Maroneia.

19 Komotiní
Κομοτηνή

A F2 **M** Thrace 🚆🚌

Only 25 km (16 miles) from the Bulgarian border to the north, and less than 100 km (62 miles) from Turkey to the east, Komotiní is a fascinating mix of Greek, Slavic and Turkish influence. First founded in the late 4th century AD, it was taken by the Turks in 1363, and remained part of the Ottoman Empire (and, briefly, Bulgaria) until 1920. Over 500 years of Turkish rule have left their mark on the town, especially since the area's Muslims were excluded from the population exchange following the Greek defeat in Asia Minor in 1922.

A feel of the town's recent past is given in the well-cared-for **Folklore Museum**. Its few rooms, in an 18th-century mansion, are crammed with costumes, local copperware and domestic items. There is also a particularly good collection of embroidery,

INSIDER TIP
Beside the Sea

If you want to get away from the ranks of hotel loungers on Alexandroúpoli's urban beach, head a little west to Agía Paraskevi or the even quieter Demir Ali beach at Makri for a refreshing dip.

including examples of a type known as Tsevrés, used in Thracian wedding ceremonies. The town's **Archaeological Museum** displays the best of the finds from the sites at ancient Abdera and Maronela, including gold jewellery found in 4th-century BC graves at Avdira. A 4th-century BC clay mask of Dionysos is on display, found at the god's sanctuary at Maroneia. The museum also has an extensive coin collection, painted sarcophagi, votive reliefs and maps.

Folklore Museum

◉ ❑ Agíou Georgíou 13 📞 25310 25931 🕐 9am–1:30pm Mon–Fri; Sat & Sun by appointment only ✖ Main public hols

Archaeological Museum

❑ Symeonídi 4 📞 25310 22411 🕐 8:30am–3:30pm Wed–Mon ✖ Main public hols

⑳
Dadiá Forest
Δάσος Δαδιάς

🅰 F2 ❑ 37km (23 miles) N of Féres, Thrace ❑ 🚌 Féres 🛈 1 km (0.5 miles) N, at Dadiá village; www.dadia-np.gr

North of the small town of Féres in the Evros valley is the lovely Dadiá pine forest. Covering a series of hills known as the Evros Mountains, it is considered to be one of the best places in Europe for observing raptors, or birds of prey; their presence here is an indication of the remote location of the forest. Out of the 39 known species of birds of prey in Europe, 26 live and nest in this region.

There is an information centre in the heart of the forest, and observation

Bust of Septimius Severus in the Komotiní Archaeological Museum

TOP
3
RARE RAPTORS IN DADIÁ

Eurasian Black Vulture
One of the world's heaviest flying birds, distinguished by its dark plumage.

Eastern Imperial Eagle
This eagle with downy legs and dark feathers is increasingly rare.

Red-Footed Falcon
The population of this bird with beautiful blue-grey plumage is declining rapidly.

huts have been placed near feeding stations, built to help preserve the rarer species that nest here. This is one of the Eurasian black vulture's last refuges in eastern Europe. The forest is home to a huge number of protected and endangered species, including imperial eagles, golden eagles, griffon vultures, sparrowhawks and peregrines. Early morning is the best time to watch the different birds as they fly on the first thermals of the day.

NEED TO KNOW

Coastal road at Igoumenitsa, northwest Greece

BEFORE
YOU GO

Things change, so plan ahead to make the most of your trip. Be prepared for all eventualities by considering the following points before you travel.

AT A GLANCE

CURRENCY
Euro (EUR)

AVERAGE DAILY SPEND

SAVE	SPEND	SPLURGE
€70	€120	€200+

BOTTLED WATER	COFFEE	BEER	DINNER FOR TWO
€1	€4	€4	€40+

ESSENTIAL PHRASES

Hello	Geiá sas
Goodbye	Antío
Please	Parakaló
Thank you	Efcharistó
Do you speak English	Miláte Angliká?
I don't understand	Den katálavaíno

ELECTRICITY SUPPLY
Power sockets are types C and F, fitting two-pronged plugs. Standard voltage is 220–240 volts.

Passports and Visas

For entry requirements, including visas, consult your nearest Greek embassy or check the **Greek Ministry of Foreign Affairs** website. EU nationals and citizens of the UK, US, Canada, Australia and New Zealand do not need visas for stays of up to three months.
Greek Ministry of Foreign Affairs
w mfa.gr/en/visas

Government Advice

Now more than ever, it is important to consult both your and the Greek government's advice before travelling. The **UK Foreign and Commonwealth Office,** the **US Department of State**, the **Australian Department of Foreign Affairs and Trade** and the **Greek Ministry of Foreign Affairs** offer the latest information on security, health and local regulations.
Australian Department of Foreign Affairs and Trade
w smarttraveller.gov.au
Greek Ministry of Foreign Affairs
w mfa.gr/en
UK Foreign and Commonwealth Office
w gov.uk/foreign-travel-advice
US State Department
w travel.state.gov

Customs Information

You can find information on the laws relating to goods and currency taken in or out of Greece on the **Greek Ministry of Tourism** website.
Greek Misistry of Tourism
w mintour.gov.gr/en/archiki-english

Insurance

We recommend taking out a comprehensive insurance policy covering theft, loss of belongings, medical care, cancellations and delays, and read the small print carefully. UK citizens are eligible for free emergency medical care in state-run clinics or hospitals, provided they have a valid European Health

Insurance Card (**EHIC**) or UK Global Health Insurance Card (**GHIC**) and enter via the casualty ward. Comprehensive travel insurance covering private clinics is highly recommended, particularly for those without an EHIC or GHIC.
EHIC
ⓦ ec.europa.eu
EHIC
ⓦ ec.europa.eu

Vaccinations

No vaccinations are required for travel in Greece. For information regarding COVID-19 vaccination requirements, consult government advice (p250).

Booking Accommodation

Booking accommodation in advance is highly recommended in high season, especially for Athens, Thessaloníki and popular holiday resorts. If travelling to more remote places it is less essential. Visitors during low season should note that some hotels close for the winter.

Money

Major credit and debit cards are accepted in most shops and restaurants, while pre-paid currency cards and contactless payments are accepted in some. It is always worth carrying some cash.

It is customary to tip up to ten per cent in restaurants; when paying for a taxi, it is the norm to round the fare up to the nearest euro.

Language

Greek is the official language but English is widely spoken and taught from primary school, along with a second European language at secondary school. Locals do appreciate visitors' efforts to speak Greek, and a phrasebook may be helpful in more rural areas.

Travellers with Specific Requirements

Greece has made some progress in meeting the needs of travellers with accessibility requirements in recent years. As of 2018, all hotels must by law provide at least one wheelchair-adapted en-suite room, though compliance, particularly

in less touristed areas, varies. Most museums have disabled access. Announcements for the visually impaired to cross streets safely are rare.

Disability NOW is a useful directory for visitors with specific requirements travelling Greece. It includes information for the visually impaired and deaf.
Disability NOW
ⓦ disabled.gr

Opening Hours

> **COVID-19** Increased rates of infection may result in temporary opening hours and/or closures. Always check ahead before visiting museums, attractions and hospitality venues.

Opening hours vary from day to day and season to season. Although the opening times have been checked at the time of going to print, it is advisable to use these as a rough guideline only.
Afternoon Many shops close after 2:30pm but are open from 5:30 to 8:30pm on Tuesday, Thursday and Friday.
Tuesdays Many archaeological museums and minor sites are closed for the day.
Sundays Most shops outside of major tourist resorts are closed.
Public holidays Major sights, shops and restaurants are closed.
Low season Many hotels, restaurants and attractions in tourist areas close over winter.

PUBLIC HOLIDAYS

1 Jan	New Year's Day
6 Jan	Epiphany
25 Mar	Greek Independence Day
April/May	Orthodox Easter
25 Apr	Liberation Day
1 May	May Day/Labour Day
Early June	Whit (Pentecost) Monday
15 Aug	Dormition Day
28 Oct	Ohi Day
25 Dec	Christmas Day
26 Dec	Gathering of the Mother of God

GETTING
AROUND

Whether you are visiting for a weekend escape to Athens or touring the country, discover how best to reach your destination and travel like a pro.

AT A GLANCE

PUBLIC TRANSPORT COSTS

ATHENS AIRPORT TO CENTRE

€6

Bus ticket

ATHENS TO THESSALONÍKI

€35

Bus ticket

ATHENS TO PÁTRA

€21

Bus ticket

SPEED LIMITS

BUILT-UP AREAS

50 km/h (30 mph)

COUNTRY ROADS

80 km/h (50 mph)

MOTORWAYS

130 km/h (80 mph)

Arriving by Air

The main airlines operating direct scheduled flights from the UK to Athens are **Aegean Airlines** and **British Airways**; several budget airlines also connect the UK to mainland Greece, especially seasonally, including **easyJet** and **Ryanair**. All the major European carriers also operate scheduled flights.

On the mainland, Athens and Thessaloníki handle most scheduled flights. The other mainland international airports – such as Préveza, Kavála and Vólos – are mainly reached by charter flights. Kalamáta is served seasonally by British Airways and easyJet. All scheduled long-haul flights to Greece land in Athens, although many are not direct and will require changing at a connecting European city.

There are direct flights to Athens from Beijing, New York, Montreal and Toronto, and seasonally from Chicago and Philadelphia. Although there are no direct flights to Athens from Australia or New Zealand, both countries offer several daily flights that involve changing at a connecting Middle Eastern hub.

In Athens, Metro line 3 (blue line) links the airport to Syntágma and Monastiráki in the city centre every 30 minutes 6:30am–11:30pm. The X95 bus runs from the airport to Sytnágma Square every 15-20 minutes. You can look up timetables on the **Athens Transport** website.

Aegean Airlines
w aegeanair.com
Athens Transport
w athenstransport.com
British Airways
w britishairways.com
easyJet
w easyjet.com
Ryanair
w ryanair.com

Arriving by Sea

There are ferry crossings from the Italian ports of Ancona, Bari, Brindisi, Venice and Trieste to Igoumenítsa in Epirus and Pátra in the Peloponnese. Minoan, ANEK and Superfast are

the main Greek companies on these routes. In summer it is advisable to book ahead, especially if you have a car or want a cabin.

Greek Ferry Service

Athens's port, Piraeus, is the largest passenger port in Europe. There are frequent ferry services to the islands of the Argo-Saronic, the Cyclades, the Northeast Aegean, the Dodecanese and Crete. The smaller port of Rafína sees ferry departures for Evia and islands in the Cyclades.

Southeast of Athens, Lávrio offers services to the Cyclades and to the Northeast Aegean with Hellenic Seaways, ANEK and Blue Star. Their fleets comprise a limited number of conventional ferries and hydrofoils, plus many more high-speed ferries and catamarans. Hydrofoils get cancelled in adverse weather, so they are confined to relatively sheltered routes. Tickets can be bought online or from travel agents in Athens. Advanced bookings are recommended for ferries in high season and are essential for high-speed catamarans and hydrofoils. Out of season, services are reduced. **Greek Travel Pages** is the most comprehensive source of information on ferry departures.
Greek Travel Pages
w gtp.gr

GETTING TO AND FROM THE AIRPORT

Airport	Distance to city	Taxi fare	Public Transport	Journey Time
Athens	35 km (22 miles)	€40-50	Bus/Metro	45-60 mins
Thessaloníki	16 km (10 miles)	€20-30	Bus	30 mins
Pátra	40 km (25 miles)	€50	Bus	45 mins

ROAD JOURNEY PLANNER

This map is a handy reference for driving between some of Greece's main towns and cities. Journey times given below are for normal travel conditions.

··· Direct train routes

Athens to Delphi	2 hrs 30 mins
Athens to Náfplio	2 hrs
Athens to Pátra	2 hrs 30 mins
Athens to Thessaloníki	5 hrs
Athens to Vólos	3 hrs 30 mins
Delphi to Ioánnina	4 hrs
Ioánnina to Kastoriá	2 hrs
Náfplio to Spárti	2 hrs
Pátra to Kalamáta	3 hrs
Thessaloníki to Kavála	2 hrs

Train Travel

International Train Travel

Two international train services connect Greece with mainland Europe. One is a daily service between Thessaloníki and Sofia (year-round), the other connects Thessaloníki to Skopje and Belgrade (summer only).

Domestic Train Travel

Greece's railway infrastructure is owned by **OSE** (Organismós Sidirodrómon Elládos), and train services are run by **TrainOSE**. Safety and hygiene measures, ticket information, transport maps and timetables can be found on the TrainOSE website. Athens forms the hub of the system. Five daily departures from Athens' main railway station, Sidirodromikós Stathmós Athinón, connect the capital with Thessaloníki. The journey takes just under four and a half hours. From Thessaloníki, there are lines travelling west to Flórina and east to Alexandroúpoli.

A new standard-gauge line is being built linking Piraeus with Pátra, the only passenger service on the Peloponnese. The latest extension takes the service as far as Rododafni. Passengers heading for Pátra then change to a TrainOSE bus to reach their final destination. Check the TrainOSE website for the latest updates.

There are two picturesque heritage routes. On the Peloponnese the dramatic rack-and-pinion line runs between Diakoftó and Kalávryta. The narrow-gauge To Trenáki on Mount Pílio runs from Ano Lechónia and Miliés daily during weekends and holidays from Easter to October.
TrainOSE
w trainose.gr

Long-Distance Bus Travel

Greece has an excellent bus network, not just between cities but in rural areas too. Due to the minimal rail network, it is often the only way to get around if you are not driving. Greece's bus system is operated by **KTEL** (Koinó Tameío Eispráxeon Leoforeíon), a syndicate of many regional private companies. Every community is provided with services of some sort, though the frequency of these varies greatly.

Larger cities such as Athens, Thessaloníki and Lamía have more than one terminal, each serving a different set of destinations. Ticket sales are computerized for all major routes, with reserved seating on modern coaches. It is wise to buy your ticket in advance, since seats often sell out and coaches tend to leave early. In country villages, the local *kafeneío* (café) often serves as the coach station. Tickets can be bought here; if not, it is possible to buy a ticket upon boarding.
KTEL
w ktelbus.com

Public Transport

Athens has a three-line metro system, which shares tickets with the small tramway network and extensive bus routes. The metro has three lines: Line 1 (green line) runs north to south with several central stops, and offers visitors the fastest way of reaching Piraeus. Line 2 (red line) runs from northwest Athens to the southeast. At Sýntagma it intersects with Line 3 (blue line), which runs from Agía Marína in western Athens to Doukíssis Plakentías in the northeast, with some trains continuing on to Elefthérios Venizélos airport. Tickets must be validated before boarding the train – use the machines at the entrances to all platforms. **ATH.ENA** cards are reusable and give discounts the more journeys you load onto them.

No other Greek cities have metro systems though one is being built in Thessaloníki and after several delays it is due to be completed in 2023. For information on bus services in Thessaloníki visit the **OASTH** website.

Athens is served by an extensive bus network, covering over 300 routes. Journeys are inexpensive but can be slow and crowded, especially in the city centre and during rush hours. Timetables and route maps (in Greek only) are available from **OASA**, the Athens Urban Transport Organization.

Athens also has a good network of trolley-buses that run on electricity on over 20 routes, connecting many of the main sights. Tickets can be bought at machines or windows at metro stations, and must be validated when boarding.

The rudimentary tram system in Athens connects the city centre and the coast. There are just three lines, confusingly numbered 3, 4 and 5. Tickets can be bought at tram stops, and must be validated at a machine at the stop before boarding.

Most communities have good bus services and this is the main form of public transport. However, even in the biggest cities, many of the main sites are probably reached more quickly on foot than by bus. For information on Greece's buses, it's best to check the KTEL website.
ATH.ENA
w athenacard.gr
OASA
w oasa.gr
OASTH
w oasth.gr

Taxis

Yellow taxis can be seen cruising the streets of Athens at most times of the day or night. Getting one to stop, however, can be a difficult task, especially between 2pm and 3pm, when drivers usually change shifts. To hail a taxi, stand on the edge of the pavement and shout out your destination to any cab that slows down. You can also find taxi ranks around the city, especially near major squares.

Athenian taxis are cheap compared to other European cities; depending on traffic, you should not pay more than €5 to travel to any destination within the downtown area, and about €15 from the centre to Piraeus. Higher tariffs come into effect between midnight and 5am and for journeys that exceed certain distances from the city centre. There are also surcharges for extra luggage weighing more than 10 kg (22 lbs), and for journeys from the ferry or railway terminals. Fares increase during holiday periods, such as Christmas and Easter.

Taxi companies can also be booked online or over the phone. In Athens, the Uber service using private cars is currently suspended, though you can use the **UberTAXI** service to book a taxi and pay through the Uber app. The situation is the same in Thessaloníki and Pátra.
UberTAXI
w uber.com

Driving

Driving in Athens can be a nerve-racking experience and is best avoided, especially if you are not accustomed to Greek road habits. Many streets in the centre are pedestrianized, and there are also plenty of one-way streets, so you need to plan your route carefully. Finding a parking space can be very difficult too. Contrary to appearances, parking in front of a no-parking sign or on a single yellow line is illegal. There are pay-and-display machines for legal on-street parking, as well as underground car parks and unofficial parking lots, although these tend to fill up quickly.

In an attempt to reduce high air pollution levels, Athens enforces a strict "odd-even" driving system. Cars that have an odd number at the end of their licence plates can enter the central grid (*daktýlios*) only on dates with an odd number, while cars ending in an even number are allowed into it only on even-numbered dates. To avoid being unable to access the *daktýlios*, some people have two cars – with odd and even plates. The "odd–even" rule does not apply to foreign cars, although you should still avoid taking your car into the city centre if possible. Driving in the rest of the country is a less fraught experience, though you may wish to avoid bigger cities like Thessaloníki and Pátra.

Major motorways are usually in good condition, but be prepared for potholes and other hazards if you go into more rural areas. Watch out for animals, too; it's not unusual to come across a flock of sheep or goats wandering along the road.

Car Rental

The minimum age for car rental is 21 years, although some companies require drivers to be over 25. In low season, rental cars can be arranged on the spot, but in summer it is advisable to reserve one online in advance. All the major international chains have local affiliates in Athens and main towns and cities. Take out a policy insuring you for the collision damage waiver excess beforehand.

Licences

Driving licences issued by any of the European Union member states are valid throughout the EU. If visiting from outside the EU, you will need to apply for an International Driving Permit. Check with your local automobile association before you travel.

Rules of the Road

The blood alcohol limit is 0.5 g per litre, and driving under the influence will result in fines, possible loss of licence and prosecution. Seatbelts must be worn in front seats, with a €350 fine and ten days' loss of licence for non-compliance. Children under ten must sit in the back seat and under-threes must ride in approved child seats (rental agencies supply these). Fines for minor infractions must be paid within ten days to avoid court proceedings. It's an offence to leave an accident involving another car or to move the vehicles before the police arrive, who will write an accident report. This will be required by your car-hire company and your insurer.

Cycling

As with driving, cycling in Athens is only for the brave. Local drivers have little respect for cyclists, and cycle lanes are non-existent. Bike-users have increased in the capital, however, and cyclists are now allowed to ride in the bus lanes. Outside the cities, things are better and some beautiful (if mountainous) scenery awaits. Bicycle hire isn't widely available, but main tourist resorts will have bikes available for rent.

Walking and Hiking

With a vast network of clearly way-marked footpaths both on the coast and further inland, mainland Greece is a fantastic destination for walkers and hikers. Ensure you have good hiking boots, plenty of water, a map and a compass – and stick to your route. Tell someone where you're going and when you plan to return.

Walking is also an enjoyable way to explore compact city centres such as Athens and Thessaloníki, where most of the key sites are within a short distance of one another.

PRACTICAL
INFORMATION

A little local know-how goes a long way in Greece. Here you will find all the essential advice and information you will need during your stay.

EMERGENCY NUMBERS

TOURIST POLICE (ATHENS ONLY)

1571

POLICE

100

FIRE

199

AMBULANCE

166

TIME ZONE
EET/EEST: Eastern European Summer Time runs from the last Sunday in March to the last Sunday in October.

TAP WATER
Unless you're told otherwise, tap water in Athens and the mainland is safe to drink.

WEBSITES AND APPS

National Tourist Board
Check out Greece's national tourist board for useful travel tips and advice (www.visitgreece.gr).

Urban Rail Transport
Find travel times across metro, tramway and railway in Athens (www.stasy.gr)

Odysseus
Check opening times of archaeological sites, monuments and state-run museums (www.odysseus.culture.gr).

Personal Security

Overall crime rates are low, although car break-ins are an increasing problem, so try not to leave belongings on display. If you suffer a theft or are assaulted, report the crime as soon as possible to the nearest police station or to the tourist police, if a branch exists. The tourist police – often just one person inside the main police station – should be consulted for any issues with taxi drivers, hoteliers, shops and tavernas.

Pickpocketing in Athens and Thessaloníki is rife, particularly on crowded buses such as the X95 bus from the airport in Athens to Sýntagma. Monastiráki station on the Piraeus–Kifisiá metro line is also notorious as a spot targeted by thieves, as are Omonia Square and Omonia station. If you are coming from Piraeus (the port) towards the centre with luggage, alight at Néo Fáliro, walk the short distance to the SEF (Stathmós Irínis ke Filías) station, and continue into town on a tram. Your ticket will be valid for both journeys.

While the majority of the country holds conservative values due to the strong influence of the Orthodox Church, Greeks are generally accepting of all people, regardless of their race, gender or sexuality. Homosexuality was legalized in Greece in 1951, and though same-sex marriage is still not legal (the issue remains somewhat divisive), the country's popularity as a gay destination goes hand in hand with the fact that LGBTQ+ rights are fairly well advanced. Athens's LGBTQ+ scene, which is centred around the fashionable Gazi neighbourhood, is where most of the city's gay and lesbian bars and clubs are situated.

However, despite the many freedoms the LGBTQ+ community enjoy, acceptance is not always a given. Rural communities and older generations tend to be less tolerant of public displays of affection from same-sex couples travelling together. If you do at any point feel unsafe or threatened, the **Safe Space Alliance** pinpoints your nearest place of refuge. Alternatively head for the nearest police station.
Safe Space Alliance
🔲 safespacealliance.com

Health

Greece's National Healthcare Service is still recvering from the economic crisis in 2007.

Emergency medical care is free for EU nationals with an EHIC or GHIC *(p251)* at state-run clinics or hospitals, provided you enter via the casualty ward. If you have an EHIC or GHIC, be sure to present this as soon as possible. For visitors from outside the EU, payment of medical expenses is the patient's responsibility. Organizing comprehensive medical insurance before your trip is essential, as private doctors or clinics within Greece are expensive.

Seek medicinal supplies and advice for minor ailments from pharmacies, which are indicated by a green cross. Greek pharmacies have over-the-counter remedies available at accessible prices without prescriptions. When they are shut, there will be a sign on the door directing you to the nearest 24-hour service).

Smoking, Alcohol and Drugs

In 2010, Greece introduced a law making smoking illegal in enclosed public spaces, including in restaurants, bars and cafés; Locals often ignore this law. Smoking in outdoor areas such as café terraces is permitted.

Greek police will not tolerate rowdy or indecent behaviour, especially when fuelled by excessive alcohol consumption; Greek courts impose heavy fines or even prison sentences on people who behave indecently. Possession of narcotics is prohibited and could result in a prison sentence.

ID

Both locals and foreigners are required to have identification (either a national ID card or passport) on them at all times.

Local Customs

The afternoon *mikró ýpno* ("little sleep") is sacrosanct, particularly in rural towns and villages: no public noise is allowed 3–5:30pm, and even making phone calls during these hours is frowned upon. Topless sunbathing is tolerated except in front of "family" tavernas, but nudity is restricted.

Visiting Places of Worship

Modest attire (shoulders and knees should be covered) is required at Greek Orthodox churches and monasteries. Many monasteries have "modesty" wraps available for free at the door. Photography inside places of worship is often forbidden, so check first.

Mobile Phones and Wi-Fi

Many visitors travelling to Greece with EU tariffs will be able to use their devices without being affected by data roaming charges; instead they will be charged the same rates for data, SMS and voice calls as they would pay at home.

All hotels and most *domátia* (rooms) or apartments have Wi-Fi signal. Ofen it's free; otherwise, ascertain charges. Most tavernas, bars or cafés have password protected Wi-Fi.

Post

Greece's postal service **ELTA** (Elliniká Tahydromía) has full-service branches (open 7:30am–2pm Monday–Friday) in cities and most decent-sized towns. Post boxes are bright yellow (ordinary) or red (express), but collection frequencies are obscure.
ELTA
🌐 elta.gr

Taxes and Refunds

Usually included in the price, the top rate of FPA (Fóros Prostitheménis Axías) – the equivalent of VAT or sales tax – is 24 percent in Greece, though taverna meals are assessed at 17 percent. Visitors from outside the EU staying fewer than three months may claim this money back on purchases over €120. A Tax-Free form must be completed in the store, a copy of which is then given to the customs authorities on departure, along with proof of purchase.

Discount Cards

Purchasing an Athens City Pass is a good way to save money on transportation and see the city's main attractions for free or with priority access.
Athens City Pass
🌐 turbopass.com/athens-city-pass

INDEX

PHRASE BOOK

There is no universally accepted system for representing the modern Greek language in the Roman alphabet. The system of transliteration adopted in this guide is the one used by the Greek Government. Though not yet fully applied throughout Greece, most of the street and place names have been transliterated according to this system. For Classical names, this guide uses the k, os, on and f spelling, in keeping with the modern system of transliteration. In a few cases, such as Socrates, the more familiar Latin form has been used. Classical names and ancient sites do not have accents. Where a well-known English form of a name exists, such as Athens or Corfu, this has been used. Variations in transliteration are given in the index.

GUIDELINES FOR PRONUNCIATION

The accent over Greek and transliterated words indicates the stressed syllable. In this guide, the accent is not written over monosyllables, except for question words and the conjunction ή (meaning "or"). In the right-hand "Pronunciation" column below, the syllable to stress is given in bold type.

On the following pages, the English is given in the left-hand column with the Greek and its transliteration in the middle column. The right-hand column provides a literal system of pronunciation and indicates the stressed syllable in bold.

THE GREEK ALPHABET

Α α	A a	*arm*
Β β	V v	*vote*
Γ γ	G g	*year (when followed by e and i sounds); otherwise, glove)*
Δ δ	D d	*that*
Ε ε	E e	*egg*
Ζ ζ	Z z	*zoo*
Η η	I i	*ski*
Θ θ	Th th	*think*
Ι ι	I i	*ski*
Κ κ	K k	*kid*
Λ λ	L l	*land*
Μ μ	M m	*man*
Ν ν	N n	*no*
Ξ ξ	X x	*taxi*
Ο ο	O o	*toad*
Π π	P p	*port*
Ρ ρ	R r	*room*
Σ σ	S s	*sorry (zero when followed by μ or y)*
ς	s	*(used at end of word)*
Τ τ	T t	*tea*
Υ υ	Y y	*barely*
Φ φ	F f	*fish*
Χ χ	Ch ch	*loch in most cases, but he when followed by a, e or i sounds*
Ψ ψ	Ps ps	*maps*
Ω ω	O o	*toad*

COMBINATIONS OF LETTERS

In Greek, there are two-letter vowels that are pronounced as one sound:

Αι αι	Ai ai	*hey*
Ει ει	Ei ei	*ski*
Οι οι	Oi oi	*believe*
Ου ου	Ou ou	*tourist*

There are also some two-letter consonant clusters that yield predictable or unusual results:

Μπ μπ	Mp mp	*but if initial; number in the middle of a word*
Ντ ντ	Nt nt	*desk if initial; under in the middle of a word*
Γκ γκ	Gk gk	*go if initial; bingo in the middle of a word*
Γξ γξ	Nx	*anxiety*
Τζ τζ	Tz tz	*judge*
Τσ τσ	Ts ts	*hits*
ΥΥ	gg	*bingo in the middle of a word*

IN AN EMERGENCY

Help!	Βοήθεια! Voítheia	*vo-ee-theea*
Stop!	Σταματήστε! Stamatíste	*sta-ma-tee-steh*
Call a doctor!	Φωνάξτε ένα γιατρό Fonáxte éna giatró	*fo-nak-steh e-na ya-trol*
Call an ambulance/ the police/ the fire brigade!	Καλέστε το ασθενοφόρο/την αστυνομία/την πυροσβεστική! Kaléste to asthenofóro/tin astynomía/tin pyrosvestikí	*ka-le-steh to as-the-no-fo-ro/teen a-sti-no-mía/teen pee-ro-zve-stee-kee*
Where is the nearest telephone/ hospital/ pharmacy?	Πού είναι το πλησιέστερο τήλεφωνο/-νοσοκο μείο/ ιφαρμακείο; Poú eínai to plisiés-tero tiléfono/nosoko-meío/farmakeío?	*poo ee-ne to plee-see-e-ste-ro tee-le-pho-no/no-so-ko-mee-o/far-ma-kee-o?*

COMMUNICATION ESSENTIALS

Yes	Ναι Nai	*neh*
No	Όχι Ochi	*o-chee*
Please	Παρακαλώ Parakaló	*pa-ra-ka-lo*
Thank you	Ευχαριστώ Efcharistó	*ef-cha-ree-sto*
You are welcome	Παρακαλώ Parakaló	*pa-ra-ka-lo*
OK/alright	Εντάξει Entáxei	*en-dak-zee*
Excuse me	Με συγχωρείτε Me synchoreíte	*me seen-cho-ree-teh*
Hello	Γειά σας Geiá sas	*yeea sas*
Goodbye	Αντίο Antío	*an-dee-o*
Good morning	Καλημέρα Kaliméra	*ka-lee-me-ra*
Good night	Καληνύχτα Kalinýchta	*ka-lee-neech-ta*
Morning	Πρωί Proí	*pro-ee*
Afternoon	Απόγευμα Apógevma	*a-po-yev-ma*
Evening	Βράδυ Vrádi	*vrath-i*
This morning	Σήμερα το πρωί Símera to proí	*see-me-ra to pro-ee*
Yesterday	Χθές Chthés	*chthes*
Today	Σήμερα Símera	*see-me-ra*
Tomorrow	Αύριο Avrio	*av-ree-o*
Here	Εδώ Edó	*ed-o*
There	Εκεί Ekeí	*e-kee*
What?	Τί; Tí?	*tee?*
Why?	Γιατί; Giatí?	*ya-tee?*
Where?	Πού; Poú?	*poo?*
How?	Πώς; Pós?	*pos?*
Wait!	Περίμενε! Perímene!	*pe-ree-me-neh*

USEFUL PHRASES

How are you?	Τί κάνετε;	tee ka-ne teh
	Τί κάνete?	
Very well, thank you	Πολύ καλά,	po-lee ka-la, ef-cha-
	ευχαριστώ	ree-sto
	Poly kalá, efcharistó	
How do you do?	Πώς είστε;	pos ees-te?
	Pós eíste?	
Pleased to meet you	Χαίρω πολύ	che-ro po-lee
	Chaíro polý	
What is your name?	Πώς λέγεστε;	pos le-ye-ste?
	Pós légeste?	
Where is/are...?	Πού είναι;	poo ee-ne?
	Poú eínai?	
How far is it to...?	Πόσο απέχει...;	po-so a-pe-chee?
	Póso apéchei...?	
How do I get to?	Πώς μπορώ να	pos bo-ro-na pa-o?
	πάω...;	
	Pós proró na ráo...?	
Do you speak English?	Μιλάτε Αγγλικά;	mee-la-te an-glee-ka?
	Miláte Angliká?	
I understand	Καταλαβαίνω	ka-ta-la-ve-no
	Katalavaíno	
I don't understand	Δεν καταλαβαίνω	then ka-ta-la-ve-no
	Den katalavaíno	
Could you speak slowly?	Μιλάτε λίγο πιο	mee-la-te lee-go pyo
	αργά παρακαλώ;	ar-ga pa-ra-ka-lo?
	Miláte lígo pio argá parakaló?	
I'm sorry	Με συγχωρείτε	me seen-cho-ree teh
	Me synchoreíte	
Does anyone have a key?	Έχει κανένας	e-chee ka-ne-nas
	κλειδί;	klee-dee?
	Echei kanénas kleidí?	

USEFUL WORDS

big	Μεγάλο	me-ga-lo
	Megálo	
small	Μικρό	mi-kro
	Mikró	
hot	Ζεστό	zes-to
	Zestó	
cold	Κρύο	kree-o
	Krýo	
good	Καλό	ka-lo
	Kaló	
bad	Κακό	ka-ko
	Kakó	
enough	Αρκετά	ar-ke-ta
	Arketá	
well	Καλά	ka-la
	Kalá	
open	Ανοιχτά	a-neech-ta
	Anoichtá	
closed	Κλειστά	klee-sta
	Kleistá	
left	Αριστερά	a-ree-ste-ra
	Aristerá	
right	Δεξιά	dek-see-a
	Dexiá	
straight on	Ευθεία	ef-thee-a
	Eftheía	
between	Ανάμεσα / Μεταξύ	a-na-me-sa/me-tak-see
	Anámesa / Metaxý	
on the corner of...	Στη γωνία του...	stee go-nee-a too
	Sti gonía tou...	
near	Κοντά	kon-da
	Kontá	
far	Μακριά	ma-kree-a
	Makriá	
up	Επάνω	e-pa-no
	Epáno	
down	Κάτω	ka-to
	Káto	
early	Νωρίς	no-rees
	Norís	
late	Αργά	ar-ga
	Argá	
entrance	Η είσοδος	ee ee-so-thos
	I eísodos	
exit	Η έξοδος	ee-ex-o-dos
	I éxodos	
toilet	Οι τουαλέτες /WC	ee-too-a-le-tes
	Oi toualétes / WC	
occupied/engaged	Κατειλημμένη	ka-tee-lee-me-nee
	Kateiliméni	

unoccupied/vacant	Ελεύθερη	e-lef-the-ree
	Eléftheri	
free/no charge	Δωρεάν	tho-re-an
	Doreán	
in/out	Μέσα/Έξω	me-sa/ek-so
	Mésa/Exo	

MAKING A TELEPHONE CALL

Where is the nearest telephone booth?	Πού βρίσκεται ο πλησιέστερος τηλεφωνικός θάλαμος;	poo vrees-ke-teh o plee-see-e-ste-ros tee-le-fo-ni-kos tha-la-mos?
	Poú vrísketai o plisiésteros tilefonikós thálamos?	
I would like to place a long-distance call	Θα ήθελα να κάνω ένα υπεραστικό τηλεφώνημα	tha ee-the-la na ka-no e-na pe-ra-sti-ko tee-le-fo-nee-ma
	Tha íthela na káno éna yperastikó tilefónima	
I would like to reverse the the charges	Θα ήθελα να χρεώσω το τηλεφώνημα στον παραλήπτη	tha ee-the-la na chre-o-so to tee-le-fo-nee-ma ston pa-ra-leep-tee
	Tha íthela na chreóso to tilefónima ston paralípti	
I will try again later	Θα ξανατηλεφωνήσω αργότερα	tha ksa-na-tee-le-fo-ni-so ar-go-te-ra
	Tha xanatilefoníso argótera	
Can I leave a message?	Μπορείτε να του αφήσετε ένα μήνυμα;	bo-ree-te na too a-fee-se-teh e-na mee-nee-ma?
	Mporeíte na tou afísete éna mínyma?	
Could you speak up a little please?	Μιλάτε δυνατότερα, παρακαλώ;	mee-la-teh dee-na-to-te-ra, pa-ra-ka-lo
	Miláte dynatótera, parakaló	
Local call	Τοπικό τηλεφώνημα	to-pí-ko tee-le-fo-nee-ma
	Topikó tilefónima	
Hold on	Περιμένετε	pe-rí-me-ne-teh
	Periménete	
Phone box/kiosk	Ο τηλεφωνικός θάλαμος	o tee-le-fo-ni-kos tha-a-mos
	O tilefonikós thálamos	
Phone card	Η τηλεκάρτα	ee tee-le-kar-ta
	I tilekárta	

SHOPPING

How much does this cost?	Πόσο κάνει;	po-so ka-nee?
	Póso kánei?	
I would like...	Θα ήθελα...	tha ee-the-la...
	Tha íthela...	
Do you have...?	Έχετε...;	e-che-teh
	Echete...?	
I am just looking	Απλώς κοιτάω	a-plos kee-ta-o
	Aplós koitáo	
Do you take credit cards?	Δέχεστε πιστωτικές κάρτες;	the-ches-teh pee-sto-tee-kes kar-tes?
	Décheste pistotikés kártes?	
What time do you open/close?	Πότε ανοίγετε/ κλείνετε;	po-teh a-nee-ye-teh/ klee-ne-teh?
	Póte anoígete/ kleínete?	
Can you ship this overseas?	Μπορείτε να το στείλετε στο εξωτερικό;	bo-ree-teh na to stee-le-teh sto e-xo-te-ree ko?
	Mporeíte na to steílete sto exoterikó?	
This one	Αυτό εδώ	af-to e-do
	Aftó edó	
That one	Εκείνο	e-kee-no
	Ekeíno	
expensive	Ακριβό	a-kree-vo
	Akrivó	
cheap	Φθηνό	fthee-no
	Fthinó	
size	Το μέγεθος	to me-ge-thos
	To mégethos	
white	Λευκό	lef-ko
	Lefkó	

black	Μαύρο Μάβρο	mav-ro
red	Κόκκινο Κόκκινο	ko-kee-no
yellow	Κίτρινο Κίτρινο	kee-tree-no
green	Πράσινο Πράσινο	pra-see-no
blue	Μπλε Μple	bleh

TYPES OF SHOP

antique shop	Μαγαζί με αντίκες Magazí me antíkes	ma-ga-zee me an-dee-kes
bakery	Ο φούρνος O foúrnos	o foor-nos
bank	Η τράπεζα I trápeza	ee tra-pe-za
bazaar	Το παζάρι To pazári	to pa-za-ree
bookshop	Το βιβλιοπωλείο To vivliopoleío	to vee-vlee-o-po-lee-o
butcher	Το κρεοπωλείο To kreopoleío	to kre-o-po-lee-o
cake shop	Το ζαχαροπλαστείο To zacharoplasteío	to za-cha-ro-pla-stee-o
delicatessen	Μαγαζί με αλλαντικά Magazi me allantiká	ma-ga-zee me a-lan-dee-ka
department store	Πολυκατάστημα Polykatástima	Po-lee-ka-ta-stee-ma
fishmarket	Το ιχθυοπωλείο/ ψαράδικο To ichthyopoleío/ psarádiko	to eech-thee-o-po-lee-o/ psa-rá-dee-ko
greengrocer	Το μανάβικο To manáviko	to ma-na-vee-ko
hairdresser	Το κομμωτήριο To kommotírio	to ko-mo-tee-ree-o
kiosk	Το περίπτερο To períptero	to pe-reep-te-ro
leather shop	Μαγαζί με δερμάτινα είδη Magazí me dermátina eídi	ma-ga-zee me ther-ma-tee-na ee-ethee
street market	Η λαϊκή αγορά I laïkí agorá	ee la-ee-kee a-go-ra
newsagent	Ο εφημεριδοπώλης O efimeridopólis	O e-fee-me-ree-tho-po-lees
pharmacy	Το φαρμακείο To farmakeío	to far-ma-kee-o
post office	Το ταχυδρομείο To tachydromeío	to ta-chee-thro-mee-o
shoe shop	Κατάστημα υποδημάτων Katástima ypodimáton	ka-ta-stee-ma ee-po-dee-ma-ton
souvenir shop	Μαγαζί "souvenir" Magazí me "souvenir"	ma-ga-zee meh "souvenir"
supermarket	Σουπερμάρκετ/ Υπεραγορά "Supermarket"/ Yperagorá	"Supermarket" /ee-per-a-go-ra
tobacconist	Είδη καπνιστού Eídi kapnistoú	Ee-thee kap-nees
travel agent	Το ταξειδιωτικό πρακτορείο To taxeidiotikó praktoreío	to tak-see-thy-o-tee-ko prak-to-ree-o

SIGHTSEEING

tourist information	Ο ΕΟΤ O ΕΟΤ	o E-OT
tourist police	Η τουριστική αστυνομία I touristikí astynomía	ee too-rees-tee-kee a-stee-no-mee-a
archaeological	αρχαιολογικός archaiologikós	ar-che-o-lo-yee-kos
art gallery	Η γκαλερί I gkalerí	ee ga-le-ree
beach	Η παραλία I paralía	ee pa-ra-lee-a
Byzantine	βυζαντινός vyzantinós	vee-zan-dee-nos
castle	Το κάστρο To kástro	to ka-stro
cathedral	Η μητρόπολη I mitrópoli	ee mee-tro-po-lee
cave	Το σπήλαιο To spílaio	to spee-le-o
church	Η εκκλησία I ekklisía	ee e-klee-see-a
folk art	λαϊκή τέχνη laïkí téchni	la-ee-kee tech-nee
fountain	Το συντριβάνι To syntriváni	to seen-dree-va-nee
garden	Ο κήπος O kípos	o kee-pos
gorge	Το φαράγγι To farággi	to fa-ran-gee
grave of...	Ο τάφος του... O táfos tou...	o ta-fos too
hill	Ο λόφος O lófos	o lo-fos
historical	ιστορικός istorikós	ee-sto-ree-kos
island	Το νησί To nisí	to nee-see
lake	Η λίμνη I límni	ee leem-nee
library	Η βιβλιοθήκη I vivliothíki	ee veev-lee-o-thee-kee
mansion	Το αρχοντικό To archontikó	to ar-chon-di-ko
monastery	Μονή moní	mo-ni
mountain	Το βουνό To vounó	to voo-no
municipal	δημοτικός dimotikós	thee-mo-tee-kos
museum	Το μουσείο To mouseío	to moo-see-o
national	εθνικός ethnikós	eth-nee-kos
park	Το πάρκο To párko	to par-ko
river	Το ποτάμι To potámi	to po-ta-mee
road	Ο δρόμος O drómos	o thro-mos
saint	άγιος/άγιοι/ αγία/αγίες ágios/ágioi/ agía/agíes	a-yee-os/a-yee-ee/ a-yee-a/a-yee-es
spring	Η πηγή I pigí	ee pee-yee
square	Η πλατεία I plateía	ee pla-tee-a
stadium	Το στάδιο To stádio	to sta-thee-o
statue	Το άγαλμα To ágalma	to a-gal-ma
theatre	Το θέατρο To théatro	to the-a-tro
town hall	Το δημαρχείο To dimarcheío	To thee-mar-chee-o
closed on public holidays	κλειστό τις αργίες kleistó tis argíes	klee-sto tees ar-yee-es

TRANSPORT

When does the ... leave?	Πότε φεύγει το ...; Póte févgei to ...?	po-teh fev-yee to ...?
Where is the bus stop?	Πού είναι η στάση του λεωφορείου; Poú eínai i stási tou leoforeíou?	poo ee-neh ee sta-see too le-o-fo-ree-oo?
Is there a bus to...?	Υπάρχει λεωφορείο για...; Ypárchei leoforeío gia...?	ee-par-chee le-o-fo-ree-o yia...?
ticket office	Εκδοτήριο εισιτηρίων Ekdotírio eisitiríon	Ek-tho-tee-ree-o ee-see-tee-ree-on
return ticket	Εισιτήριο με επιστροφή Eisitírio me epistrofí	ee-see-tee-ree-o meh e-pee-stro-fee
single journey	Απλό εισιτήριο Apló eisitírio	a-plo ee-see-tee-reeo
bus station	Ο σταθμός λεωφορείων O stathmós leoforeíon	o stath-mos leo-fo-ree-on
bus ticket	Εισιτήριο λεωφορείου Eisitírio leoforeíou	ee-see-tee-ree-o leo-fo-ree-oo
trolley bus	Το τρόλλεϋ To trólley	to tro-le-ee

port	Το λιμάνι To limáni	to lee-ma-nee
train	Το τρένο To tréno	to tre-no
railway station	σιδηροδρομικός σταθμός sidirodromikós stathmós	see-thee-ro-thro- mee-kos stath-mos
motorbike	το μηχανάκι To michanáki	to mee-cha-na-kee
bicycle	Το ποδήλατο To podílato	to po-thee-la-to
taxi	Το ταξί To taxí	to tak-see
airport	Το αεροδρόμιο To aerodrómio	to a-e-ro-thro-mee-o
ferry	Το φερυμπότ To "ferry-boat"	to fe-ree-bot
fast ferry	Το ταχυπλοΰ To tachypló	to ta-hee-plo
hydrofoil	Το δελφίνι / Το υδροπτέρυγο To delfíni / Το ydroptérygo	to del-fee-nee/To ee-throp-te-ree-go
catamaran	Το καταμαράν To katamarán	to catamaran
for hire/rent	Ενοικιάζονται Enoikiázontai	e-nee-kya-zon-deh

STAYING IN A HOTEL

Do you have a vacant room?	Έχετε δωμάτιο Echete domátio?	e-che-teh tho- ma-tee-o?
double room with double bed	Δίκλινο με διπλό κρεβάτι Díklino me dipló kreváti	thee-klee-no meh thee-plo kre-va-tee
twin room	Δίκλινο με μονά κρεβάτια Díklino me moná krevátia	thee-klee-no meh mo-na kre-vat-ya
single room	Μονόκλινο Monóklino	mo-no-klee-no
room with a bath	Δωμάτιο με μπάνιο Domátio me mpánio	tho-ma-tee-o meh ban-yo
shower	Το ντουζ To douz	To dooz
key	Το κλειδί To kleidí	to klee-dee
I have a reservation	Έχω κάνει κράτηση Echo káni krátisi	e-cho ka-nee kra- tee-see
room with a sea view/balcony	Δωμάτιο με θέα στη θάλασσα/ μπαλκόνι Domátio me théa sti thálassa/mpalkóni	tho-ma-tee-o meh the-a stee tha-la- sa/bal-ko-nee
Does the price include breakfast?	Το πρωινό συμπεριλαμβάνεται στην τιμή; To proïnó symperi- lamvánetai stin timí?	to pro-ee-no seem- be-ree-lam-va-ne- teh steen tee-mee?

EATING OUT

Have you got a table?	Έχετε τραπέζι; Echete trapézi?	e-che-te tra-pe-zee?
want to reserve a table	Θέλω να κρατήσω ένα τραπέζι Thélo na kratíso éna trapézi	the-lo na kra-tee-so e-na tra-pe-zee
The bill, please	Τον λογαριασμό, παρακαλώ Ton logariasmó parakaló	ton lo-gar-yaz-mo pa-ra-ka-lo
I am a vegetarian	Είμαι χορτοφάγος Eímai chortofágos	ee-meh chor- to-fa-gos
What is today's special?	Πιό είναι το πιάτο ημέρας; Pió eínai to piáto iméras?	pyó ee-neh to-pi-a-to ee me-ras?
waiter/waitress	Κύριε / Γκαρσόν / Κυρία (female) Kýrie/Garson/Kyría	Kee-ree-eh/Gar- son/Kee-ree-a
menu	Ο κατάλογος O katálogos	o ka-ta-lo-gos
cover charge	Το κουβέρ Το "couvert"	to koo-ver
wine list	Ο οινοκατάλογος O oinokatálogos	o ee-no-ka-ta-lo-gos
glass	Το ποτήρι Το potíri	to po-tee-ree

bottle	Το μπουκάλι Το mpoukáli	to bou-ka-lee
knife	Το μαχαίρι Το machaíri	to ma-che-ree
fork	Το πηρούνι Το piroúni	to pee-roo-nee
spoon	Το κουτάλι Το koutáli	to koo-ta-lee
breakfast	Το πρωινό Το proïnó	to pro-ee-no
lunch	Το μεσημεριανό Το mesimerianó	to me-see-mer-ya-no
dinner	Το δείπνο Το deípno	to theep-no
main course	Το κύριο πιάτο Το kýrio piáto	to kee-ri-o piato
starters/first courses	Τα ορεκτικά Ta orektiká	ta o-rek-tee-ka
dessert	Το γλυκό Το glykó	to ylee-ko
dish of the day	Το πιάτο της ημέρας Το piáto tis iméras	to pya-to tees ee-me-ras
bar	Το μπαρ Το "bar"	To bar
taverna	Η ταβέρνα I tavérna	ee ta-ver-na
café	Το καφενείο Το kafeneío	to ka-fe-nee-o
fish taverna	Η ψαροταβέρνα I psarotavérna	ee psa-ro-ta-ver-na
grill house	Η ψησταριά I psistariá	ee psee-sta-rya
wine shop	Το οινοπωλείο Το oinopoleío	to ee-no-po-lee-o
dairy shop	Το γαλακτοπωλείο Το galaktopoleío	to ga-lak-to-po-lee-o
restaurant	Το εστιατόριο Το estiatório	to e-stee-a-to-ree-o
ouzeri	Το ουζερί Το ouzerí	to oo-ze-ree
meze shop	Το μεζεδοπωλείο Το mezedopoleío	To me-ze- do-po-lee-o
take away kebabs	Το σουβλατζίδικο Το souvlatzídiko	To soo-vlat- zee-dee-ko
rare	Ελάχιστα ψημένο Eláchista psiméno	e-lach-ees-ta psee-me-no
medium	Μέτρια ψημένο Métria psiméno	met-ree-a psee- me-no
well done	Καλοψημένο Kalopsiméno	ka-lo-psee-me-no

BASIC FOOD AND DRINK

coffee	Ο καφές O Kafés	o ka-fes
with milk	με γάλα me gála	me ga-la
black coffee	σκέτος skétos	ske-tos
without sugar	χωρίς ζάχαρη chorís záchari	cho-rees za-cha-ree
medium sweet	μέτριος métrios	me-tree-os
very sweet	γλυκύς glykýs	glee-kees
tea	τσάι tsái	tsa-ee
hot chocolate	ζεστή σοκολάτα zestí sokoláta	ze-stee so-ko-la-ta
wine	κρασί krasí	kra-see
red	κόκκινο kókkino	ko-kee-no
white	λευκό lefkó	lef-ko
rosé	ροζέ rozé	ro-ze
raki	Το ρακί Το rakí	to ra-kee
ouzo	Το ούζο Το oúzo	to oo-zo
retsina	Η ρετσίνα I retsína	ee ret-see-na
water	Το νερό Το neró	to ne-ro
octopus	Το χταπόδι Το chtapódi	to chta-po-dee
fish	Το ψάρι Το psári	to psa-ree
cheese	Το τυρί Το tyrí	to tee-ree

English	Greek	Pronunciation
mastello	Το μαστέλο / Το mastélo	to mas-te-lo
feta	Η φέτα / I féta	ee fe ta
bread	Το ψωμί / Το psomí	to pso-mee
bean soup	Η φασολάδα / I fasoláda	ee fa-so-la-da
houmous	Το χούμους / Το houmous	to choo-moos
halva	Ο χαλβάς / O chalvás	o chal-vas
thin meat slabs	Ο γύρος / O gýros	o yee-ros
Turkish delight	Το λουκούμι / Το loukoúmi	to loo-koo-mee
baklava	Ο μπακλαβάς / O mpaklavás	o bak-la-vas
kleftiko	Το κλέφτικο / Το kléftiko	to klef-tee-ko

NUMBERS

	Greek	Pronunciation
1	ένα / éna	e-na
2	δύο / dýo	thee-o
3	τρία / tría	tree-a
4	τέσσερα / téssera	te-se-ra
5	πέντε / pénte	pen-deh
6	έξι / éxi	ek-si
7	επτά / eptá	ep-ta
8	οχτώ / ochtó	och-to
9	εννέα / ennéa	e-ne-a
10	δέκα / déka	the-ka
11	έντεκα / énteka	en-de-ka
12	δώδεκα / dódeka	tho-the-ka
13	δεκατρία / dekatría	de-ka-tree-a
14	δεκατέσσερα / dekatéssera	the-ka-tes-se-ra
15	δεκαπέντε / dekapénte	the-ka-pen-de
16	δεκαέξι / dekaéxi	the-ka-ek-si
17	δεκαεπτά / dekaeptá	the-ka-ep-ta
18	δεκαοχτώ / dekaochtó	the-ka-och-to
19	δεκαεννέα / dekaennéa	the-ka-e-ne-a
20	είκοσι / eíkosi	ee-ko-see
21	εικοσιένα / eikosiéna	ee-ko-see-e-na
30	τριάντα / triánta	tree-an-da
40	σαράντα / saránta	sa-ran-da
50	πενήντα / penínta	pe-neen-da
60	εξήντα / exínta	ek-seen-da
70	εβδομήντα / evdomínta	ev-tho-meen-da
80	ογδόντα / ogdónta	og-thon-da
90	ενενήντα / enenínta	e-ne-neen-da
100	εκατό / ekató	e-ka-to
200	διακόσια / diakósia	thya-kos-ya
1,000	χίλια / chília	cheel-ya
2,000	δύο χιλιάδες / dýo chiliádes	thee-o cheel-ya-thes
1,000,000	ένα εκατομμύριο / éna ekatommýria	e-na e-ka-to-mee-ree-o

TIME, DAYS AND DATES

English	Greek	Pronunciation
one minute	ένα λεπτό / éna leptó	e-na lep-to
one hour	μία ώρα / mía óra	mee-a o-ra
half an hour	μισή ώρα / misí óra	mee-see o-ra
quarter of an hour	ένα τέταρτο / éna tétarto	e-na te-tar-to
half past one	μία και μισή / mía kai misí	mee-a keh mee-see
quarter past one	μία και τέταρτο / mía kai tétarto	mee-a keh te-tar-to
ten past one	μία και δέκα / mía kai déka	mee-a keh the-ka
quarter to two	δύο παρά τέταρτο / dýo pará tétarto	thee-o pa-ra te-tar-to
ten to two	δύο παρά δέκα / dýo pará déka	thee-o pa-ra the-ka
a day	μία μέρα / mía méra	mee-a me-ra
a week	μία εβδομάδα / mía evdomáda	mee-a ev-tho-ma-tha
a month	ένας μήνας / énas mínas	e-nas mee-nas
a year	ένας χρόνος / énas chrónos	e-nas chro-nos
Monday	Δευτέρα / Deftéra	thef-te-ra
Tuesday	Τρίτη / Tríti	tree-tee
Wednesday	Τετάρτη / Tetárti	te-tar-tee
Thursday	Πέμπτη / Pémpti	pemp-tee
Friday	Παρασκευή / Paraskeví	pa-ras-ke-vee
Saturday	Σάββατο / Sávvato	sa-va-to
Sunday	Κυριακή / Kyriakí	keer-ee-a-kee
January	Ιανουάριος / Ianouários	ee-a-noo-a-ree-os
February	Φεβρουάριος / Fevrouários	fev-roo-a-ree-os
March	Μάρτιος / Mártios	mar-tee-os
April	Απρίλιος / Aprílios	a-pree-lee-os
May	Μάιος / Máios	ma-ee-os
June	Ιούνιος / Ioúnios	ee-oo-nee-os
July	Ιούλιος / Ioúlios	ee-oo-lee-os
August	Αύγουστος / Avgoustos	av-goo-stos
September	Σεπτέμβριος / Septémvrios	sep-tem-vree-os
October	Οκτώβριος / Októvrios	ok-to-vree-os
November	Νοέμβριος / Noémvrios	no-em-vree-os
December	Δεκέμβριος / Dekémvrios	the-kem-vree-os

DK would like to thank the following for their contribution to the previous edition: Mike Gerrard, Robin Gauldie, Marc Dubin, Andy Harris, Tanya Tsikas

The publisher would like to thank the following for their kind permission to reproduce their photographs:

Key: a-above; b-below/bottom; c-centre; f-far; l-left; r-right; t-top

123RF.com: dimaberkut 236–7t; Pavel Dudek 13t, 13cr; freeartist 27tl; Syrbu Igor 238b; Anton Ivanov 215b; Engin Korkmaz 120tr; Viacheslav Lopatin 118–19b; Tomas Marek 22bl; Andrei Nekrassov 218clb; saiko3p 86bl; Birute Vijeikiene 88b.

4Corners: Massimo Ripani 69bl, 126l; Reinhard Schmid 19, 142–3, 220–21.

Aeschylia Festival: 52clb.

akg-images: 62tl; De Agostini Picture Library 62–3t.

Alamy Stock Photo: Adam 204bl; AF archive 163br; AGE Fotostock / Aristidis Vafeiadakis 135cla; Allstar Picture Library 63bl; Ancient Art and Architecture 58br, 199br; Andronosh 156bl, 156–7t; Arco Images GmbH / R. Müller 239crb (Purple Heron); Art Directors & TRIP / Helene Rogers / ArkReligion.com 109cra; Artokoloro Quint Lox Limited 78clb, 78bc, 79cra, 194br, / liszt collection 79cr; Vadim Arzyukov 233clb; Ashley Cooper pics 47cr; George Atsametakis 46cla; Azoor Photo 155clb; Erin Babnik 77br; BasilT 45tr; Fero Bednar 246–47t; Bilwissedition Ltd. & Co. KG 36cb, 36crb, 36fcrb; blickwinkel / McPHOTO / MAS 239crb, 239br; Sergey Borisov 95t; Chronicle 58tl, 58clb, 59bc; Classic Image 55tr, 56cl; Cultural Archive 79br; Ian Dagnall 8cla, 11t, 105ca, 111t; Ian G Dagnall 20cl; Danita Delimont / Jim Engelbrecht 154bl; Darling Archive 78cra; Mark Delete 151br; Dimitris K. 113br; Adam Eastland 75, 82bl, 101cl; Peter Eastland 33br, 50b,173cra, 232–3t, 242t; Everett Collection Inc 61bc; Falkensteinfoto 36clb, 55br; Michele Falzone 197cr; Adam Ján Figel 176cl; Kirk Fisher 153cra; Stuart Forster 236br; funkyfood London - Paul Williams 12–13b, 175tr; Glyn Genin 85br, 86–7t; Nikolas Georgiou 49cb; Gibon Art 78crb; Milan Gonda 41crb, 103t, 110b, 114crb, 123tc, 136–7t; Karsten Hamre 120bl; Terry Harris 133tl, 133cr; Brian Hartshorn 188bl; Chris Hellier 235cra; hemis.fr / Marc Dozier 51tl, / Franck Guiziou 11br, 54br, / Lionel Montico 46tr; Heritage Image Partnership Ltd / Ashmolean Museum of Art and Archaeology 79cb,79bl, / © Fine Art Images 59clb; Marc Hill 209br; Historical image collection by Bildagentur-online 55cra; Andrew Holt 140br; Peter Horree 240bl; Constantinos Iliopoulos 159br; imageBROKER / Katja Kreder 39clb, / Wolfgang Weinhäupl 171t, / Konrad Wothe 41bl; incamerastock / ICP 164–5b; INTERFOTO / Fine Arts 129tl, / Personalities 37clb; Anton Ivanov 226tl; Izzet Keribar 82–3t; Panagiotis Kotsovolos 39–9b, 158–9t, 159cl, 180t, 216bl; Lanmas 37tr; Melvyn Longhurst 74cra; De Luan 55clb; Ioannis Mantas 136bl, 141cr, 176bl, 214br; Markets / Peter Erik Forsberg 122bl; mauritius images GmbH / Philochrome 89cra; Violeta Meletis 87bl, 141t; Hercules Milas 39crb, 57tl, 69tr, 74bl, 90–91, 115tr, 132bl, 139tr, 153t, 154t, 166bl, 173tl, 184bl, 185tl, 199tr, 213tc, 224b, 228b, 239bl, 241br, 247bl; Stanislav Moroz 201t; MShieldsPhotos 56–7b; Juan Carlos Muñoz 76–7t; National Geographic Image Collection / H.M. Herget 200bl; North Wind Picture Archives 59tr; B.O'Kane 177tr; Iordanis Pallikaras 51br; Dimitris Pan 134–5b; Theodoros Papageorgiou 157clb; Papilio / Robert Pickett 239cr; Stefano Paterna 205cl; Kim Petersen 172–3b; Photo12 / Ann Ronan Picture Library 139br; Greek photonews 121b; Pictorial Press Ltd 61cr; The Picture Art Collection 60cb, 83crb, 243tr; Pictures Now 36cra; The Print Collector / Heritage-Images 165tr, / Ann Ronan Picture Library 155cr, / Oxford Science Archive 61crb; Prisma Archivo 37cra, 37cr; Quagga Media 172cla; ReligiousStock 176clb; Robertharding 32tl, / Bestravelvideo 45crb, / Neil Farrin 160clb, / Michael Runkel 12t, / Lizzie Shepherd 31tr, 219; Science History Images 37fcrb, / Photo Researchers 56clb; Rosanne Tackaberry 105tr; Konstantinos Tsakalidis 52crb; Georgios Tsichlis 188t; Nevena Tsvetanova 58–9t; Ivan Vdovin 234bl; Vasilis Ververidis 245tl; Joe Vogan 76bl, 156cb; Edward Webb / Percy Ryall 53cr; Westend61 GmbH / Maria Maar 105crb; Jan Wlodarczyk 117tr, 163cr,196bl; Emma Wood 12clb; World History Archive 37cb, 185bc, 242br; World History Archive / Desmond Morris Collection 131bc; Xinhua 52cl; Ariadne Van Zandbergen 202tl; Zoonar GmbH / Serghei Starus 30tl; ZUMA Press; Inc. / SOPA Images / Ioannis Alexopoulos 63tr, / Aristidis Vafeiadakis 49bl.

AWL Images: Peter Adams 68c, 70–71l Hemis 8–9b; Stefano Politi Markovina 6–7; Nave Orgad 203b.

Dreamstime.com: Absente 45cra, 161t; Vassilis Anastasiou 101ca; Charalambos Andronos 27tr, 94bl; Vangelis Aragiannis 53crb; Arsty 211b;

This edition updated by
Contributors Amber Charmei, Jane Foster
Senior Editor Alison McGill
Senior Designers Ben Hinks, Stuti Tiwari
Project Editors Dipika Dasgupta, Danielle Watt
Project Art Editor Ankita Sharma
Editor Manjari Thakur
Assistant Picture Research Administrator
Vagisha Pushp
Jacket Coordinator Bella Talbot
Jacket Designers Ben Hinks, Jordan Lambley
Senior Cartographer Subhashree Bharati
Cartography Manager Suresh Kumar
Senior DTP Designer Tanveer Zaidi
Senior Production Editor Jason Little
Production Controller Kariss Ainsworth
Producer Kariss Ainsworth
Deputy Managing Editor Beverly Smart
Managing Editors Shikha Kulkarni,
Hollie Teague
Managing Art Editor Bess Daly
Senior Managing Art Editor Priyanka Thakur
Art Director Maxine Pedliham
Publishing Director Georgina Dee

First edition 1997

Published in Great Britain by Dorling Kindersley Limited,
DK, One Embassy Gardens, 8 Viaduct Gardens,
London SW11 7BW

The authorised representative in the EEA is
Dorling Kindersley Verlag GmbH. Arnulfstr.
124, 80636 Munich, Germany

Published in the United States by DK Publishing,
1450 Broadway, Suite 801, New York, NY 10018

A CIP catalogue record for this book
is available from the British Library.

A catalogue record for this book is available
from the Library of Congress.

ISSN: 1542 1554
ISBN: 978 0 2415 6596 4

Printed and bound in China.

www.dk.com

A NOTE FROM DK EYEWITNESS

The rapid rate at which the world is changing is
constantly keeping the DK Eyewitness team on our
toes. While we've worked hard to ensure that this
edition of Greece is accurate and up-to-date, we know
that opening hours alter, standards shift, prices
fluctuate, places close and new ones pop up in their
stead. So, if you notice we've got something wrong
or left something out, we want to hear about it.
Please get in touch at travelguides@dk.com